Better Homes and Gardens.

3
books in one

Meredith® Books
Des Moines, Iowa

Meredith Books
1716 Locust Street
Des Moines, Iowa 50309–3023
meredithbooks.com

First Edition.

Printed in China.
ISBN-13: 978-0-696-23523-8
ISBN-10: 0-696-23523-4

Our seal assures you that every recipe in *3 Books in One* has been tested in the
Better Homes and Gardens® Test Kitchen. This means that each recipe is practical and
reliable, and meets our high standards of taste appeal. We guarantee your satisfaction
with this book for as long as you own it.

Compiled from Better Homes and Gardens® *Biggest Book of Grilling,* Better Homes and Gardens® *Biggest
Book of 30-Minute Meals,* and Better Homes and Gardens® *500 Five-Ingredient Recipes.*

table of contents

introduction

Three complete Better Homes and Gardens® cookbooks, all in one! Yes, you read it right. Three hot-topic books in one comprehensive volume just for you. With the variety of recipes you'll find here, this might just become your everyday go-to cookbook.

30-minute meals
Let's face it, everyone is busy these days. From hauling kids to soccer or piano lessons to increasingly crazy workloads, we are constantly on the lookout for ways to get dinner on the table quickly while still serving tasty, healthful fare. For these busy nights, turn to the section featuring recipes from *The Biggest Book of 30-Minute Meals*. This collection features more than a hundred ready-in-a-flash recipes. We also give you timesaving tips, pantry-stocking advice, and a menu idea with every main-dish recipe.

grilling
We are a nation of grillers. And not just in the summer; many of us grill year round. For inspiration and fabulous recipes, turn the pages to the part of the book featuring recipes from the *Biggest Book of Grilling*. This jam-packed section includes recipes for both gas and charcoal grilling and its repertoire boasts chapters for main dish meats of all varieties, burgers, side dishes, and desserts—all prepared on the grill. Plus, look for amazingly simple sauces, rubs, and marinades to jazz up your grilled fare.

5-ingredient recipes
One, two, three, four, five! That's how many ingredients every recipe pulled from the pages of the *500 Five-Ingredient Recipes* section features. You'll love how quickly these family-friendly dishes come together. Most can be prepared in under 30 minutes and for those with longer start to finish times, the prep can typically be done quickly and then it's hands off for the cook while a recipe bakes, freezes, or marinates. Chapters include everything from main dishes to sides and desserts. Many of the recipes take advantage of the growing market of convenience products out there on the market—all designed, like this book—to make your life easier!

Every recipe in this flavor-filled book has been tested and been given the Better Homes and Gardens® Test Kitchen seal, which means we guarantee its success every single time you make it.

Now get to cooking!

grilling
recipes

peppered rib roast

A simple, five-ingredient rub adds outstanding flavor to a beef rib roast.

PREP: 10 minutes **GRILL:** 2¼ hours **STAND:** 15 minutes
MAKES: 10 to 12 servings

1	6-pound beef rib roast
2	tablespoons finely chopped shallots
4	teaspoons coarsely ground black pepper
1	teaspoon coarse salt
1	teaspoon dried basil, crushed
1	teaspoon dried thyme, crushed
1	tablespoon olive oil

one Trim fat from roast. For rub, in a small bowl combine shallots, pepper, salt, basil, and thyme. Brush meat with oil. Sprinkle rub evenly over roast; rub in with your fingers.

two For a charcoal grill, arrange medium coals around drip pan. Test for medium-low heat above pan. Place roast, bone side down, on grill rack over pan. Cover and grill until desired doneness. Allow 2¼ to 2¾ hours for medium-rare doneness (135°F) or 2¾ to 3¼ hours for medium doneness (150°F). Add coals as necessary to maintain heat. (For a gas grill, preheat grill. Reduce heat to medium-low. Adjust for indirect cooking. Place roast on rack in roasting pan, place on grill rack, and grill as above.)

three Remove meat from grill. Cover with foil; let stand for 15 minutes before carving. The meat's temperature after standing should be 145°F for medium-rare or 160°F for medium.

NUTRITION FACTS PER SERVING: 310 cal., 18 g total fat (7 g sat. fat), 100 mg chol., 305 mg sodium, 1 g carbo., 0 g fiber, 34 g pro.

three-pepper beef tenderloin roast

Fork-tender beef tenderloin, seasoned with a trio of peppers, will make guests feel you've gone the extra mile for them.

PREP: 15 minutes **GRILL:** 1 hour **STAND:** 15 minutes
MAKES: 9 or 10 servings

1	3- to 3½-pound beef tenderloin roast
1	teaspoon salt
1	teaspoon dried oregano, crushed
1	teaspoon dried thyme, crushed
1	teaspoon paprika
½	teaspoon garlic powder
½	teaspoon onion powder
½	teaspoon ground white pepper
½	teaspoon freshly ground black pepper
¼	teaspoon cayenne pepper

one Trim the fat from roast. For rub, in a small bowl combine salt, oregano, thyme, paprika, garlic powder, onion powder, white pepper, black pepper, and cayenne pepper. Sprinkle rub evenly over roast; rub in with your fingers.

two For a charcoal grill, arrange hot coals around a drip pan. Test for medium-hot heat above the pan. Place meat on grill rack over drip pan. Cover and grill for 1 to 1¼ hours or until medium-rare doneness (135°F). Add coals as necessary to maintain heat. (For a gas grill, preheat grill. Reduce heat to medium. Adjust for indirect cooking. Place meat on a rack in a roasting pan, place on grill rack, and grill as above.)

three Transfer meat to a cutting board; tent meat with foil and let stand for 15 minutes before carving into ¼- to ½-inch slices. The meat's temperature after standing should be 145°F.

NUTRITION FACTS PER SERVING: 253 cal., 13 g total fat (5 g sat. fat), 93 mg chol., 328 mg sodium, 1 g carbo., 0 g fiber, 32 g pro.

teriyaki t-bone steaks

The tangy-sweet taste of teriyaki flavors these T-bones. Serve them with steamed rice tossed with toasted macadamia nuts and thinly sliced green onions.

PREP: 15 minutes **MARINATE:** 4 to 6 hours **GRILL:** 11 minutes
MAKES: 4 servings

2	beef T-bone steaks, cut 1 inch thick (1¼ to 2 pounds total)
⅓	cup bottled teriyaki sauce
2	tablespoons sliced green onion
1	tablespoon honey
1	tablespoon lemon juice or rice vinegar
1	tablespoon finely chopped fresh ginger
1	teaspoon toasted sesame oil
½	teaspoon bottled minced garlic (1 clove)
¼	teaspoon coarsely ground black pepper
1	small fresh pineapple, cut into wedges and cored
2	or 4 1-inch slices tomato or sweet pepper
1	tablespoon cooking oil

one Trim fat from steaks. Place steaks in a resealable plastic bag set in a shallow dish. For marinade, in a small bowl combine teriyaki sauce, green onion, honey, lemon juice, fresh ginger, sesame oil, garlic, and black pepper. Pour marinade over steaks. Seal bag; turn to coat steaks. Marinate in the refrigerator for at least 4 hours or up to 6 hours, turning bag occasionally.

two Drain steaks, reserving marinade. For a charcoal grill, grill steaks on the rack of an uncovered grill directly over medium coals until desired doneness, turning and brushing once with reserved marinade halfway through grilling. Allow 11 to 14 minutes for medium-rare doneness (145°F) or 13 to 16 minutes for medium doneness (160°F). Discard any remaining marinade.

three While the steaks are grilling, brush pineapple wedges and tomato slices with cooking oil; add pineapple and tomato slices to grill. Grill for 6 to 8 minutes or until slightly charred, turning once halfway through grilling. (For a gas grill, preheat grill. Reduce heat to medium. Place steaks, then pineapple and tomato slices on grill rack over heat. Cover and grill as above.)

four To serve, cut each steak in half. Serve with pineapple and tomato slices.

NUTRITION FACTS PER SERVING: 296 cal., 12 g total fat (4 g sat. fat), 66 mg chol., 586 mg sodium, 16 g carbo., 1 g fiber, 29 g pro.

filet mignon with portobello sauce

Just a splash of Madeira or port wine makes this buttery, meltingly tender steak and mushroom dish simply marvelous. Madeira and port are slightly sweet Spanish wines flavored with a bit of brandy.

PREP: 15 minutes **GRILL:** 11 minutes **MAKES:** 4 servings

4	beef tenderloin steaks, cut 1 inch thick (about 1¼ pounds total)
1	teaspoon olive oil
¼	teaspoon ground black pepper
2	large portobello mushrooms, halved and sliced
8	green onions, cut into 1-inch pieces
1	tablespoon butter or margarine
⅓	cup beef broth
2	tablespoons Madeira or port wine

one Trim fat from steaks. Rub both sides of each steak with oil and pepper. For charcoal grill, grill steaks on the rack of an uncovered grill directly over medium coals until desired doneness, turning once halfway through grilling. Allow 11 to 15 minutes for medium-rare doneness (145°F) or 14 to 18 minutes for medium doneness (160°F). (For a gas grill, preheat grill. Reduce heat to medium. Place steaks on grill rack over heat. Cover and grill as above.)

two Meanwhile, for sauce, in a large skillet cook and stir mushrooms and green onions in hot butter over medium heat about 5 minutes or until vegetables are tender. Stir in broth and wine. Bring to boiling. Remove from heat. Thinly slice steaks diagonally and serve with sauce.

NUTRITION FACTS PER SERVING: 260 cal., 13 g total fat (5 g sat. fat), 88 mg chol., 160 mg sodium, 4 g carbo., 1 g fiber, 29 g pro.

chipotle tenderloin steak with potatoes

These steaks have all the attributes of a classic Mexican dish—chile peppers, cilantro, garlic, and lime. Enjoy a margarita while dinner grills.

PREP: 15 minutes **GRILL:** 20 minutes **MAKES:** 4 servings

- 4 beef tenderloin or ribeye steaks, cut 1 to 1¼ inches thick
- 2 to 4 tablespoons finely chopped, drained chipotle chile peppers in adobo sauce
- 2 tablespoons snipped fresh cilantro
- 1 tablespoon lime juice
- 2 teaspoons bottled minced garlic (4 cloves)
- ½ teaspoon salt
- 3 medium potatoes, each cut lengthwise into 8 wedges
- 2 teaspoons olive oil
- 1 teaspoon coarse salt or kosher salt
- 1 lime, cut into wedges

one Trim fat from steaks. In a small bowl stir together chipotle peppers, cilantro, lime juice, garlic, and salt. Brush mixture onto both sides of each steak. Brush potato wedges with olive oil; sprinkle with salt.

two For a charcoal grill, place potatoes on the rack of a grill with a cover directly over medium coals. Cover and grill for 20 to 25 minutes or until potatoes are tender and brown, turning once halfway through grilling. While the potatoes are grilling, add steaks to grill. Cover and grill until steaks are desired doneness, turning once halfway through grilling. Allow 11 to 15 minutes for medium-rare doneness (145°F) or 14 to 18 minutes for medium doneness (160°F). (For a gas grill, preheat grill. Reduce heat to medium. Place potatoes, then steaks on grill rack over heat. Cover and grill as above.) To serve, pass lime wedges with steaks.

NUTRITION FACTS PER SERVING: 385 cal., 13 g total fat (4 g sat. fat), 96 mg chol., 959 mg sodium, 30 g carbo., 1 g fiber, 35 g pro.

blt steak

The makings of the classic summer sandwich deliciously top this belt-busting steak.

PREP: 15 minutes **GRILL:** 14 minutes **MAKES:** 4 servings

2	12-ounce beef top loin steaks, cut 1¼ inches thick
8	slices bacon
½	cup bottled balsamic vinaigrette salad dressing
12	red and/or yellow tomato slices
2	cups torn mixed salad greens

one For charcoal grill, grill steaks on the rack of an uncovered grill directly over medium coals until desired doneness, turning once halfway through grilling. Allow 14 to 18 minutes for medium-rare doneness (145°F) or 17 to 21 minutes for medium doneness (160°F). (For a gas grill, preheat grill. Reduce heat to medium. Place steaks on grill rack over heat. Cover and grill as above.)

two Meanwhile, in a skillet cook bacon until crisp. Drain bacon on paper towels, reserving 1 tablespoon drippings in skillet. Add balsamic vinaigrette salad dressing to the drippings in skillet. Cook and stir for 1 minute, scraping up any browned bits. Halve the steaks. Top steaks with tomato slices, bacon, mixed greens, and dressing mixture.

NUTRITION FACTS PER SERVING: 556 cal., 42 g total fat (14 g sat. fat), 122 mg chol., 636 mg sodium, 5 g carbo., 1 g fiber, 38 g pro.

beef steaks with tomato-garlic butter

Beef steaks take kindly to the enhancement of butter, especially this tangy, garlic-infused blend. Double the butter recipe if you want to spread it on warm bread.

PREP: 12 minutes **GRILL:** 11 minutes **MAKES:** 4 servings

½	cup butter, softened
1	tablespoon snipped oil-packed dried tomatoes
1	tablespoon chopped kalamata olives
1	tablespoon finely chopped green onion
½	teaspoon bottled minced garlic (1 clove)
4	boneless beef top loin steaks, cut 1 inch thick (about 1½ pounds total)
	Salt (optional)
	Ground black pepper (optional)

one For flavored butter, in a small bowl stir together butter, dried tomatoes, kalamata olives, green onion, and garlic. Set aside. Trim fat from steaks.

two For a charcoal grill, grill steaks on the rack of an uncovered grill directly over medium coals until desired doneness, turning once halfway through grilling. Allow 11 to 15 minutes for medium-rare doneness (145°F) or 14 to 18 minutes for medium doneness (160°F). (For a gas grill, preheat grill. Reduce heat to medium. Place steaks on grill rack over heat. Cover and grill as above.)

three If desired, sprinkle steaks with salt and pepper. To serve, spread 1 tablespoon of the butter mixture over each steak. Cover and chill the remaining butter mixture for another time (also can be used as a spread for bread).

NUTRITION FACTS PER SERVING: 383 cal., 22 g total fat (11 g sat. fat), 161 mg chol., 227 mg sodium, 0 g carbo., 0 g fiber, 45 g pro.

here's-the-beef steck & onions

The sweet mustard topper transforms grilled
steak and onions into extraordinary fare.

PREP: 10 minutes **GRILL:** 11 minutes **MAKES:** 4 servings

¼	cup Dijon-style, brown, or yellow mustard
1	tablespoon honey
1½	teaspoons snipped fresh thyme or ½ teaspoon dried thyme, crushed
½	teaspoon bottled minced garlic (1 clove)
⅛	teaspoon ground black pepper
2	boneless beef top loin steaks, cut 1 inch thick (about 12 ounces total)
2	medium onions, cut into ½-inch slices

one For glaze, in a small bowl stir together mustard, honey, thyme, garlic, and pepper. Set aside. Trim fat from steaks.

two For charcoal grill, grill steaks and onion slices on the rack of an uncovered grill directly over medium coals until steaks are desired doneness and onions are tender, turning and generously brushing steaks and onions once with glaze halfway through grilling. Allow 11 to 15 minutes for medium-rare doneness (145°F) or 14 to 18 minutes for medium doneness (160°F). (For a gas grill, preheat grill. Reduce heat to medium. Place steaks and onion slices on grill rack over heat. Cover and grill as above.) Discard any remaining glaze.

three To serve, thinly slice the steaks and arrange with the onion slices on 4 dinner plates.

NUTRITION FACTS PER SERVING: 158 cal., 4 g total fat (1 g sat. fat), 50 mg chol., 389 mg sodium, 8 g carbo., 1 g fiber, 19 g pro.

kansas city strip steaks

Cuts other than strip steaks will benefit from this peppy seasoning. Rub the mixture on T-bone or sirloin steaks too. Halve the mixture if grilling fewer steaks.

PREP: 10 minutes **CHILL:** 1 hour **GRILL:** 11 minutes **MAKES:** 8 servings

2	tablespoons prepared horseradish
2	tablespoons lemon juice
4	teaspoons sugar
2	teaspoons paprika
2	teaspoons bottled minced garlic (4 cloves)
1	teaspoon salt
1	teaspoon ground black pepper
½	teaspoon instant beef bouillon granules
4	8-ounce beef top loin steaks, cut 1 inch thick

one In a small bowl combine horseradish, lemon juice, sugar, paprika, garlic, salt, pepper, and beef bouillon granules. Trim fat from meat. Rub mixture on both sides of each steak. Cover; refrigerate steaks for 1 hour.

two For charcoal grill, grill steaks on the rack of an uncovered grill directly over medium coals until desired doneness, turning once halfway through grilling. Allow 11 to 15 minutes for medium-rare doneness (145°F) or 14 to 18 minutes for medium doneness (160°F). (For a gas grill, preheat grill. Reduce heat to medium. Place steaks on grill rack over heat. Cover and grill as above.)

NUTRITION FACTS PER SERVING: 276 cal., 19 g total fat (8 g sat. fat), 74 mg chol., 400 mg sodium, 8 g carbo., 0 g fiber, 22 g pro.

steak lover's platter

If all the food won't fit on your grill at once, cook it in two batches, vegetables first. If the vegetables get too cool, warm them on the grill while you slice the meat.

PREP: 30 minutes **MARINATE:** 4 to 6 hours **GRILL:** 20 minutes
MAKES: 6 servings

½	cup cider vinegar
¼	cup dark beer or dark or amber nonalcoholic beer
5	tablespoons snipped fresh marjoram or 1 tablespoon dried marjoram, crushed
2	tablespoons olive oil or cooking oil
½	teaspoon salt
½	teaspoon ground black pepper
½	teaspoon bottled minced garlic (1 clove)
1	2-pound boneless beef top sirloin steak, cut 1½ inches thick
3	medium baking potatoes, each cut lengthwise into 8 wedges (about 1 pound)
4	small zucchini, halved lengthwise (about 1 pound)
3	medium yellow, orange, green, or red sweet peppers, seeded and cut into 1-inch-wide rings
2	tablespoons olive oil or cooking oil
¼	teaspoon salt
¼	teaspoon ground black pepper
1	recipe Onion Sauce

one For marinade, in a small bowl combine vinegar, beer, 2 tablespoons of the fresh marjoram or 2 teaspoons of the dried marjoram, 2 tablespoons oil, the ½ teaspoon salt, the ½ teaspoon black pepper, and the garlic. Place steak in a resealable plastic bag set in a shallow dish. Pour marinade over steak. Seal bag; turn to coat steak. Marinate in the refrigerator for at least 4 hours or up to 6 hours, turning bag occasionally.

two In a covered medium saucepan cook potato wedges in a large amount of boiling water for 4 minutes; drain. In a large bowl stir together potatoes, zucchini, and sweet peppers. In a small bowl stir together 1 tablespoon of the remaining fresh marjoram or remaining 1 teaspoon dried marjoram, 2 tablespoons oil, the ¼ teaspoon salt, and the ¼ teaspoon black pepper; sprinkle over vegetables. Toss to coat.

three Drain meat, discarding marinade. For a charcoal grill, grill meat, potatoes, zucchini, and sweet peppers on the greased rack of an uncovered grill directly over medium coals until meat is desired doneness and vegetables are tender. Allow 20 to 24 minutes for medium-rare doneness (145°F) or 24 to 28 minutes for medium doneness (160°F), turning meat and vegetables once halfway through grilling. (For a gas grill, preheat grill. Reduce heat to medium. Place meat, potatoes, zucchini, and sweet peppers on grill rack over heat. Cover and grill as above.)

four Carve beef across grain into ¼-inch slices. Arrange beef, potatoes, zucchini, and peppers on serving platter.

five Drizzle with half of the Onion Sauce; pass remaining sauce. Sprinkle with remaining fresh marjoram, if using.

NUTRITION FACTS PER SERVING: 510 cal., 23 g total fat (7 g sat. fat), 106 mg chol., 445 mg sodium, 34 g carbo., 2 g fiber, 39 g pro.

onion sauce: In a small saucepan cook 1 cup chopped onion and ½ teaspoon bottled minced garlic (1 clove) in 1 tablespoon hot butter or margarine over medium heat for 4 minutes or until onions are tender. In a small bowl gradually stir ½ cup dark beer or dark or amber nonalcoholic beer, ½ cup beef broth, and 1 tablespoon Worcestershire sauce into 1 tablespoon cornstarch. Add to saucepan. Cook and stir over medium heat until thickened and bubbly. Cook and stir for 2 minutes more.

marinated steak with blue cheese

Plain steak becomes a showstopper when it's marinated and served with a chunky blue cheese topper.

PREP: 20 minutes **MARINATE:** 6 to 24 hours **GRILL:** 14 minutes
MAKES: 4 servings

1	pound boneless beef top sirloin steak, cut 1 inch thick
¼	cup olive oil
¼	cup dry red wine
1	teaspoon coarsely ground black pepper
1	teaspoon bottled minced garlic (2 cloves)
½	teaspoon salt
½	teaspoon Dijon-style mustard
¼	cup thinly sliced green onions
¼	cup crumbled blue cheese (1 ounce)
2	tablespoons soft goat cheese (chèvre)
½	teaspoon bottled minced garlic (1 clove)

one Trim fat from steak. Place steak in a resealable plastic bag set in a shallow dish. For marinade, in a small bowl stir together olive oil, red wine, pepper, the 1 teaspoon minced garlic, the salt, and mustard. Pour marinade over steak. Seal bag; turn to coat steak. Marinate in the refrigerator for at least 6 hours or up to 24 hours, turning bag occasionally.

two Drain steak, discarding marinade. For a charcoal grill, grill steak on the rack of an uncovered grill directly over medium coals until desired doneness, turning once halfway through. Allow 14 to 18 minutes for medium-rare doneness (145°F) or 18 to 22 minutes for medium doneness (160°F). (For a gas grill, preheat grill. Reduce heat to medium. Place steak on grill rack over heat. Cover and grill as above.)

three Meanwhile, in a small bowl combine green onions, blue cheese, goat cheese, and the ½ teaspoon garlic. Transfer meat to serving platter. Dollop some of the blue cheese mixture over steak. To serve, thinly slice meat across the grain. Pass remaining blue cheese mixture.

NUTRITION FACTS PER SERVING: 315 cal., 21 g total fat (7 g sat. fat), 89 mg chol., 345 mg sodium, 1 g carbo., 0 g fiber, 29 g pro.

steak with roasted garlic & herbs

When roasted, garlic turns mild and sweet–ideal for spreading on grilled steak or your favorite bread or crackers.

PREP: 15 minutes **GRILL:** 30 minutes **MAKES:** 6 servings

1	or 2 whole bulb(s) garlic
3	to 4 teaspoons snipped fresh basil or 1 teaspoon dried basil, crushed
1	tablespoon snipped fresh rosemary or 1 teaspoon dried rosemary, crushed
2	tablespoons olive oil or cooking oil
1	to 2 teaspoons cracked black pepper
½	teaspoon salt
1	1½-pound boneless beef top sirloin steak, cut 1 inch thick, or 1½ pounds beef ribeye steaks, cut 1 inch thick
	Fresh rosemary sprigs (optional)

one Remove papery outer layers from garlic bulb(s), leaving individual cloves attached to bulb(s). Cut off about ½ inch from top of bulb(s) and discard. Tear off a 20×10-inch piece of heavy foil. Fold in half to make a double thickness of foil that measures 10×10 inches. Place garlic in center of foil. Bring foil up around garlic to form a shallow bowl. Sprinkle garlic with basil and snipped or dried rosemary; drizzle with oil.

two Completely enclose garlic in foil, twisting ends of foil on top. For a charcoal grill, grill foil packet on the rack of an uncovered grill directly over medium coals about 30 minutes or until garlic cloves are soft. Remove bulb(s) from foil packet, reserving herb-oil mixture. Let cool slightly.

three Meanwhile, for rub, in a small bowl combine pepper and salt. Sprinkle rub evenly over both sides of steak; rub in with your fingers. Grill steak alongside the garlic packet until desired doneness, turning steak once halfway through grilling. For sirloin steak, allow 14 to 18 minutes for medium-rare doneness (145°F) or 18 to 22 minutes for medium doneness (160°F). For ribeye steaks, allow 11 to 15 minutes for medium-rare doneness (145°F) or 14 to 18 minutes for medium doneness (160°F). (For a gas grill, preheat grill. Reduce heat to medium. Place foil packet, then steaks on grill rack over heat. Cover and grill as above.)

four To serve, cut steak into serving-size pieces. Carefully squeeze the pulp from the garlic cloves onto the steak pieces. Mash pulp slightly with a fork and spread over steak pieces. Drizzle steaks with the reserved herb-oil mixture. If desired, garnish with rosemary sprigs.

NUTRITION FACTS PER SERVING: 251 cal., 15 g total fat (5 g sat. fat), 76 mg chol., 235 mg sodium, 2 g carbo., 0 g fiber, 26 g pro.

beer-braised beef short ribs

If you enjoy ribs with a touch of fire, add the bottled hot pepper sauce to the subtly sweet molasses basting mixture.

PREP: 30 minutes **BAKE:** 2 hours **GRILL:** 10 minutes **MAKES:** 4 to 6 servings

5	pounds beef chuck short ribs
2	12-ounce cans dark beer
1	14-ounce can beef broth
1	medium onion, sliced
1	teaspoon dried thyme, crushed
½	teaspoon salt
¼	cup molasses
2	tablespoons balsamic vinegar
½	to 1 teaspoon bottled hot pepper sauce (optional)

one Place short ribs in a 6- to 7-quart Dutch oven. Add beer, broth, onion, ½ teaspoon of the thyme, and ¼ teaspoon of the salt. Bring to boiling; remove from heat. Cover and bake in a 350°F oven about 2 hours or until ribs are very tender.

two Remove from oven; cool slightly. Remove short ribs from cooking liquid. (If desired, cover and store short ribs in the refrigerator up to 24 hours or until ready to grill.) Spoon fat from surface of cooking liquid;* discard fat. Strain cooking liquid, reserving ¼ cup; discard remaining cooking liquid and solids. Stir molasses, balsamic vinegar, hot pepper sauce (if desired), the remaining ½ teaspoon thyme, and the remaining ¼ teaspoon salt into reserved ¼ cup cooking liquid.

three For a charcoal grill, grill short ribs, bone sides down, on the rack of an uncovered grill directly over medium coals for 10 to 15 minutes or until short ribs are crisp and heated through, turning and brushing frequently with molasses mixture. (For a gas grill, preheat grill. Reduce heat to medium. Place short ribs on grill rack over heat. Cover and grill as above.)

NUTRITION FACTS PER SERVING: 371 cal., 15 g total fat (6 g sat. fat), 85 mg chol., 466 mg sodium, 17 g carbo., 0 g fiber, 37 g pro.

*NOTE: To easily remove fat from the cooking liquid, pour the liquid into a bowl. Set the bowl inside a larger bowl filled with ice cubes. Cover and refrigerate about 1 hour or until fat is solidified. (Or cover and refrigerate cooking liquid overnight.) Remove and discard fat.

beef fajitas

Mexican cowboys first created beef fajitas when they began tinkering with the lowly skirt steak. They started by marinating the tough cut to tenderize it and then cooked it over a hot wood fire to bring out its robust flavor.

PREP: 20 minutes **MARINATE:** 6 to 24 hours **GRILL:** 17 minutes
MAKES: 6 servings

1	1½-pound beef skirt steak or flank steak
½	cup bottled salsa
⅓	cup bottled Italian salad dressing
3	fresh serrano chile peppers, seeded (if desired) and finely chopped*
1	teaspoon bottled minced garlic (2 cloves)
¼	teaspoon ground black pepper
6	7- to 8-inch flour tortillas, warmed**
	Sweet pepper strips (optional)
	Shredded cheddar cheese (optional)
	Bottled salsa

one Trim fat from meat. Place meat in a resealable plastic bag set in a shallow dish. For marinade, in a small bowl stir together the ½ cup salsa, the Italian dressing, serrano chile peppers, garlic, and black pepper. Pour marinade over meat. Seal bag; turn to coat meat. Marinate in the refrigerator for at least 6 hours or up to 24 hours, turning bag occasionally.

two Drain meat, discarding marinade. For a charcoal grill, grill meat on the rack of an uncovered grill directly over medium coals for 17 to 21 minutes or until medium doneness (160°F), turning once halfway through grilling. (For a gas grill, preheat grill. Reduce heat to medium. Place meat on grill rack over heat. Cover and grill as above.)

three Transfer meat to a cutting board. Thinly slice across the grain. Divide the sliced meat among warm tortillas. If desired, top with sweet pepper strips, cheese, and additional salsa. Fold tortillas.

NUTRITION FACTS PER SERVING: 341 cal., 14 g total fat (5 g sat. fat), 45 mg chol., 350 mg sodium, 24 g carbo., 1 g fiber, 28 g pro.

*NOTE: Because chile peppers contain volatile oils that can burn your skin and eyes, avoid direct contact with them as much as possible. When working with chile peppers, wear plastic or rubber gloves. If your bare hands do touch the chile peppers, wash your hands and nails well with soap and warm water.

**NOTE: To heat the tortillas on the grill, wrap them in foil. Place on the grill rack next to the meat; heat about 10 minutes or until warm, turning once.

meat & vegetable kabobs

Start with your favorite barbecue sauce and add a medley of seasonings for a flavorful sauce that complements beef, chicken, and vegetables.

PREP: 25 minutes **MARINATE:** 6 to 24 hours **GRILL:** 8 minutes
MAKES: 4 or 5 servings

½	cup bottled barbecue sauce
¼	cup water
1	to 2 teaspoons bottled minced garlic (2 to 4 cloves)
2	tablespoons dried minced onion
2	tablespoons sugar
2	tablespoons bottled steak sauce
2	tablespoons vinegar
2	tablespoons Worcestershire sauce
2	tablespoons cooking oil
½	teaspoon salt
1½	pounds beef sirloin steak, cut 1 inch thick, and/or skinless, boneless chicken breasts and/or thighs
2	medium onions, each cut into 8 wedges
10	to 12 fresh mushrooms, stems removed
1	medium zucchini, halved and cut into ½-inch slices
1	large red or green sweet pepper, cut into 1-inch pieces
	Fresh herb sprigs (optional)

one For marinade, in a small saucepan combine barbecue sauce, the water, garlic, dried onion, sugar, steak sauce, vinegar, Worcestershire sauce, oil, and salt. Bring just to boiling. Cool.

two Cut steak into 1-inch cubes or cut chicken into 1-inch pieces. Place steak and/or chicken in a resealable plastic bag set in a deep bowl. Pour marinade over steak and/or chicken. Seal bag; turn to coat steak and/or chicken. Marinate in the refrigerator for at least 6 hours or up to 24 hours, turning bag occasionally.

three In a covered medium saucepan cook onions in a small amount of boiling water for 3 minutes. Add mushrooms; cook for 1 minute more. Drain.

four Drain meat, reserving marinade. On metal skewers, alternately thread vegetables and steak and/or chicken, leaving ¼-inch space between pieces. For a charcoal grill, grill kabobs on rack of an uncovered grill directly over medium coals for 8 to 14 minutes or until done, turning once halfway through grilling and brushing once with reserved marinade after 3 minutes of grilling. (For a gas grill, preheat grill. Reduce heat to medium. Place kabobs on grill rack over heat. Cover and grill as above.)

five In a small saucepan heat remaining marinade to boiling; serve warmed marinade with kabobs. If desired, garnish with fresh herb sprigs.

NUTRITION FACTS PER SERVING: 381 cal., 14 g total fat (3 g sat. fat), 103 mg chol., 849 mg sodium, 24 g carbo., 3 g fiber, 40 g pro.

beef & avocado tacos

In Mexican cuisine, carne asada (grilled meat) is a popular choice for tacos and burritos.

PREP: 20 minutes **GRILL:** 10 minutes **MAKES:** 4 servings

- 2 tablespoons lemon juice
- 1 avocado, pitted, peeled, and cut into ½-inch cubes
- 1 pound boneless beef sirloin steak or eye round steak, cut 1 inch thick
- 1 medium onion, cut into wedges
- 2 fresh Anaheim or poblano chile peppers, cut into 1-inch squares*
- 1 tablespoon olive oil
- ½ cup bottled picante sauce
- 2 cups shredded lettuce
- 4 7- to 8-inch flour tortillas

   Bottled picante sauce (optional)

one Drizzle lemon juice over avocado; toss gently to coat. Set aside.

two Cut steak into 2×1-inch strips. On four 12-inch metal skewers, thread steak strips (accordion-style). On four additional 12-inch metal skewers, alternately thread onion wedges and pepper squares. Brush vegetables with olive oil.

three For a charcoal grill, grill skewers on the rack of an uncovered grill directly over medium coals for 10 to 12 minutes or until steak is done, turning kabobs once halfway through grilling and brushing occasionally with the ½ cup picante sauce during the first 5 minutes of grilling. (For a gas grill, preheat grill. Reduce heat to medium. Place skewers on grill rack over heat. Cover and grill as above.) Discard remainder of the ½ cup picante sauce.

four To serve, divide the steak, onion, peppers, avocado, and lettuce among the flour tortillas. Fold tortillas over filling. If desired, serve with additional picante sauce.

NUTRITION FACTS PER SERVING: 425 cal., 24 g total fat (6 g sat. fat), 76 mg chol., 403 mg sodium, 24 g carbo., 3 g fiber, 30 g pro.

***NOTE:** Because chile peppers contain volatile oils that can burn your skin and eyes, avoid direct contact with them as much as possible. When working with chile peppers, wear plastic or rubber gloves. If your bare hands do touch the chile peppers, wash your hands and nails well with soap and warm water.

grilled beef, red onion & blue cheese salad

The natural sweetness of red onions is intensified when the onions are brushed with a balsamic vinaigrette and grilled alongside sirloin steak. Aromatic grilled herb bread makes a perfect go-along with this crisp and hearty main-dish salad.

PREP: 15 minutes **GRILL:** 14 minutes **MAKES:** 4 servings

2	tablespoons olive oil
3	tablespoons balsamic vinegar
½	teaspoon bottled minced garlic (1 clove)
½	teaspoon salt
½	teaspoon ground black pepper
1	boneless beef top sirloin steak, cut 1 inch thick (about 12 ounces)
1	tablespoon snipped fresh thyme
2	teaspoons snipped fresh rosemary
4	¼-inch-thick slices red onion
6	cups lightly packed mesclun or torn mixed salad greens
2	tablespoons crumbled blue cheese
8	yellow and/or red pear tomatoes, halved

one For vinaigrette, in a screw-top jar combine oil, balsamic vinegar, garlic, salt, and pepper; cover and shake well. Trim fat from steak. Remove 1 tablespoon of the vinaigrette from jar and brush evenly onto both sides of steak. Press thyme and rosemary onto both sides of the steak. Brush both sides of onion slices with some of the remaining vinaigrette, reserving the rest; set aside.

two For charcoal grill, grill steak on rack of an uncovered grill directly over medium coals until desired doneness, turning once halfway through grilling. Allow 14 to 18 minutes for medium-rare doneness (145°F) or 18 to 22 minutes for medium doneness (160°F). For last 10 minutes of grilling, place onions on grill rack alongside meat. Grill onions until tender, turning once. (For a gas grill, preheat grill. Reduce heat to medium. Place steaks, then onions on the grill rack over heat. Cover and grill as above.)

three Divide mesclun or mixed salad greens among 4 dinner plates. To serve, thinly slice the steak across the grain. Separate onion slices into rings. Arrange warm steak and onions on greens. Drizzle with the reserved vinaigrette. Top with cheese and tomatoes.

NUTRITION FACTS PER SERVING: 266 cal., 16 g total fat (5 g sat. fat), 59 mg chol., 373 mg sodium, 9 g carbo., 2 g fiber, 22 g pro.

bbq burgers

Zip up the sauce by adding a few dashes of bottled hot pepper sauce.

PREP: 15 minutes **GRILL:** 14 minutes **MAKES:** 4 servings

- ¼ cup ketchup
- 2 tablespoons bottled steak sauce
- 1 tablespoon water
- 1 teaspoon sugar
- 1 teaspoon vinegar
- ½ teaspoon bottled minced garlic (1 clove)
  Few dashes bottled hot pepper sauce (optional)
- 1 pound lean ground beef
- ¼ teaspoon salt
- ¼ teaspoon ground black pepper
- 4 hamburger buns, split and toasted
  Desired accompaniments (such as American cheese slices, lettuce leaves, tomato slices, onion slices, and/or pickle slices) (optional)

one For sauce, in a small saucepan combine ketchup, steak sauce, the water, sugar, vinegar, garlic, and, if desired, hot pepper sauce. Bring to boiling; reduce heat. Simmer, uncovered, for 3 minutes. Remove from heat; set aside.

two In a medium bowl combine beef, salt, and pepper. Shape mixture into four ¼-inch-thick patties.

three For a charcoal grill, grill patties on the rack of an uncovered grill directly over medium coals for 14 to 18 minutes or until meat is done (160°F),* turning once halfway through grilling and brushing once or twice with sauce during the last 5 minutes of grilling. (For a gas grill, preheat grill. Reduce heat to medium. Place patties on grill rack over heat. Cover and grill as above.)

four Reheat any remaining sauce until bubbly. Serve patties on buns. Spoon reheated sauce over patties. If desired, serve with your choice of accompaniments.

NUTRITION FACTS PER SERVING: 332 cal., 13 g total fat (5 g sat. fat), 71 mg chol., 713 mg sodium, 29 g carbo., 1 g fiber, 24 g pro.

*NOTE: The internal color of a burger is not a reliable doneness indicator. A beef patty cooked to 160°F is safe, regardless of color. To measure the doneness of a patty, insert an instant-read thermometer through the side of the patty to a depth of 2 to 3 inches.

spicy beer burgers

Add a side of seasoned grilled potato wedges and a frosty beer for a brew pub-style meal.

PREP: 20 minutes **GRILL:** 14 minutes **MAKES:** 6 servings

1	slightly beaten egg
½	cup finely chopped onion
¼	cup fine dry bread crumbs
¼	cup beer
1	tablespoon Worcestershire sauce
½	teaspoon dried thyme, crushed
¼	teaspoon dry mustard
¼	teaspoon cayenne pepper
1	pound lean ground beef
6	hamburger buns, split and toasted
	Romaine leaves (optional)
	Tomato slices (optional)

one In a large bowl combine the egg, onion, bread crumbs, beer, Worcestershire sauce, thyme, mustard, and cayenne pepper. Add ground beef; mix well. Shape meat mixture into six ¾-inch-thick patties.

two For a charcoal grill, grill patties on the rack of an uncovered grill directly over medium coals for 14 to 18 minutes or until meat is done (160°F),* turning once halfway through grilling. (For a gas grill, preheat grill. Reduce heat to medium. Place patties on grill rack over heat. Cover and grill as above.)

three Serve burgers on toasted buns. If desired, top burgers with romaine and tomato slices.

NUTRITION FACTS PER SERVING: 284 cal., 10 g total fat (4 g sat. fat), 83 mg chol., 400 mg sodium, 26 g carbo., 2 g fiber, 19 g pro.

*NOTE: The internal color of a burger is not a reliable doneness indicator. A beef patty cooked to 160°F is safe, regardless of color. To measure the doneness of a patty, insert an instant-read thermometer through the side of the patty to a depth of 2 to 3 inches.

colossal stuffed burger

What fun! This giant burger is packed with mushrooms and mozzarella, grilled, then cut into wedges to serve.

PREP: 20 minutes **GRILL:** 35 minutes **MAKES:** 6 servings

2	pounds lean ground beef or lamb
¼	cup grated Parmesan cheese (1 ounce)
2	teaspoons dried oregano, crushed
1	teaspoon lemon juice
1	teaspoon bottled teriyaki sauce
½	teaspoon garlic salt
¼	cup tomato paste
1	4-ounce can chopped mushrooms, drained
¼	cup shredded mozzarella cheese (1 ounce)

one In a large bowl combine ground meat, Parmesan cheese, oregano, lemon juice, teriyaki sauce, and garlic salt. Divide meat mixture in half. Shape each half into a ball; pat each ball onto waxed paper to form a flat patty 8 inches in diameter. Spread tomato paste in the center of 1 circle of the meat. Top tomato paste with mushrooms and mozzarella cheese. Top with the second circle of the meat. Press to seal edge.

two For a charcoal grill, arrange medium-hot coals around a drip pan. Test for medium heat above the pan. Place the burger on the grill rack over drip pan. Cover and grill about 35 minutes or until meat is done (160°F).* Cut into wedges to serve.

NUTRITION FACTS PER SERVING: 290 cal., 16 g total fat (7 g sat. fat), 102 mg chol., 334 mg sodium, 4 g carbo., 1 g fiber, 30 g pro.

*NOTE: The internal color of a burger is not a reliable doneness indicator. A beef patty cooked to 160°F is safe, regardless of color. To measure the doneness of a patty, insert an instant-read thermometer through the side of the patty into the meaty section to a depth of 2 to 3 inches.

creole carnival burgers

Add extra kick to these stuffed burgers by substituting Monterey Jack cheese with jalapeño peppers for the plain Monterey Jack cheese.

PREP: 25 minutes **GRILL:** 14 minutes **MAKES:** 6 servings

2	pounds ground beef
2	teaspoons Cajun seasoning
½	teaspoon salt
1	medium onion, chopped
1	small green sweet pepper, chopped
½	cup shredded Monterey Jack cheese (2 ounces)
6	hamburger buns, split
	Desired accompaniments (such as lettuce, sliced tomatoes, sliced cucumber, pickles, carrot sticks, and/or celery sticks) (optional)

one In a large bowl combine beef, Cajun seasoning, and salt. Shape into twelve ¼-inch-thick patties.

two In a medium bowl combine onion, sweet pepper, and cheese. Spoon ¼ cup of cheese mixture into center of each of 6 of the patties. Top with remaining 6 patties; press edges to seal. Reshape patties as necessary.

three For a charcoal grill, grill patties on the rack of an uncovered grill directly over medium coals for 14 to 18 minutes or until meat is done (160°F),* turning once halfway through grilling. (For a gas grill, preheat grill. Reduce heat to medium. Place patties on grill rack over heat. Cover and grill as above.)

four Serve on buns. If desired, serve with your choice of accompaniments.

NUTRITION FACTS PER SERVING: 461 cal., 24 g total fat (10 g sat. fat), 103 mg chol., 626 mg sodium, 25 g carbo., 2 g fiber, 35 g pro.

*NOTE: The internal color of a burger is not a reliable doneness indicator. A beef patty cooked to 160°F is safe, regardless of color. To measure the doneness of a patty, insert an instant-read thermometer through the side of the patty into the meaty section to a depth of 2 to 3 inches.

country boy pork tenderloins

Instead of serving grilled pork with applesauce, make a marinade of apple butter that sweetly coats every slice of the meat.

PREP: 10 minutes **MARINATE:** 2 to 8 hours **GRILL:** 40 minutes
MAKES: 6 to 8 servings

1	cup apple butter
½	cup white vinegar
1	tablespoon sugar
1	tablespoon Worcestershire sauce
1	tablespoon brandy
1	tablespoon soy sauce
½	teaspoon dry mustard
½	teaspoon salt
¼	teaspoon ground black pepper
¼	teaspoon paprika
	Few dashes bottled hot pepper sauce
2	1-pound pork tenderloins

one In a medium bowl stir together apple butter, vinegar, sugar, Worcestershire sauce, brandy, soy sauce, mustard, salt, black pepper, paprika, and bottled hot pepper sauce.

two Place the tenderloins in a resealable plastic bag set in a shallow dish. Pour the apple butter mixture over meat. Seal bag; turn to coat tenderloin. Marinate in the refrigerator for at least 2 hours or up to 8 hours. Drain meat, reserving marinade.

three For a charcoal grill, arrange hot coals around a drip pan. Test for medium-hot heat above the pan. Place tenderloins on grill rack over drip pan. Cover and grill for 40 to 50 minutes or until meat juices run clear (160°F), brushing occasionally with marinade during the first 20 minutes of grilling. (For a gas grill, preheat grill. Reduce heat to medium-hot. Adjust for indirect cooking. Place tenderloins on rack in a roasting pan, place on grill rack, and grill as above.) Discard any remaining marinade.

NUTRITION FACTS PER SERVING: 459 cal., 3 g total fat (1 g sat. fat), 89 mg chol., 442 mg sodium, 64 g carbo., 2 g fiber, 37 g pro.

jalapeño-stuffed pork tenderloin

This spunky grilled roast starts with a sprinkling of jalapeño peppers, tomato, and cilantro, and ends with a sassy butter brush-on.

PREP: 30 minutes **MARINATE:** 8 to 24 hours **GRILL:** 30 minutes
STAND: 10 minutes **MAKES:** 4 to 6 servings

1	1- to 1¼-pound pork tenderloin
6	fresh jalapeño chile peppers, seeded and chopped*
1	plum tomato, chopped
2	tablespoons snipped fresh cilantro
2	tablespoons lime juice
2½	teaspoons bottled minced garlic (5 cloves)
½	teaspoon salt
¼	cup butter, melted
	Ground black pepper
	Salt

one Trim fat from meat. Split tenderloin lengthwise, cutting to but not through the opposite side. Spread meat open. Cover with plastic wrap. Working from the center to the edges, pound with the flat side of a meat mallet to about ½-inch thickness. Remove plastic wrap.

two In a small bowl combine half of the jalapeño peppers, the tomato, cilantro, lime juice, garlic, and ¼ teaspoon of the salt. Sprinkle over meat. Starting from a long side, roll up into a spiral, tucking in ends. Tie at 1-inch intervals with 100-percent-cotton kitchen string; place in a shallow dish. Cover and chill in the refrigerator for at least 8 hours or up to 24 hours. Cover and refrigerate the remaining 3 chopped jalapeño peppers.

three In a small bowl combine melted butter, the remaining jalapeño peppers, and the remaining ¼ teaspoon salt. For a charcoal grill, arrange medium-hot coals around a drip pan. Test for medium heat above the pan. Place meat on grill rack over drip pan. Cover and grill for 30 to 45 minutes or until meat juices run clear (160°F), brushing occasionally with butter mixture during the first 20 minutes of grilling. (For a gas grill, preheat grill. Reduce heat to medium. Adjust for indirect cooking. Place meat on a rack in a roasting pan, place on the grill rack, and grill as above.) Discard any remaining butter mixture.

four Remove meat from grill. Cover with foil; let stand for 10 minutes. Remove string from meat. Slice meat. Sprinkle with black pepper and additional salt.

NUTRITION FACTS PER SERVING: 260 cal., 16 g total fat (9 g sat. fat), 106 mg chol., 543 mg sodium, 4 g carbo., 1 g fiber, 25 g pro.

*NOTE: Because chile peppers contain volatile oils that can burn your skin and eyes, avoid direct contact with them as much as possible. When working with chile peppers, wear plastic or rubber gloves. If your bare hands do touch the chile peppers, wash your hands and nails well with soap and warm water.

pork chops with grilled vegetables

Season the chops with your choice of lemon-pepper seasoning or garlic-pepper seasoning.

PREP: 20 minutes **GRILL:** 35 minutes **MAKES:** 4 servings

4	pork loin chops, cut 1¼ inches thick
2	teaspoons olive oil
1	teaspoon lemon-pepper seasoning or garlic-pepper seasoning
⅓	cup plain low-fat yogurt
1¼	teaspoons snipped fresh thyme or rosemary
¼	teaspoon salt
¼	teaspoon ground black pepper
1	medium Vidalia or other sweet onion, cut into ½-inch slices
1	green or yellow sweet pepper, seeded and cut into quarters
4	plum tomatoes, halved lengthwise
1	tablespoon balsamic vinegar
1	tablespoon olive oil

one Trim fat from chops. Brush chops on both sides with the 2 teaspoons oil; sprinkle with lemon-pepper seasoning. In a small bowl combine yogurt, ¾ teaspoon of the thyme, ⅛ teaspoon of the salt, and ⅛ teaspoon of the black pepper. Cover and chill yogurt mixture.

two For a charcoal grill, arrange medium-hot coals around a drip pan. Test for medium heat above pan. Place chops on grill rack over drip pan. Cover and grill for 35 to 40 minutes or until meat juices run clear (160°F). Place onions on grill rack directly over coals for the last 15 minutes of grilling or until crisp-tender, turning once. Place sweet peppers and tomatoes directly over coals for the last 5 to 8 minutes of grilling or until peppers are crisp-tender and tomatoes begin to soften, turning once. (For a gas grill, preheat grill. Reduce heat to medium. Adjust for indirect cooking. Grill chops, onion, and peppers as above.)

three Meanwhile, in a large bowl combine vinegar, the 1 tablespoon olive oil, the remaining ½ teaspoon thyme, the remaining ⅛ teaspoon salt, and the remaining ⅛ teaspoon black pepper. Add onions, sweet peppers, and tomatoes; toss gently to coat. To serve, spoon vegetables over chops. Serve with yogurt mixture.

NUTRITION FACTS PER SERVING: 225 cal., 13 g total fat (4 g sat. fat), 64 mg chol., 353 mg sodium, 2 g carbo., 1 g fiber, 22 g pro.

south carolina barbecued chops

Even from region to region within a state, the way meat is barbecued is different—and so are the sauces. True to form, this simmered South Carolina-style sauce is sweet, mustardy, and the color of sunshine.

PREP: 20 minutes **GRILL:** 25 minutes **MAKES:** 4 servings

4	boneless pork top loin chops, cut 1 to 1¼ inches thick
⅓	cup yellow mustard
⅓	cup red wine vinegar
4	teaspoons brown sugar
1	tablespoon butter or margarine
1	teaspoon Worcestershire sauce
½	teaspoon freshly ground black pepper
¼	to ½ teaspoon bottled hot pepper sauce

one Trim fat from pork chops; set chops aside. For sauce, in a small saucepan whisk together mustard, vinegar, brown sugar, butter, Worcestershire sauce, black pepper, and hot pepper sauce. Bring to boiling; reduce heat. Simmer, uncovered, for 5 minutes; remove from heat. Cool slightly. Set aside half of the sauce to serve with chops.

two For charcoal grill, arrange medium-hot coals around drip pan. Test for medium heat above the pan. Place chops on grill rack over drip pan. Cover and grill for 25 to 35 minutes or until meat juices run clear (160°F), turning and brushing once with remaining sauce halfway through grilling. (For a gas grill, preheat grill. Reduce heat to medium. Adjust for indirect cooking. Grill as above.) Discard remainder of sauce used for brushing chops. Serve the pork chops with reserved sauce.

NUTRITION FACTS PER SERVING: 356 cal., 19 g total fat (6 g sat. fat), 107 mg chol., 379 mg sodium, 4 g carbo., 0 g fiber, 37 g pro.

zesty chops

In Midwestern states, thick-cut pork top loin chops are sometimes called Iowa chops. Elsewhere, the boneless version may be called America's cut. No matter what they're called, these slow-cooked beauties will impress your family and friends.

PREP: 5 minutes **GRILL:** 18 minutes **MAKES:** 4 servings

- 4   12- to 14-ounce pork top loin chops, cut 1¼ to 1½ inches thick

     Bottled Italian salad dressing

- 1   recipe Rice Pilaf (optional)

one For a charcoal grill, grill chops on the rack of an uncovered grill directly over medium coals for 18 to 22 minutes or until meat juices run clear (160°F), turning once and brushing frequently with Italian dressing during the last 5 minutes of grilling. (For a gas grill, preheat grill. Reduce heat to medium. Place chops on grill rack over heat. Cover and grill as above.)

two Pass additional Italian dressing with the chops. If desired, serve with Rice Pilaf.

NUTRITION FACTS PER SERVING: 510 cal., 27 g total fat (7 g sat. fat), 148 mg chol., 342 mg sodium, 3 g carbo., 0 g fiber, 60 g pro.

rice pilaf: In a medium saucepan melt 1 tablespoon butter or margarine over medium heat. Add ½ cup chopped onion, ½ cup sliced fresh mushrooms, ¼ cup chopped celery, and ½ teaspoon bottled minced garlic (1 clove); cook until tender. Carefully stir in 1½ cups water, ¾ cup uncooked long grain rice, 1½ teaspoons instant chicken bouillon granules, and ¼ teaspoon ground black pepper. Bring to boiling; reduce heat. Cover and simmer about 15 minutes or until rice is tender and liquid is absorbed. Makes 4 servings.

savory pork steaks

What an unlikely combination! Italian salad dressing, beer, maple syrup, and barbecue sauce create a marinade for these pork shoulder steaks. The result is a savory-sweet entrée that's sure to please.

PREP: 10 minutes **MARINATE:** 6 to 24 hours **GRILL:** 15 minutes
MAKES: 5 to 7 servings

1	8-ounce bottle zesty Italian salad dressing
¾	cup lemon juice
¾	cup beer
⅔	cup maple syrup
½	cup bottled barbecue sauce
⅓	cup dried minced onion
1½	teaspoons bottled minced garlic (3 cloves)
5	to 7 pork shoulder steaks, cut ¾ inch thick (4½ to 5 pounds total)

one For the marinade, in a medium bowl stir together salad dressing, lemon juice, beer, maple syrup, barbecue sauce, dried minced onion, and garlic.

two Place the pork steaks in a resealable plastic bag set in a very large bowl. Pour marinade over steaks. Seal bag; turn to coat steaks. Marinate in refrigerator for at least 6 hours or up to 24 hours, turning bag occasionally.

three Drain, discarding marinade. For a charcoal grill, grill steaks on the rack of an uncovered grill directly over medium coals for 15 to 20 minutes or until juices run clear (160°F), turning steaks once halfway through grilling. (For a gas grill, preheat grill. Reduce heat to medium. Place pork steaks on grill rack over heat. Cover and grill as above.)

NUTRITION FACTS PER SERVING: 438 cal., 20 g total fat (6 g sat. fat), 147 mg chol., 358 mg sodium, 15 g carbo., 0 g fiber, 46 g pro.

polish sausage foil dinner

Try this recipe with slices of smoked turkey kielbasa, smoked Italian sausage with fennel, or your favorite smoked sausage. If you want to serve more than one person, increase the ingredients and make a packet for each serving.

PREP: 5 minutes **GRILL:** 15 minutes **STAND:** 5 minutes **MAKES:** 1 serving

- 1 cup frozen loose-pack diced hash brown potatoes with onion and peppers, thawed
- 3 ounces smoked sausage, sliced (½ cup)
- 1 tablespoon bottled Italian salad dressing
- 2 tablespoons shredded cheddar cheese

one Fold a 24×12-inch piece of heavy foil in half to make a 12-inch square. Place potatoes and sausage in center of the foil square. Drizzle Italian salad dressing over potatoes and sausage. Bring up 2 opposite edges of foil; seal with a double fold. Fold remaining edges to completely enclose the mixture, leaving space for steam to build.

two For a charcoal grill, grill packet on the rack of an uncovered grill directly over medium coals about 15 minutes or until potatoes are tender, turning once. (For a gas grill, preheat grill. Reduce heat to medium. Place packet on grill rack over heat. Cover and grill as above.)

three Remove from grill; carefully open packet. Sprinkle mixture with cheese. Reseal packet; let stand about 5 minutes or until cheese is melted.

NUTRITION FACTS PER SERVING: 577 cal., 40 g total fat (14 g sat. fat), 73 mg chol., 1,499 mg sodium, 29 g carbo., 0 g fiber, 25 g pro.

barbecued baby back bibs

A rub featuring paprika, garlic salt, onion powder, sage, celery seeds, and cayenne pepper spices up these pork loin back ribs.

PREP: 15 minutes **GRILL:** 1½ hours **MAKES:** 8 servings

3½	to 4 pounds pork loin back ribs
1	tablespoon paprika
1½	teaspoons garlic salt
1	teaspoon onion powder
1	teaspoon dried sage, crushed
½	teaspoon celery seeds
¼	teaspoon cayenne pepper
½	cup apple juice or apple cider

one Trim fat from ribs. For rub, in a small bowl combine paprika, garlic salt, onion powder, sage, celery seeds, and cayenne pepper. Sprinkle evenly over both sides of ribs; rub in with your fingers.

two For a charcoal grill, arrange medium-hot coals around drip pan. Test for medium heat above the pan. Place ribs, bone sides down, on grill rack over pan. (Or place ribs in a rib rack; place on grill rack.) Cover and grill for 1½ to 1¾ hours or until tender, brushing occasionally with apple juice after the first hour of grilling. Add coals as necessary to maintain heat. (For a gas grill, preheat grill. Reduce heat to medium. Adjust for indirect cooking. Place ribs in a roasting pan, place on grill rack, and grill as above.)

NUTRITION FACTS PER SERVING: 324 cal., 14 g total fat (5 g sat. fat), 94 mg chol., 253 mg sodium, 3 g carbo., 0 g fiber, 43 g pro.

maple-glazed country ribs

If you have a grill rack, use it to hold the ribs
for grilling.

PREP: 15 minutes **GRILL:** 1½ hours **MAKES:** 4 servings

½	cup apple jelly
½	cup pure maple syrup or maple-flavored syrup
1	tablespoon cider vinegar
1	tablespoon coarse-grain brown mustard
½	teaspoon bottled minced garlic (1 clove)
2½	to 3 pounds pork country-style ribs

one For sauce, in a small saucepan combine apple jelly, maple syrup, vinegar, mustard, and garlic. Bring to boiling; reduce heat. Simmer, uncovered, about 10 minutes or until desired consistency, stirring frequently. Remove from heat. Trim fat from ribs.

two For a charcoal grill, arrange medium-hot coals around a drip pan. Test for medium heat above the pan. Place ribs, bone sides down, on grill rack over drip pan. (Or place ribs in a rib rack; place on grill rack.) Cover and grill for 1½ to 2 hours or until ribs are tender, brushing occasionally with sauce during the last 10 minutes of grilling. Add coals as necessary to maintain heat. (For a gas grill, preheat grill. Reduce heat to medium. Adjust for indirect cooking. Place ribs in a roasting pan, place on grill rack, and grill as above.) Pass remaining sauce with ribs.

NUTRITION FACTS PER SERVING: 572 cal., 21 g total fat (7 g sat. fat), 98 mg chol., 155 mg sodium, 53 g carbo., 0 g fiber, 41 g pro.

apple-glazed pork kabobs

There's a hint of cinnamon and cloves in the sweet jelly-based glaze used on the kabobs.

PREP: 20 minutes **GRILL:** 12 minutes **MAKES:** 4 servings

8	12-inch wooden skewers
1	cup apple jelly
2	tablespoons honey
2	tablespoons lemon juice
2	tablespoons butter or margarine
1	teaspoon ground cinnamon
¼	teaspoon ground cloves
1	pound boneless pork loin, cut into 1-inch cubes
1	teaspoon garlic powder
½	teaspoon celery salt
½	to 1 teaspoon ground black pepper
1	large onion, cut into 1-inch pieces
2	large green sweet peppers, cut into 1-inch pieces
1	tablespoon olive oil

one In a shallow dish soak wooden skewers in enough warm water to cover for 30 minutes. In a small saucepan combine apple jelly, honey, lemon juice, butter, cinnamon, and cloves. Bring to boiling; reduce heat. Simmer, uncovered, 4 to 5 minutes or until of glaze consistency, stirring frequently.

two Sprinkle pork with garlic powder, celery salt, and black pepper. Thread pork, onion, and sweet peppers alternately onto soaked skewers, leaving ¼-inch space between pieces. Drizzle with oil.

three For a charcoal grill, place kabobs on grill rack directly over medium coals for 12 to 15 minutes or until meat juices run clear and vegetables are tender, turning frequently and brushing with glaze after 6 minutes of grilling. (For a gas grill, preheat grill. Reduce heat to medium. Place kabobs on grill rack over heat. Cover and grill as above.)

NUTRITION FACTS PER SERVING: 521 cal., 15 g total fat (6 g sat. fat), 83 mg chol., 266 mg sodium, 73 g carbo., 3 g fiber, 26 g pro.

blackberry-glazed smoked ham

At your next family reunion or for a neighborhood block party, serve this smoky ham dressed up with a blackberry-and-mustard brush-on.

PREP: 10 minutes **GRILL:** 2¼ hours **STAND:** 15 minutes
MAKES: 20 to 28 servings

1	6- to 8-pound cooked ham shank
1½	cups seedless blackberry jam or other seedless berry jam
¼	cup coarse-grain brown mustard
2	tablespoons balsamic vinegar

one Score ham on both sides in a diamond pattern by cutting diagonally at 1-inch intervals.

two For a charcoal grill, arrange medium coals around edge of grill, leaving center of grill without coals. Test for medium-low heat above center of grill (not over coals). Place ham on a rack in a roasting pan. Place pan on grill rack over center of grill (not over coals). Cover and grill for 2 to 2½ hours or until heated through (135°F). Add coals as necessary to maintain heat. (For a gas grill, preheat grill. Reduce heat to medium-low. Adjust for indirect cooking. Place ham on rack in a roasting pan; place on grill rack. Cover and grill as above.)

three Meanwhile, for berry sauce, in a medium saucepan stir together jam, mustard, and vinegar. Bring just to boiling; reduce heat. Simmer, uncovered, for 5 minutes.

four Brush ham with some of the sauce. Cover and grill for 15 minutes more, brushing once or twice with sauce. Remove ham from grill. Cover with foil; let stand for 15 minutes before carving. The meat's temperature after standing should be 140°F.

five To serve, slice ham. Reheat any remaining sauce until bubbly and pass with ham.

NUTRITION FACTS PER SERVING: 210 cal., 6 g total fat (2 g sat. fat), 51 mg chol., 1,202 mg sodium, 19 g carbo., 0 g fiber, 20 g pro.

down island burgers

Grilled onions and a mango-mayonnaise sauce top the subtly spiced pork burgers.

PREP: 25 minutes **GRILL:** 14 minutes **MAKES:** 6 servings

1½	pounds ground pork
2	tablespoons dry white wine or water
1	to 2 tablespoons bottled hot pepper sauce
2	tablespoons fine dry bread crumbs
3	to 4 teaspoons grated fresh ginger
3	to 4 teaspoons curry powder
2	teaspoons bottled minced garlic (4 cloves)
½	teaspoon salt
½	teaspoon ground allspice
6	¼-inch slices sweet onion (such as Vidalia or Maui)
6	hamburger buns, split
	Lettuce leaves or 1 bunch stemmed watercress
1	recipe Mango Mayonnaise

one In a large bowl combine pork, wine, hot pepper sauce, bread crumbs, ginger, curry powder, garlic, salt, and allspice; mix well. Shape into six ¾-inch-thick patties.

two For a charcoal grill, grill patties and onion slices on the rack of an uncovered grill directly over medium coals for 14 to 18 minutes or until meat is done (160°F)* and onions are crisp-tender, turning once halfway through grilling. (For a gas grill, preheat grill. Reduce heat to medium. Place patties and onions on grill rack over heat. Cover and grill as above.)

three For the last 2 minutes of grilling, place buns, cut sides down, on grill to toast.

four To serve, place lettuce leaves on bottom halves of buns. Top with burgers, onion slices, and Mango Mayonnaise. Add bun tops.

NUTRITION FACTS PER SERVING: 360 cal., 18 g total fat (5 g sat. fat), 56 mg chol., 590 mg sodium, 29 g carbo., 2 g fiber, 19 g pro.

*NOTE: The internal color of a burger is not a reliable doneness indicator. A pork patty cooked to 160°F is safe, regardless of color. To measure the doneness of a patty, insert an instant-read thermometer through the side of the patty to a depth of 2 to 3 inches.

mango mayonnaise: In a small bowl stir together ¼ cup mayonnaise, salad dressing, or fat-free mayonnaise dressing; ½ cup finely chopped mango or sliced peaches; and 2 tablespoons lime juice. Cover and refrigerate until serving time.

honey-mustard pork sandwiches

Stirred together straight from the jars, Dijon-style mustard and honey create a glossy, hot-sweet sauce that clings to pork.

PREP: 10 minutes **GRILL:** 12 minutes **MAKES:** 4 servings

1	1-pound pork tenderloin
	Ground black pepper
2	tablespoons honey
2	tablespoons Dijon-style mustard
4	kaiser rolls or hamburger buns, split and toasted
¼	cup mayonnaise or salad dressing
4	tomato slices

one Trim fat from meat. Cut meat into ¾-inch slices. Sprinkle with pepper. For glaze, in a small bowl combine honey and mustard; set aside.

two For a charcoal grill, grill meat on the rack of an uncovered grill directly over medium coals for 12 to 15 minutes or until meat juices run clear (160°F), turning and brushing once with honey-mustard mixture halfway through grilling. (For a gas grill, preheat grill. Reduce heat to medium. Place meat on grill rack over heat. Cover and grill as above.) Discard any remaining honey-mustard mixture.

three To serve, spread cut sides of toasted rolls with mayonnaise. Top bottoms of rolls with meat and tomato slices.

NUTRITION FACTS PER SERVING: 459 cal., 18 g total fat (3 g sat. fat), 89 mg chol., 639 mg sodium, 41 g carbo., 0 g fiber, 32 g pro.

brats deluxe

The sauerkraut-onion topping is equally delicious on Polish sausage.

PREP: 15 minutes **COOK:** 20 minutes **GRILL:** 20 minutes
MAKES: 10 servings

10	uncooked bratwursts (about 4 ounces each)
2	medium onions, halved and thinly sliced
1	tablespoon cooking oil
1	32-ounce jar sauerkraut, undrained
1	12-ounce can beer
10	hoagie buns, split and toasted (optional)
	Mustard (optional)

one Pierce bratwursts in several places with tines of fork. For a charcoal grill, arrange medium-hot coals around a drip pan. Test for medium heat above the pan. Place brats on grill rack over drip pan. Cover and grill for 20 to 30 minutes or until meat juices run clear (160°F),* turning occasionally. (For a gas grill, preheat grill. Reduce heat to medium. Adjust for indirect cooking. Grill as above.)

two Meanwhile, in a Dutch oven cook onions in hot oil until tender. Stir in sauerkraut and beer. Bring to boiling; reduce heat. Simmer, uncovered, for 20 minutes. Add cooked bratwursts; heat through.

three If desired, serve bratwursts on hoagie buns with mustard. Serve with the sauerkraut mixture.

NUTRITION FACTS PER SERVING: 430 cal., 35 g total fat (17 g sat. fat), 68 mg chol., 1,421 mg sodium, 9 g carbo., 3 g fiber, 15 g pro.

*NOTE: The internal color of a fresh bratwurst is not a reliable doneness indicator. A bratwurst cooked to 160°F is safe, regardless of color. To measure the doneness of a bratwurst, insert an instant-read thermometer from an end into the center of the bratwurst.

picnic hot dog platter

Setting out a platter loaded with a variety of hot dogs and sausages will please everyone at your gathering.

PREP: 10 minutes **GRILL:** 20 minutes (fresh) or 10 minutes (cooked)
MAKES: 12 servings

- 12   frankfurters, uncooked bratwursts, smoked pork sausages, veal sausages, turkey sausages, vegetarian frankfurters, and/or other favorites
- 1   dozen frankfurter or bratwurst buns or French-style rolls, split
- 1   recipe Tart Apple Mustard, 1 recipe Bacon Brown-Sugar Mustard, and/or 1 recipe Tomato Mustard

  Desired condiments (such as chopped pickled peppers, sliced tomatoes, pickle relish, and/or crumbled cooked bacon) (optional)

one Pierce uncooked sausages all over with a fork.

two For a charcoal grill, arrange medium-hot coals around a drip pan. Test for medium heat above the pan. Place uncooked sausages on grill rack over drip pan. Cover and grill for 20 to 30 minutes or until meat is done (160°F),* turning once halfway through grilling. Add frankfurters and cooked sausage to the grill after the first 10 minutes; grill until heated through, turning once. (For a gas grill, preheat grill. Reduce heat to medium. Adjust for indirect cooking. Grill as above.) Serve with buns and desired mustards and condiments.

NUTRITION FACTS PER FRANKFURTER WITH BUN AND 1 TABLESPOON TART APPLE MUSTARD: 281 cal., 16 g total fat (6 g sat. fat), 24 mg chol., 757 mg sodium, 24 g carbo., 1 g fiber, 9 g pro.

*NOTE: The internal color of an uncooked sausage is not a reliable doneness indicator. A sausage cooked to 160°F is safe, regardless of color. To measure doneness, insert instant-read thermometer from end into center of sausage.

tart apple mustard: Stir together ½ cup honey mustard; 2 tablespoons shredded, unpeeled tart green apple; and ½ teaspoon ground black pepper. Cover; refrigerate at least 2 hours or up to 24 hours.

MAKES: About ⅔ cup.

NUTRITION FACTS PER TABLESPOON: 23 cal., 0 g total fat (0 g sat. fat), 0 mg chol., 11 mg sodium, 5 g carbo., 0 g fiber, 0 g pro.

bacon brown-sugar mustard: Stir together ¾ cup yellow mustard; 3 slices bacon, crisp-cooked, drained, and finely crumbled; and 4 teaspoons brown sugar. Cover; refrigerate at least 8 hours or up to 2 days.

MAKES: 1 cup.

NUTRITION FACTS PER TABLESPOON: 22 cal., 1 g total fat (0 g sat. fat), 1 mg chol., 161 mg sodium, 1 g carbo., 0 g fiber, 1 g pro.

tomato mustard: Stir together ⅓ cup creamy Dijon-style mustard blend and ½ teaspoon dry mustard. Gently stir in ½ cup peeled, seeded, and chopped tomatoes. Cover; refrigerate for up to 24 hours.

MAKES: About ⅔ cup.

NUTRITION FACTS PER TABLESPOON: 20 cal., 2 g total fat (0 g sat. fat), 0 mg chol., 102 mg sodium, 2 g carbo., 0 g fiber, 0 g pro.

garlic-studded veal chops & asparagus

The grilled asparagus also pairs well with grilled chicken or pork.

PREP: 15 minutes **STAND:** 30 minutes **GRILL:** 11 minutes + 3 minutes
MAKES: 4 servings

- 1 pound fresh asparagus spears
- 2 tablespoons dry sherry
- 2 tablespoons olive oil
- ½ teaspoon bottled minced garlic (1 clove)
- 4 boneless veal top loin chops, cut ¾ inch thick
- 3 or 4 cloves garlic, cut into thin slivers
- 1 tablespoon snipped fresh thyme or 1 teaspoon dried thyme, crushed
- ⅛ teaspoon salt
- ⅛ teaspoon ground black pepper

one Snap off and discard woody stems from asparagus spears. In a medium skillet bring a small amount of water to boiling; add asparagus. Cover and simmer about 3 minutes or until crisp-tender; drain. Place asparagus in a resealable plastic bag; add sherry, 1 tablespoon of the olive oil, and the minced garlic. Let stand at room temperature for 30 minutes.

two Meanwhile, trim fat from chops. With the tip of a sharp knife, make a few small slits in each veal chop; insert garlic slivers in slits. In a small bowl combine the remaining 1 tablespoon olive oil, the thyme, salt, and pepper; brush over chops.

three For a charcoal grill, grill chops on the rack of an uncovered grill directly over medium coals for 11 to 13 minutes or until medium doneness (160°F), turning once halfway through grilling.

four Add asparagus spears to grill (lay spears perpendicular to wires on grill rack so they won't fall into coals). Grill for 3 to 4 minutes or until crisp-tender and lightly browned, turning occasionally. (For a gas grill, preheat the grill. Reduce heat to medium. Place chops, then asparagus on grill rack over heat. Cover and grill as above.) Serve asparagus with chops.

NUTRITION FACTS PER SERVING: 237 cal., 11 g total fat (3 g sat. fat), 92 mg chol., 131 mg sodium, 5 g carbo., 2 g fiber, 27 g pro.

sweet & sour veal chops

Orange juice and vinegar, with the flavorful additions of ginger and cinnamon, become the perfect marinade for these veal chops. Toasted sesame oil, either drizzled or brushed over the chops after grilling, adds a delicious finishing touch.

PREP: 15 minutes **MARINATE:** 2 hours **GRILL:** 12 minutes
MAKES: 4 servings

4	veal loin chops, cut 1 inch thick (about 2 pounds total)
½	cup frozen orange juice concentrate, thawed
½	cup rice vinegar or cider vinegar
3	tablespoons olive oil or peanut oil
2	tablespoons soy sauce
2	tablespoons grated fresh ginger
2	teaspoons bottled minced garlic (4 cloves)
¼	teaspoon ground cinnamon
½	teaspoon toasted sesame oil
	Freshly ground black pepper

one Trim fat from veal chops. Place veal chops in a resealable plastic bag set in a shallow dish. For marinade, in a small bowl combine orange juice concentrate, vinegar, oil, soy sauce, ginger, garlic, and cinnamon. Pour marinade over veal chops. Seal bag; turn to coat veal chops. Marinate in the refrigerator for 2 hours, turning bag occasionally.

two Drain veal chops, reserving marinade. For a charcoal grill, grill veal chops on the rack of an uncovered grill directly over medium coals for 12 to 15 minutes or until juices run clear (160°F), turning once and brushing occasionally with reserved marinade during the first 15 minutes of grilling. (For a gas grill, preheat grill. Reduce heat to medium. Place veal chops on grill rack over heat. Cover and grill as above.) Discard any remaining marinade.

three To serve, brush veal chops with sesame oil and sprinkle with freshly ground black pepper.

NUTRITION FACTS PER SERVING: 345 cal., 17 g total fat (4 g sat. fat), 135 mg chol., 511 mg sodium, 13 g carbo., 0 g fiber, 35 g pro.

greek lamb chops

Grilled tomatoes, sliced and tossed with a kalamata olive and feta cheese mixture, add an authentic Greek touch to the lamb.

PREP: 20 minutes **MARINATE:** 8 to 24 hours **GRILL:** 14 minutes
MAKES: 6 servings

6	lamb sirloin chops, cut ¾ to 1 inch thick
1	tablespoon finely shredded lemon peel
⅔	cup lemon juice
6	tablespoons olive oil
⅓	cup snipped fresh oregano
½	teaspoon salt
⅛	teaspoon ground black pepper
½	cup snipped fresh parsley
½	cup crumbled feta cheese (2 ounces)
¼	cup pitted sliced kalamata olives
¼	teaspoon ground cinnamon
¼	teaspoon ground black pepper
2	pounds plum tomatoes

one Place lamb chops in a resealable plastic bag set in a shallow dish. For marinade, in a medium bowl stir together the lemon peel, half of the lemon juice, 4 tablespoons of the oil, the oregano, salt, and the ⅛ teaspoon pepper. Pour marinade over lamb. Seal bag; turn to coat meat. Marinate in the refrigerator for at least 8 hours or up to 24 hours, turning bag occasionally.

two In a large bowl combine remaining ⅓ cup lemon juice, 1 tablespoon of the remaining oil, the parsley, feta cheese, olives, cinnamon, and the ¼ teaspoon pepper; set aside.

three Drain lamb chops, discarding marinade. Brush tomatoes with the remaining 1 tablespoon oil. For charcoal grill, grill lamb chops on the rack of an uncovered grill directly over medium coals for 14 to 17 minutes or until lamb is medium doneness (160°F), turning once halfway through grilling. Grill tomatoes alongside lamb chops for last 8 to 10 minutes of grilling or until tomatoes are slightly charred, turning once. (For a gas grill, preheat grill. Reduce heat to medium. Place lamb, then tomatoes on the grill rack over heat. Cover and grill as above.)

four Transfer tomatoes to cutting board; cool slightly and slice. Toss sliced tomatoes with the feta cheese mixture; serve with the lamb.

NUTRITION FACTS PER SERVING: 263 cal., 15 g total fat (4 g sat. fat), 72 mg chol., 292 mg sodium, 10 g carbo., 2 g fiber, 23 g pro.

lamb chops with mint marinade

Lamb and mint are longtime partners. Fresh mint in this marinade is a refreshing change from the traditional mint jelly.

PREP: 10 minutes **MARINATE:** 30 minutes to 24 hours **GRILL:** 12 minutes
MAKES: 4 servings

8	lamb loin chops, cut 1 inch thick (about 2 pounds total)
2	tablespoons lemon juice
2	tablespoons olive oil
¼	cup snipped fresh mint
1½	teaspoons bottled minced garlic (3 cloves)
¼	teaspoon ground black pepper
¼	teaspoon salt

one Trim fat from chops. Place chops in a resealable plastic bag set in a shallow dish. For marinade, combine lemon juice, oil, 3 tablespoons of the mint, the garlic, and pepper. Pour marinade over the chops. Seal bag; turn to coat chops. Marinate in the refrigerator for at least 30 minutes or up to 24 hours.

two Drain chops, discarding marinade. Sprinkle chops with the salt. For charcoal grill, grill chops on rack of an uncovered grill directly over medium coals until desired doneness, turning once halfway through grilling. Allow 12 to 14 minutes for medium-rare doneness (145°F) or 15 to 17 minutes for medium doneness (160°F). (For a gas grill, preheat grill. Reduce heat to medium. Place chops on grill rack over heat. Cover and grill as above.) Sprinkle with remaining 1 tablespoon mint.

NUTRITION FACTS PER SERVING: 310 cal., 18 g total fat (5 g sat. fat), 107 mg chol., 229 mg sodium, 2 g carbo., 0 g fiber, 34 g pro.

aloha chicken

Marinate chicken with the island seasonings of soy and ginger, then grill.

PREP: 15 minutes **MARINATE:** 4 to 24 hours **GRILL:** 50 minutes
MAKES: 6 servings

3	whole large chicken breasts (about 4 pounds total), halved lengthwise
1/3	cup soy sauce
1/4	cup packed brown sugar
1/4	cup sliced green onions
2	tablespoons grated fresh ginger
2	teaspoons bottled minced garlic (4 cloves)

one Skin chicken, if desired. Place chicken in a resealable plastic bag set in a shallow dish. For marinade, in a small bowl combine soy sauce, brown sugar, green onions, ginger, and garlic. Pour marinade over chicken. Seal bag; turn to coat chicken. Marinate in refrigerator for at least 4 hours or up to 24 hours, turning bag occasionally.

two Drain chicken, discarding marinade.

three For a charcoal grill, arrange medium-hot coals around drip pan. Test for medium heat above the pan. Place chicken, bone sides down, on grill rack over the drip pan. Cover and grill for 50 to 60 minutes or until chicken is no longer pink (170°F). Watch chicken closely because the sweet marinade may cause overbrowning. (For a gas grill, preheat grill. Reduce heat to medium. Adjust for indirect cooking. Grill as above.)

NUTRITION FACTS PER SERVING: 310 cal., 17 g total fat (5 g sat. fat), 113 mg chol., 299 mg sodium, 2 g carbo., 0 g fiber, 35 g pro.

apricot-and-mustard-glazed chicken

Apricot spreadable fruit is the foundation for this glaze, while rosemary and mustard add interesting flavor.

PREP: 15 minutes **GRILL:** 50 minutes **MAKES:** 6 servings

½	cup apricot spreadable fruit
1	tablespoon white vinegar
1	tablespoon Dijon-style mustard
1	tablespoon snipped fresh rosemary or 1 teaspoon dried rosemary, crushed
1	teaspoon bottled minced garlic (2 cloves)
¼	teaspoon ground black pepper
3	whole medium chicken breasts (about 3 pounds total), halved lengthwise

one For glaze, in a small saucepan combine spreadable fruit, vinegar, mustard, rosemary, garlic, and pepper. Cook and stir over low heat until heated through. Remove from heat.

two For a charcoal grill, arrange medium-hot coals around a drip pan. Test for medium heat above the pan. Place chicken, skin sides down, on grill rack over drip pan. Cover and grill for 50 to 60 minutes or until chicken is no longer pink (170°F), brushing with some of the glaze during the last 15 minutes of grilling. (For a gas grill, preheat grill. Reduce heat to medium. Adjust for indirect cooking. Grill as above.)

NUTRITION FACTS PER SERVING: 255 cal., 8 g total fat (2 g sat. fat), 83 mg chol., 132 mg sodium, 17 g carbo., 0 g fiber, 29 g pro.

chicken caribbean

Experience the islands without venturing from your patio. Fresh basil (try cinnamon basil if you can find it) infuses aroma and peppery-clove flavor into the slightly sweet coconut-orange sauce—perfect with the spicy jerk-seasoned grilled chicken.

PREP: 10 minutes **GRILL:** 12 minutes **MAKES:** 4 servings

4	skinless, boneless chicken breast halves (about 1¼ pounds total)
½	teaspoon Jamaican jerk seasoning
½	cup purchased unsweetened coconut milk*
¼	cup orange juice
2	tablespoons snipped fresh basil
1	teaspoon finely shredded orange peel (optional)
2	cups hot cooked rice

one Rub both sides of chicken with jerk seasoning. For a charcoal grill, grill chicken on the rack of an uncovered grill directly over medium coals for 12 to 15 minutes or until chicken is no longer pink (170°F), turning once halfway through grilling. (For a gas grill, preheat grill. Reduce heat to medium. Place chicken on grill rack over heat. Cover and grill as above.)

two Meanwhile, for sauce, in a small saucepan combine coconut milk, orange juice, and 1 tablespoon of the basil. Bring to boiling; reduce heat. Simmer, uncovered, about 5 minutes or until reduced to ½ cup.

three If desired, stir the orange peel into cooked rice. Serve chicken and sauce over rice. Sprinkle with the remaining 1 tablespoon basil.

NUTRITION FACTS PER SERVING: 319 cal., 9 g total fat (6 g sat. fat), 75 mg chol., 100 mg sodium, 25 g carbo., 0 g fiber, 31 g pro.

*NOTE: Look for canned coconut milk in the Asian food section of your supermarket or at an Asian specialty store.

chicken with corn salsa

During the summer, use fresh corn for the salsa. Just cut enough corn off the cobs to measure 2 cups of kernels.

PREP: 30 minutes **MARINATE:** 2 to 4 hours **GRILL:** 12 minutes
MAKES: 6 servings

6	skinless, boneless chicken breast halves (about 2 pounds total)
½	cup light beer
1	tablespoon reduced-sodium soy sauce
1	tablespoon snipped fresh cilantro
2	teaspoons lime juice
2	teaspoons finely chopped seeded fresh jalapeño chile pepper*
1	10-ounce package frozen whole kernel corn, thawed (2 cups)
¼	cup chopped red onion
¼	cup chopped red sweet pepper
¼	cup snipped fresh cilantro
2	tablespoons lime juice
2	tablespoons finely chopped seeded fresh jalapeño chile pepper*
½	teaspoon salt

one Place chicken in a resealable plastic bag set in a shallow dish. For marinade, in a small bowl combine the beer, soy sauce, the 1 tablespoon cilantro, the 2 teaspoons lime juice, and the 2 teaspoons jalapeño pepper. Pour marinade over the chicken. Seal bag; turn to coat chicken. Marinate in the refrigerator for at least 2 hours or up to 4 hours, turning bag occasionally.

two Meanwhile, for corn salsa, in a small bowl combine corn, red onion, sweet pepper, the ¼ cup cilantro, the 2 tablespoons lime juice, the 2 tablespoons jalapeño pepper, and the salt. Cover; refrigerate for at least 2 hours or up to 4 hours. Remove corn salsa from refrigerator about 30 minutes before serving.

three Drain chicken, discarding marinade. For a charcoal grill, grill chicken on the rack of an uncovered grill directly over medium coals for 12 to 15 minutes or until chicken is no longer pink (170°F), turning once halfway through grilling. (For a gas grill, preheat grill. Reduce heat to medium. Place chicken on grill rack over heat. Cover and grill as above.) Serve with corn salsa.

NUTRITION FACTS PER SERVING: 215 cal., 5 g total fat (1 g sat. fat), 81 mg chol., 277 mg sodium, 12 g carbo., 1 g fiber, 32 g pro.

*NOTE: Because chile peppers contain volatile oils that can burn your skin and eyes, avoid direct contact with them as much as possible. When working with chile peppers, wear plastic or rubber gloves. If your bare hands do touch the chile peppers, wash your hands and nails well with soap and warm water.

honey-rosemary chicken

Opt for bone-in or boneless chicken breasts. The honey, mustard, and herb marinade is great with either choice.

PREP: 20 minutes **MARINATE:** 4 to 24 hours **GRILL:** 50 minutes
MAKES: 8 servings

⅓	cup honey
¼	cup olive oil
2	tablespoons coarse-grain mustard
1½	teaspoons bottled minced garlic (3 cloves)
1	tablespoon snipped fresh rosemary
2	teaspoons lemon juice
½	teaspoon salt
¼	teaspoon ground black pepper
4	whole medium chicken breasts (about 4 pounds total), halved lengthwise, or 8 skinless, boneless chicken breast halves

one For marinade, in a small bowl combine honey, olive oil, mustard, garlic, rosemary, lemon juice, salt, and pepper.

two If desired, skin bone-in chicken. Place chicken in a resealable plastic bag set in a shallow dish. Pour marinade over chicken. Seal bag; turn to coat chicken. Marinate in the refrigerator for at least 4 hours or up to 24 hours, turning bag occasionally.

three Drain chicken, reserving marinade. For a charcoal grill, arrange medium-hot coals around a drip pan. Test for medium heat above the pan. Place chicken on grill rack over drip pan. Cover and grill for 50 to 60 minutes for bone-in chicken breasts or 15 to 18 minutes for boneless chicken breasts or until chicken is no longer pink (170°F), brushing once with reserved marinade halfway through grilling. (For a gas grill, preheat grill. Reduce heat to medium. Adjust for indirect cooking. Grill as above.) Discard any remaining marinade.

NUTRITION FACTS PER SERVING: 354 cal., 17 g total fat (4 g sat. fat), 105 mg chol., 286 mg sodium, 12 g carbo., 0 g fiber, 38 g pro.

italian-seasoned chicken

A marinade made with wine, olive oil, Italian seasoning, and garlic—now that's Italian!

PREP: 10 minutes **MARINATE:** 8 to 24 hours **GRILL:** 50 minutes
MAKES: 4 to 6 servings

- 2 to 3 whole medium chicken breasts (2 to 3 pounds total), halved lengthwise
- 1½ cups dry white wine
- ½ cup olive oil
- 1 tablespoon dried Italian seasoning, crushed
- 2 teaspoons bottled minced garlic (4 cloves)

  Fresh herb sprigs (optional)

one If desired, skin chicken. Place chicken in a resealable plastic bag set in a shallow dish.

two For marinade, in a small bowl combine wine, olive oil, Italian seasoning, and garlic. Pour marinade over chicken. Seal bag; turn to coat chicken. Marinate in the refrigerator for at least 8 hours or up to 24 hours, turning bag occasionally.

three Drain chicken, reserving marinade. For a charcoal grill, arrange medium-hot coals around a drip pan. Test for medium heat above the pan. Place chicken, bone sides down, on grill rack over drip pan. Cover and grill for 50 to 60 minutes or until chicken is no longer pink (170°F), brushing with some of the reserved marinade during the first 40 minutes of grilling. (For a gas grill, preheat grill. Reduce heat to medium. Adjust for indirect cooking. Grill as above.) Discard any remaining marinade. If desired, garnish with fresh herbs.

NUTRITION FACTS PER SERVING: 276 cal., 11 g total fat (2 g sat. fat), 90 mg chol., 87 mg sodium, 1 g carbo., 0 g fiber, 36 g pro.

fusion chicken

For an easy, tasty side dish, serve wild rice pilaf made from a mix.

PREP: 15 minutes **MARINATE:** 1 to 2 hours **GRILL:** 50 minutes
MAKES: 4 servings

2	whole medium chicken breasts (about 2 pounds total), halved lengthwise
1	cup dry red wine
¼	cup bottled hoisin sauce
¼	cup chopped onion
1	tablespoon soy sauce
1	teaspoon bottled minced garlic (2 cloves)
½	teaspoon grated fresh ginger
½	teaspoon five-spice powder
¼	teaspoon crushed red pepper
	Wild rice pilaf (optional)

one Place chicken in a resealable plastic bag set in a shallow dish. For marinade, in a medium bowl combine wine, hoisin sauce, onion, soy sauce, garlic, ginger, five-spice powder, and crushed red pepper. Pour marinade over chicken. Seal bag; turn to coat chicken. Marinate in refrigerator for at least 1 hour or up to 2 hours.

two Drain chicken, reserving marinade. For a charcoal grill, arrange medium-hot coals around a drip pan. Test for medium heat above the pan. Place chicken, bone sides down, on grill rack over drip pan. Cover and grill for 50 to 60 minutes or until chicken is no longer pink (170°F). (For a gas grill, preheat grill. Reduce heat to medium. Adjust for indirect cooking. Grill as above.)

three Meanwhile, place reserved marinade in a small saucepan. Bring to boiling; reduce heat. Simmer, uncovered, for 10 minutes. If desired, strain marinade. If desired, serve chicken with rice pilaf. Drizzle hot marinade over chicken.

NUTRITION FACTS PER SERVING: 333 cal., 12 g total fat (4 g sat. fat), 90 mg chol., 620 mg sodium, 12 g carbo., 0 g fiber, 30 g pro.

raspberry chicken with plantains

Cousins of bananas, plantains must be cooked before eating. Here a brown sugar glaze adds a touch of sweetness to the plantain slices.

PREP: 20 minutes **GRILL:** 12 minutes **MAKES:** 4 servings

1	cup fresh raspberries or one 10-ounce package frozen lightly sweetened raspberries
2	tablespoons granulated sugar
1	teaspoon butter or margarine
2	ripe plantains or firm bananas, sliced
2	tablespoons brown sugar
2	tablespoons white wine vinegar
2	green onions, thinly sliced
1	small fresh jalapeño chile pepper, seeded and finely chopped*
1	pound skinless, boneless chicken breast halves
	Salt
	Ground black pepper

one For sauce, in a small saucepan combine raspberries and granulated sugar. Heat over low heat about 3 minutes or until the berries are softened. Press berries through a fine-mesh sieve; discard seeds.

two In a large nonstick skillet melt butter over medium heat. Add the plantains (if using); cook and stir about 2 minutes or until plantains are lightly browned and slightly softened. Stir in brown sugar and vinegar; heat through. Remove from heat; stir in green onions and jalapeño pepper. (Or if using bananas, melt butter. Stir in bananas, brown sugar, and vinegar; heat through. Remove from heat; stir in the green onions and the jalapeño pepper.)

three Sprinkle chicken with salt and black pepper. For a charcoal grill, grill chicken on the rack of an uncovered grill directly over medium coals for 12 to 15 minutes or until chicken is no longer pink (170°F), turning once halfway through grilling. (For a gas grill, preheat grill. Reduce heat to medium. Place chicken on grill rack over heat. Cover and grill as above.)

four If desired, place each chicken breast on a ti leaf. Spoon sauce over chicken. Serve with plantain or banana mixture.

NUTRITION FACTS PER SERVING: 300 cal., 5 g total fat (1 g sat. fat), 62 mg chol., 103 mg sodium, 45 g carbo., 4 g fiber, 23 g pro.

*NOTE: Because chile peppers contain volatile oils that can burn your skin and eyes, avoid direct contact with them as much as possible. When working with chile peppers, wear plastic or rubber gloves. If your bare hands do touch the chile peppers, wash your hands and nails well with soap and warm water.

sesame-ginger barbecued chicken

Oriental chile sauce makes this robust barbecue sauce downright awesome.

PREP: 10 minutes **GRILL:** 12 minutes **MAKES:** 6 servings

⅓	cup bottled plum sauce or sweet-sour sauce
¼	cup water
3	tablespoons bottled hoisin sauce
1½	teaspoons sesame seeds (toasted, if desired)
1	teaspoon grated fresh ginger or ¼ teaspoon ground ginger
½	teaspoon bottled minced garlic (1 clove)
¼	to ½ teaspoon Oriental chile sauce or several dashes bottled hot pepper sauce
6	skinless, boneless chicken breast halves and/or thighs (about 2 pounds total)

one For sauce, in a small saucepan combine plum sauce, the water, hoisin sauce, sesame seeds, ginger, garlic, and chile sauce. Bring to boiling over medium heat, stirring frequently; reduce heat. Cover and simmer for 3 minutes. Set aside.

two For a charcoal grill, grill chicken on the rack of an uncovered grill directly over medium coals for 12 to 15 minutes or until chicken is no longer pink (170°F), turning once halfway through grilling and brushing with some of the sauce during the last 5 minutes of grilling. (For a gas grill, preheat grill. Reduce heat to medium. Place chicken on grill rack over heat. Cover and grill as above.)

three To serve, reheat the remaining sauce until bubbly; pass with chicken.

NUTRITION FACTS PER SERVING: 209 cal., 5 g total fat (1 g sat. fat), 81 mg chol., 237 mg sodium, 9 g carbo., 0 g fiber, 31 g pro.

barbara bush's barbecued chicken

This former First Lady's lemon-marinated chicken is brushed with a homemade barbecue sauce and grilled to perfection.

PREP: 30 minutes **MARINATE:** 4 to 24 hours **COOK:** 20 minutes + 50 minutes **GRILL:** 50 minutes **MAKES:** 4 servings

1	2½- to 3-pound broiler-fryer chicken, quartered
3	tablespoons lemon juice
1	tablespoon cooking oil
1	teaspoon salt
½	teaspoon freshly ground black pepper
½	teaspoon bottled minced garlic (1 clove)
2½	cups water
1	cup coarsely chopped onion
½ to ¾	cup sugar
½	cup butter or margarine
⅓	cup prepared mustard
¼	cup cider vinegar
½	teaspoon freshly ground black pepper
2½	cups ketchup
½	cup Worcestershire sauce
6 to 8	tablespoons lemon juice
½	teaspoon cayenne pepper

one Place chicken in a resealable plastic bag set in a shallow dish. For marinade, stir together the 3 tablespoons lemon juice, the cooking oil, salt, ½ teaspoon black pepper, and garlic. Pour over chicken. Seal bag; turn to coat chicken. Marinate in the refrigerator for at least 4 hours or up to 24 hours, turning bag occasionally.

two For sauce, in a large saucepan combine the water, onion, sugar, butter, mustard, vinegar, and ½ teaspoon black pepper. Bring to boiling; reduce heat. Simmer, uncovered, for 20 minutes. Stir in ketchup, Worcestershire sauce, the 6 to 8 tablespoons lemon juice, and the cayenne pepper. Return to boiling; reduce heat. Simmer, uncovered, for 50 to 60 minutes or until reduced to about 4 cups.

three Meanwhile, drain chicken, discarding marinade. For a charcoal grill, arrange medium-hot coals around a drip pan. Test for medium heat above the pan. Place chicken, bone sides down, on grill rack over drip pan. Cover and grill for 50 to 60 minutes or until chicken is no longer pink (170°F for breast portions; 180°F for drumstick portions), brushing with some of the sauce during the last 15 minutes of grilling. (For a gas grill, preheat grill. Reduce heat to medium. Adjust for indirect cooking. Grill as above.)

four To serve, pass the remaining sauce* with the chicken.

NUTRITION FACTS PER SERVING: 433 cal., 25 g total fat (9 g sat. fat), 115 mg chol., 1,307 mg sodium, 21 g carbo., 1 g fiber, 32 g pro.

*****NOTE:** Cover and chill any leftover sauce in the refrigerator for up to 1 week.

sweet-and-smoky chicken

A mixture of vinegar, brown sugar, Worcestershire sauce, and liquid smoke makes an easy basting sauce that's luscious on chicken and pork.

PREP: 15 minutes **GRILL:** 50 minutes **MAKES:** 4 servings

2½	to 3 pounds chicken breast halves and thighs
½	cup vinegar
⅓	cup packed brown sugar
2	tablespoons Worcestershire sauce
¾	teaspoon liquid smoke
½	teaspoon salt
¼	teaspoon ground black pepper

one Skin chicken. For basting sauce, in a small saucepan stir together vinegar, brown sugar, Worcestershire sauce, liquid smoke, salt, and pepper. Bring to boiling; reduce heat. Simmer, uncovered, for 5 to 8 minutes or until sauce is reduced to ⅔ cup.

two For a charcoal grill, arrange medium-hot coals around a drip pan. Test for medium heat above the pan. Place chicken, bone sides down, on grill rack over drip pan. Cover and grill for 50 to 60 minutes or until chicken is no longer pink (170°F for breast halves; 180°F for thighs), brushing with the basting sauce during the last 15 minutes of grilling. (For a gas grill, preheat grill. Reduce heat to medium. Adjust for indirect cooking. Grill as above.) Discard any remaining basting sauce.

NUTRITION FACTS PER SERVING: 500 cal., 27 g total fat (8 g sat. fat), 161 mg chol., 518 mg sodium, 22 g carbo., 0 g fiber, 40 g pro.

sticky-sloppy barbecue chicken

Country meets city in this finger-lickin' barbecue recipe. Dry sherry supplies the uptown flavor.

PREP: 15 minutes **MARINATE:** 2 to 4 hours **COOK:** 30 minutes
GRILL: 50 minutes **MAKES:** 6 servings

3	to 4 pounds meaty chicken pieces (breast halves, thighs, and drumsticks)
1½	cups dry sherry
1	cup finely chopped onion
¼	cup lemon juice
1	tablespoon bottled minced garlic (6 cloves)
2	bay leaves
1	15-ounce can tomato puree
¼	cup honey
3	tablespoons molasses
1	teaspoon salt
½	teaspoon dried thyme, crushed
¼	to ½ teaspoon cayenne pepper
¼	teaspoon ground black pepper
2	tablespoons white vinegar

one Place chicken in a resealable plastic bag set in a shallow dish. For marinade, in a medium bowl stir together sherry, onion, lemon juice, garlic, and bay leaves. Pour marinade over chicken. Seal bag; turn to coat chicken. Marinate in the refrigerator for at least 2 hours or up to 4 hours, turning bag occasionally.

two Drain chicken, reserving marinade. Cover and chill chicken until ready to grill. For sauce, in a large saucepan combine the reserved marinade, the tomato puree, honey, molasses, salt, thyme, cayenne pepper, and black pepper. Bring to boiling; reduce heat. Simmer, uncovered, about 30 minutes or until reduced to 2 cups. Remove from heat. Discard bay leaves. Stir in white vinegar.

three For a charcoal grill, arrange medium-hot coals around a drip pan. Test for medium heat above the pan. Place chicken pieces, bone sides down, on grill rack over drip pan. Cover and grill for 50 to 60 minutes or until tender and no longer pink (170°F for breast halves; 180°F for thighs and drumsticks), brushing with some of the sauce during the last 15 minutes of grilling. (For a gas grill, preheat grill. Reduce heat to medium. Adjust for indirect cooking. Grill as above.)

four To serve, reheat remaining sauce until bubbly; pass with chicken.

NUTRITION FACTS PER SERVING: 446 cal., 13 g total fat (4 g sat. fat), 104 mg chol., 735 mg sodium, 33 g carbo., 2 g fiber, 35 g pro.

chicken drumsticks extraordinaire

Drumsticks become company fare when brushed with a pestolike mixture made with aromatic fresh basil and pecans.

PREP: 15 minutes **GRILL:** 35 minutes **MAKES:** 4 servings

1	cup lightly packed fresh basil leaves
½	cup broken pecans
¼	cup olive oil
1	teaspoon bottled minced garlic (2 cloves)
¼	teaspoon salt
¼	teaspoon ground black pepper
8	meaty chicken drumsticks

one In a blender container or small food processor bowl combine basil leaves, broken pecans, olive oil, garlic, salt, and pepper. Cover and blend or process until pureed, scraping down side as needed. Divide mixture in half; chill half of the mixture.

two Skin chicken, if desired. Before grilling, brush chicken with the unchilled basil mixture; discard remainder of the basil mixture used as a brush-on. For a charcoal grill, grill chicken on the rack of an uncovered grill directly over medium coals for 35 to 45 minutes or until chicken is no longer pink (180°F), turning once halfway through grilling and brushing with the chilled basil mixture during the last 5 minutes of grilling. (For a gas grill, preheat grill. Reduce heat to medium. Place chicken on grill rack over heat. Cover and grill as above.) (Watch carefully for flare-ups after turning chicken. Move chicken to a different area of the grill until the flare-up ends.)

NUTRITION FACTS PER SERVING: 451 cal., 36 g total fat (6 g sat. fat), 118 mg chol., 243 mg sodium, 3 g carbo., 2 g fiber, 30 g pro.

greek chicken thighs

Chicken thighs are an often-overlooked cut. They're a good dark meat alternative to breasts and usually less expensive too.

PREP: 20 minutes **MARINATE:** 4 to 24 hours **GRILL:** 35 minutes
STAND: 2 minutes **MAKES:** 4 to 6 servings

8	chicken thighs (about 2½ pounds)
¼	cup dry red wine
2	tablespoons olive oil
2	tablespoons finely chopped red onion
1	teaspoon finely shredded lemon peel
1	teaspoon snipped fresh rosemary
1	teaspoon snipped fresh oregano
½	teaspoon bottled minced garlic (1 clove)
¼	teaspoon salt
¼	teaspoon ground black pepper
½	cup crumbled basil-and-tomato-flavored feta cheese or plain feta cheese

one Skin chicken thighs. Place chicken in a resealable plastic bag set in a shallow dish. For marinade, in a small bowl combine red wine, olive oil, onion, lemon peel, rosemary, oregano, garlic, salt, and pepper. Pour marinade over chicken. Seal bag; turn to coat chicken. Marinate in the refrigerator for at least 4 hours or up to 24 hours, turning bag occasionally.

two Drain chicken, reserving marinade. For a charcoal grill, grill chicken on the rack of an uncovered grill directly over medium coals for 35 to 40 minutes or until chicken is no longer pink (180°F), turning once halfway through grilling and brushing with reserved marinade frequently during the first 20 minutes of grilling. (For a gas grill, preheat grill. Reduce heat to medium. Place chicken on grill rack over heat. Cover and grill as above.) Discard any remaining marinade.

three Sprinkle chicken with feta cheese. Cover loosely with foil; let stand for 2 minutes before serving.

NUTRITION FACTS PER SERVING: 389 cal., 19 g total fat (6 g sat. fat), 205 mg chol., 512 mg sodium, 2 g carbo., 0 g fiber, 47 g pro.

buffalo chicken wings

Although these zesty wings make a great appetizer, you also can serve them as a main dish for four.

PREP: 15 minutes **GRILL:** 18 minutes **MAKES:** 32 appetizer servings

- 16 chicken wings (about 3 pounds total)
- 2 tablespoons butter or margarine
- 1 2-ounce bottle hot pepper sauce (¼ cup)
- 1 recipe Blue Cheese Dip
  Celery sticks

one Cut off and discard wing tips. Bend the 2 larger sections of each wing back and forth, breaking the cartilage connecting them. Use a knife or cleaver to cut through the cartilage and skin, cutting each wing into 2 sections.

two In a small saucepan melt butter. Stir in hot pepper sauce. Brush the butter mixture generously over wing pieces.

three For a charcoal grill, grill wing pieces on the rack of an uncovered grill directly over medium coals for 18 to 20 minutes or until chicken is no longer pink (170°F), turning once and brushing with the remaining butter mixture during the first 5 minutes of grilling. (For a gas grill, preheat grill. Reduce heat to medium. Place wing pieces on grill rack over heat. Cover and grill as above.) Discard any remaining butter mixture. Serve wing pieces with Blue Cheese Dip and celery sticks.

blue cheese dip: In a blender container or food processor bowl combine ½ cup dairy sour cream; ½ cup crumbled blue cheese; ¼ cup mayonnaise or salad dressing; 1 teaspoon bottled minced garlic (2 cloves); 2 tablespoons lemon juice; 2 tablespoons thinly sliced green onion; and 1 tablespoon milk. Cover and blend or process just until combined. Transfer to a small bowl; cover and chill in refrigerator until serving time or up to 1 hour.

NUTRITION FACTS PER SERVING WITH 2 TEASPOONS DIP: 71 cal., 6 g total fat (2 g sat. fat), 19 mg chol., 55 mg sodium, 0 g carbo., 0 g fiber, 4 g pro.

garlic-grilled chicken

A mixture of garlic and basil inserted under the skin and a combination of lemon, sweet pepper, and additional garlic in the cavity flavor every bite of this grilled chicken.

PREP: 20 minutes **GRILL:** 1 hour **STAND:** 15 minutes **MAKES:** 5 servings

- 1   2½- to 3-pound whole broiler-fryer chicken
- 3   cloves garlic, peeled
- ½   of a lemon, sliced
- ½   of a red sweet pepper, sliced
- 1   tablespoon snipped fresh basil or 1 teaspoon dried basil, crushed
- ⅛   teaspoon salt
- 1   tablespoon olive oil or cooking oil
- 1   tablespoon lemon juice
     Steamed new potatoes (optional)
     Fresh oregano (optional)

one Soak several wooden toothpicks in enough water to cover for 15 minutes; drain before using. Remove the neck and giblets from chicken. Twist wing tips under the back. Cut one of the garlic cloves lengthwise in half. Rub skin of chicken with cut edge of garlic. Place garlic halves, lemon slices, and sweet pepper slices in cavity of chicken.

two Mince remaining 2 cloves garlic. In a small bowl combine minced garlic, basil, and salt; set aside. Starting at the neck on one side of the breast, slip your fingers between skin and meat, loosening the skin as you work toward the tail end. Once your entire hand is under the skin, free the skin around the thigh and leg area up to, but not around, the tip of the drumstick. Repeat on the other side of the breast. Rub garlic mixture over entire surface under skin. Securely fasten opening with water-soaked toothpicks.

three Stir together oil and lemon juice; brush over chicken. Reserve remaining lemon juice mixture. Insert an oven-going meat thermometer into the center of an inside thigh muscle, making sure bulb does not touch bone.

four For a charcoal grill, arrange medium-hot coals around a drip pan. Test for medium heat above the pan. Place chicken, breast side up, on grill rack over drip pan. Cover and grill for 1 to 1¼ hours or until thermometer registers 180°F, brushing occasionally with oil-lemon mixture during first 30 minutes of grilling. Add coals as necessary to maintain heat. (For a gas grill, preheat grill. Reduce heat to medium. Adjust for indirect cooking. Grill as above.) Discard any remaining oil-lemon mixture.

five Remove chicken from grill and cover with foil. Let stand for 15 minutes before carving. If desired, serve on a platter with steamed new potatoes and garnish with fresh oregano.

NUTRITION FACTS PER SERVING: 253 cal., 15 g total fat (4 g sat. fat), 82 mg chol., 193 mg sodium, 2 g carbo., 0 g fiber, 26 g pro.

herbed chicken

During grilling, the flavorful juices get locked in to make the meat tender and moist.

PREP: 15 minutes **GRILL:** 1 hour **STAND:** 15 minutes **MAKES:** 4 to 6 servings

1	2½- to 3-pound whole broiler-fryer chicken
2	tablespoons butter or margarine
3	tablespoons lemon juice
1½	teaspoons bottled minced garlic (3 cloves)
1	teaspoon dried thyme, savory, or sage, crushed
¼	teaspoon salt
¼	teaspoon ground black pepper
	Fresh thyme sprigs (optional)

one Remove the neck and giblets from chicken. Skewer neck skin to back. Tie legs to tail. Twist wing tips under back. Insert an oven-going meat thermometer into the center of an inside thigh muscle, making sure bulb does not touch bone. In a small saucepan melt butter; stir in lemon juice, garlic, dried herb, salt, and black pepper. Brush chicken with some of the butter and herb mixture.

two For a charcoal grill, arrange medium-hot coals around a drip pan. Test for medium heat above the pan. Place chicken, breast side up, on grill rack over drip pan. Cover and grill for 1 to 1¼ hours or until thermometer registers 180°F, brushing with the remaining butter mixture during the first 45 minutes of grilling. Add coals as necessary to maintain heat. (For a gas grill, preheat grill. Reduce heat to medium. Adjust for indirect cooking. Grill as above.) Discard any remaining butter mixture.

three Remove chicken from grill and cover with foil. Let stand for 15 minutes before carving. If desired, garnish with fresh thyme sprigs.

NUTRITION FACTS PER SERVING: 237 cal., 16 g total fat (6 g sat. fat), 81 mg chol., 262 mg sodium, 2 g carbo., 0 g fiber, 21 g pro.

potato & chicken kabobs

To assure that the chicken and potatoes cook evenly, be sure to leave a ¼-inch space between pieces. Use the same general guideline for other kabobs.

PREP: 20 minutes **GRILL:** 12 minutes **MAKES:** 4 servings

12	whole tiny new potatoes (about 1 pound total)
12	ounces skinless, boneless chicken breast halves, cut into 1½-inch pieces
1	lemon, cut into 4 wedges
3	tablespoons olive oil
1	tablespoon snipped fresh oregano or 1 teaspoon dried oregano, crushed
½	teaspoon bottled minced garlic (1 clove)

one In a small saucepan bring a small amount of water to boiling; add potatoes. Cover and simmer about 10 minutes or until almost tender. Drain well; halve potatoes lengthwise.

two On 4 long metal skewers, alternately thread chicken and potatoes, leaving ¼-inch space between pieces. Add a lemon wedge to the end of each skewer. In a small bowl combine olive oil, oregano, and garlic; brush kabobs with oil mixture.

three For a charcoal grill, grill kabobs on the rack of an uncovered grill directly over medium coals for 12 to 15 minutes or until chicken is no longer pink, turning kabobs once and brushing once with remaining oil mixture halfway through grilling. (For a gas grill, preheat grill. Reduce heat to medium. Place kabobs on grill rack over heat. Cover and grill as above.) Discard any remaining oil mixture.

four To serve, remove chicken and potatoes from skewers; squeeze lemon over chicken and potatoes.

NUTRITION FACTS PER SERVING: 293 cal., 13 g total fat (2 g sat. fat), 45 mg chol., 49 mg sodium, 26 g carbo., 1 g fiber, 19 g pro.

margarita fajitas with sub-lime salsa

To boost the heat in the salsa, stir in some of the adobo sauce from the chipotles or add more jalapeños.

PREP: 20 minutes **MARINATE:** 1 hour **GRILL:** 12 minutes **MAKES:** 4 servings

1	15-ounce can black beans, rinsed and drained
1	8-ounce can pineapple tidbits (juice pack), drained
¼	cup finely chopped red onion
2	fresh jalapeño chile peppers, seeded and finely chopped*
2	tablespoons snipped fresh cilantro
1	canned chipotle chile pepper in adobo sauce, drained and finely chopped*
4	teaspoons lime juice
¼	teaspoon salt
1¼	pounds skinless, boneless chicken breast halves
¼	cup tequila
¼	cup lime juice
1	tablespoon cooking oil
¼	teaspoon salt
¼	teaspoon ground black pepper
8	6- to 7-inch flour tortillas

one For salsa, in a medium bowl stir together beans, pineapple, onion, jalapeño peppers, cilantro, chipotle pepper, the 4 teaspoons lime juice, and ¼ teaspoon salt. Cover and chill in the refrigerator while chicken marinates.

two Place the chicken in a resealable plastic bag set in a shallow dish. For marinade, in a small bowl stir together tequila, the ¼ cup lime juice, the oil, ¼ teaspoon salt, and the ground black pepper. Pour marinade over chicken. Seal bag; turn to coat chicken. Marinate in the refrigerator for 1 hour, turning bag occasionally. Meanwhile, wrap tortillas in heavy foil; set aside.

three Drain chicken, discarding marinade. For a charcoal grill, grill chicken on the rack of an uncovered grill directly over medium coals for 12 to 15 minutes or until chicken is no longer pink (170°F), turning once halfway through grilling. During the last 5 minutes of grilling, place foil-wrapped tortillas alongside chicken on the grill rack; heat through, turning once. (For a gas grill, preheat grill. Reduce heat to medium. Place chicken, then tortillas on grill rack over heat. Cover and grill as above.) Remove chicken to a cutting board.

four Cut chicken into ½-inch slices. Divide chicken among tortillas and top with salsa. Roll up.

NUTRITION FACTS PER SERVING: 489 cal., 7 g total fat (2 g sat. fat), 82 mg chol., 835 mg sodium, 61 g carbo., 8 g fiber, 46 g pro.

*NOTE: Because chile peppers contain volatile oils that can burn your skin and eyes, avoid direct contact with them as much as possible. When working with chile peppers, wear plastic or rubber gloves. If your bare hands do touch the chile peppers, wash your hands and nails well with soap and warm water.

grilled chicken salad

Steak seasoning adds just the right touch of spiciness to the chicken.

PREP: 20 minutes **STAND:** 1 hour **GRILL:** 12 minutes **MAKES:** 4 servings

- ¼ cup olive oil
- 3 tablespoons balsamic vinegar
- 1 tablespoon dried dillweed
- ½ teaspoon bottled minced garlic (1 clove)
- ¼ teaspoon freshly ground black pepper
- ¼ teaspoon dried oregano, crushed
- 1 pound skinless, boneless chicken breast halves

  Montreal steak seasoning or Kansas City steak seasoning
- 8 cups mesclun or spring salad greens or fresh spinach
- ¾ cup seedless red grapes, halved
- ⅓ cup crumbled goat cheese
- ¼ cup pine nuts, toasted

one For dressing, in a screw-top jar combine oil, balsamic vinegar, dillweed, garlic, pepper, and oregano. Cover and shake well; let stand for 1 hour.

two Meanwhile, sprinkle chicken breast halves lightly with steak seasoning. For a charcoal grill, grill chicken on the rack of an uncovered grill directly over medium coals for 12 to 15 minutes or until chicken is no longer pink (170°F), turning once halfway through grilling. (For a gas grill, preheat grill. Reduce heat to medium. Place chicken on grill rack over heat. Cover and grill as above.) Cool slightly.

three Divide mesclun or salad greens among 4 dinner plates; top with grapes, goat cheese, and pine nuts. Slice chicken breast halves and arrange sliced chicken on top of salads. Shake dressing and drizzle over the salads.

NUTRITION FACTS PER SERVING: 400 cal., 23 g total fat (4 g sat. fat), 86 mg chol., 167 mg sodium, 12 g carbo., 2 g fiber, 38 g pro.

blackberry-glazed smoked ham

Recipe on page 36

steak-lover's platter
Recipe on page 14

garlic and shrimp pasta toss
Recipe on page 108

mango and pepper bbq sauce
Recipe on page 117

honey-peach sauce
Recipe on page 121

sesame-ginger barbecued chicken
Recipe on page 53

sticky-sloppy barbecue chicken
Recipe on page 56

mahi mahi with vegetable slaw
Recipe on page 99

south-of-the-border potato skins
Recipe on page 135

grilled turkey piccata

A dish done piccata-style always includes lemon, parsley, and capers in it. Another time, try making this Italian specialty with boneless chicken breasts in place of the turkey breast tenderloin pieces.

PREP: 15 minutes **GRILL:** 15 minutes **MAKES:** 4 servings

1¼	to 1½ pounds turkey breast tenderloins
2	lemons
4	teaspoons olive oil
2	teaspoons snipped fresh rosemary or ½ teaspoon dried rosemary, crushed
¼	teaspoon salt
¼	teaspoon freshly ground black pepper
1	tablespoon drained capers
1	tablespoon snipped fresh flat-leaf parsley

one Split each turkey breast tenderloin in half horizontally. Finely shred enough peel from 1 of the lemons to make 1 teaspoon; set aside. Halve and squeeze the juice from that lemon (should have about 3 tablespoons); set aside. Cut the other lemon into very thin slices; set aside.

two For rub, in a small bowl combine the shredded lemon peel, 2 teaspoons of the olive oil, the rosemary, salt, and pepper. Sprinkle the mixture evenly over both sides of each turkey piece; rub in with your fingers.

three For a charcoal grill, arrange medium-hot coals around a drip pan. Test for medium heat above the pan. Place turkey on grill rack over drip pan. Cover and grill for 8 minutes. Turn turkey. Arrange lemon slices on top of turkey, overlapping if necessary. Cover and grill for 7 to 10 minutes more or until turkey is no longer pink (170°F). (For a gas grill, preheat grill. Reduce heat to medium. Adjust for indirect cooking. Grill as above.)

four Meanwhile, in a small saucepan combine the remaining 2 teaspoons olive oil, the lemon juice, and the capers. Heat caper mixture through.

five Remove turkey to a serving platter. Drizzle with the warm caper mixture. Sprinkle with parsley.

NUTRITION FACTS PER SERVING: 159 cal., 5 g total fat (1 g sat. fat), 71 mg chol., 269 mg sodium, 1 g carbo., 0 g fiber, 26 g pro.

stuffed turkey tenderloins

Turkey tenderloins stuffed with spinach and goat cheese make a delicious headliner for a party.

PREP: 15 minutes **GRILL:** 16 minutes **MAKES:** 4 servings

- 2   8-ounce turkey breast tenderloins
- 2   cups chopped fresh spinach leaves
- 3   ounces semisoft goat cheese (chèvre) or feta cheese, crumbled (about ¾ cup)
- ½   teaspoon ground black pepper
- 1   tablespoon olive oil
- 1   teaspoon paprika
- ½   teaspoon salt
- ⅛   to ¼ teaspoon cayenne pepper

one Make a pocket in each turkey breast tenderloin by cutting horizontally from one side almost to, but not through, the opposite side; set aside. In a medium bowl combine spinach, goat cheese, and black pepper. Spoon spinach mixture into pockets. Tie 100 percent-cotton kitchen string around each tenderloin in 3 or 4 places to hold in stuffing. In a small bowl combine oil, paprika, salt, and cayenne pepper; brush evenly over tenderloins.

two For a charcoal grill, grill turkey on the rack of an uncovered grill directly over medium coals for 16 to 20 minutes or until turkey is no longer pink (170°F), turning once halfway through grilling. (For a gas grill, preheat grill. Reduce heat to medium. Place turkey on grill rack over heat. Cover and grill as above.) Remove and discard strings; slice tenderloins crosswise.

NUTRITION FACTS PER SERVING: 220 cal., 12 g total fat (4 g sat. fat), 68 mg chol., 458 mg sodium, 1 g carbo., 1 g fiber, 26 g pro.

peppered turkey steaks

These spicy turkey steaks have a kick reminiscent of Buffalo wings.

PREP: 15 minutes **MARINATE:** 4 to 6 hours **GRILL:** 15 minutes
MAKES: 5 to 7 servings

1½	pounds turkey breast tenderloins
1	cup bottled Italian salad dressing
½	cup finely chopped onion
⅓	cup lemon juice
2	teaspoons bottled minced garlic (4 cloves)
1½	to 2 teaspoons cayenne pepper
1	teaspoon taco seasoning
1	teaspoon Cajun seasoning
⅛	to ¼ teaspoon ground black pepper

one Split each turkey breast tenderloin in half horizontally. Place turkey pieces in a resealable plastic bag set in a shallow dish. For marinade, in a medium bowl combine Italian salad dressing, onion, lemon juice, garlic, cayenne pepper, taco seasoning, Cajun seasoning, and black pepper. Pour marinade over turkey. Seal bag; turn to coat turkey. Marinate in refrigerator for at least 4 hours or up to 6 hours, turning bag occasionally.

two Drain turkey, discarding marinade. For a charcoal grill, arrange medium-hot coals around a drip pan. Test for medium heat above the pan. Place turkey on grill rack over drip pan. Cover and grill for 15 to 18 minutes or until turkey is no longer pink (170°F). (For a gas grill, preheat grill. Reduce heat to medium. Adjust for indirect cooking. Grill as above.)

NUTRITION FACTS PER SERVING: 234 cal., 10 g total fat (2 g sat. fat), 81 mg chol., 209 mg sodium, 3 g carbo., 0 g fiber, 32 g pro.

turkey steaks & vegetables

Vegetable juice—with a few added ingredients—doubles as a basting sauce for turkey steaks. Serve these savory grilled turkey steaks and grilled vegetables with chewy Italian bread and a glass of Chianti.

PREP: 10 minutes **GRILL:** 12 minutes **MAKES:** 4 servings

1	pound turkey breast tenderloins
¼	cup vegetable juice
3	tablespoons mayonnaise or salad dressing
1	tablespoon snipped fresh chives or green onion tops
2	teaspoons snipped fresh thyme or ½ teaspoon dried thyme, crushed
½	teaspoon bottled minced garlic (1 clove)
	Salt
	Ground black pepper
2	small zucchini, halved lengthwise
2	large plum tomatoes, halved lengthwise

one Split each turkey breast tenderloin in half horizontally. For sauce, in a small bowl gradually stir vegetable juice into mayonnaise; stir in chives or green onion tops, thyme, and garlic. Set aside.

two Sprinkle turkey with salt and pepper. For a charcoal grill, grill turkey and halved zucchini and tomatoes, cut sides down, on the rack of an uncovered grill directly over medium coals for 12 to 15 minutes or until turkey is no longer pink (170°F), zucchini is tender, and tomatoes are heated through,* turning once halfway through grilling and brushing with some of the sauce during the last 3 minutes of grilling. (For a gas grill, preheat grill. Reduce heat to medium. Place turkey, zucchini, and tomatoes on grill rack over heat. Cover and grill as above.)

three Serve with any remaining sauce.

NUTRITION FACTS PER SERVING: 209 cal., 11 g total fat (2 g sat. fat), 56 mg chol., 200 mg sodium, 6 g carbo., 1 g fiber, 22 g pro.

*NOTE: If the zucchini and tomatoes are done before the turkey, remove them from the grill and keep warm.

chili-mustard turkey breast

Spreading a mustard mixture under the skin gives turkey another flavor dimension.

PREP: 20 minutes **GRILL:** 1¼ hours **STAND:** 15 minutes
MAKES: 6 to 8 servings

3	tablespoons honey mustard
1	tablespoon packed brown sugar
½	teaspoon chili powder
⅛	teaspoon ground cumin
⅛	teaspoon ground black pepper
1	2- to 2½-pound bone-in turkey breast half

one In a small bowl stir together the mustard, brown sugar, chili powder, cumin, and black pepper.

two Starting at the edge of the turkey breast, slip your fingers between the skin and meat, loosening the skin to make a pocket. Using your fingers or a spoon, spread mustard mixture evenly over the meat under the skin. Secure with wooden skewers or toothpicks, if necessary. Insert an oven-going meat thermometer into the thickest portion of the turkey breast, making sure bulb does not touch bone.

three For a charcoal grill, arrange medium-hot coals around a drip pan. Test for medium heat above the pan. Place turkey, bone side down, on grill rack over drip pan. Cover and grill for 1¼ to 2 hours or until meat thermometer registers 170°F. Add coals as necessary to maintain heat. (For a gas grill, preheat grill. Reduce heat to medium. Adjust for indirect cooking. Place turkey on rack in a roasting pan, place on grill rack, and grill as above.)

four Remove turkey from grill; cover with foil. Let stand for 15 minutes before carving.

NUTRITION FACTS PER SERVING: 217 cal., 9 g total fat (2 g sat. fat), 83 mg chol., 120 mg sodium, 4 g carbo., 0 g fiber, 28 g pro.

hazelnut-pesto turkey breast

Spread the savory mixture of nuts, spinach, basil, garlic, and Parmesan cheese between the skin and meat of the turkey breast half.

PREP: 25 minutes **GRILL:** 1¼ hours **STAND:** 15 minutes
MAKES: 6 to 8 servings

- ¼ cup chopped hazelnuts or almonds, toasted
- 1 egg yolk
- 1 cup loosely packed fresh spinach leaves
- 1 cup loosely packed fresh basil leaves
- 2 tablespoons cooking oil
- ½ teaspoon bottled minced garlic (1 clove)
- ¼ cup grated Parmesan or Romano cheese (1 ounce)
- 1 2½- to 3-pound bone-in turkey breast half
  Cooking oil

one For pesto, blend nuts in a covered blender container until very finely chopped. Add egg yolk, spinach, basil, the 2 tablespoons oil, and garlic to blender. Cover and blend until nearly smooth. Stir in Parmesan cheese.

two Remove bone from turkey. Starting at the edge of the turkey breast, slip your fingers between skin and meat, loosening the skin to make a pocket. Using your fingers or a spoon, spread pesto evenly over the meat under the skin. Secure with wooden skewers or toothpicks. Tuck thinner portion of breast half under thicker portion. Tie with 100 percent-cotton kitchen string. Insert an oven-going meat thermometer into the thickest portion of the turkey breast.

three For a charcoal grill, arrange medium-hot coals around a drip pan. Test for medium heat above the pan. Place turkey, skin side up, on grill rack over drip pan. Brush skin with cooking oil. Cover and grill for 1¼ to 2 hours or until meat thermometer registers 170°F. Add coals as necessary to maintain heat. (For a gas grill, preheat grill. Reduce heat to medium. Adjust for indirect cooking. Place turkey on rack in a roasting pan, place on grill rack, and grill as above.)

four Remove turkey from grill; cover with foil. Let stand for 15 minutes before carving.

NUTRITION FACTS PER SERVING: 324 cal., 18 g total fat (4 g sat. fat), 154 mg chol., 127 mg sodium, 2 g carbo., 1 g fiber, 38 g pro.

cranberry margarita turkey legs

Look for chipotle chile peppers in adobo sauce in the Mexican food section of your supermarket or at a Mexican market.

PREP: 20 minutes **MARINATE:** 2 to 24 hours **GRILL:** 45 minutes
MAKES: 6 servings

6	turkey drumsticks (about 3 pounds total)
¼	cup cranberry juice
¼	cup tequila
1	tablespoon finely shredded lime peel
¼	cup lime juice
1	teaspoon bottled minced garlic (2 cloves)
1	teaspoon salt
¼	teaspoon cayenne pepper (optional)
1	16-ounce can whole cranberry sauce
2	or 3 canned chipotle chile peppers in adobo sauce, mashed

one Place turkey in a resealable plastic bag set in a shallow dish. For marinade, in a small bowl stir together cranberry juice, 2 tablespoons of the tequila, 1½ teaspoons of the lime peel, 2 tablespoons of the lime juice, the garlic, salt, and, if desired, cayenne pepper. Pour marinade over turkey. Seal bag; turn to coat turkey. Marinate in the refrigerator for at least 2 hours or up to 24 hours, turning bag occasionally.

two For sauce, in a small saucepan combine remaining 2 tablespoons tequila, remaining 1½ teaspoons lime peel, remaining 2 tablespoons lime juice, the cranberry sauce, and chipotle peppers. Bring to boiling; reduce heat. Simmer, uncovered, for 5 minutes. Transfer 1¼ cups of the sauce to a small bowl; chill in refrigerator. Reserve remaining sauce for brush-on.

three Drain turkey, discarding marinade. For a charcoal grill, arrange medium-hot coals around a drip pan. Test for medium heat above the pan. Place turkey on grill rack over drip pan. Cover and grill for 45 minutes to 1¼ hours or until turkey is no longer pink (180°F), brushing with remaining sauce during the last 10 minutes of grilling. (For a gas grill, preheat grill. Reduce heat to medium. Adjust for indirect cooking. Grill as above.) Discard remainder of sauce used as a brush-on.

four To serve, reheat the chilled sauce; pass with turkey.

NUTRITION FACTS PER SERVING: 372 cal., 9 g total fat (3 g sat. fat), 105 mg chol., 290 mg sodium, 32 g carbo., 1 g fiber, 36 g pro.

behemoth drumsticks

For a medieval twist, eat the huge turkey drumsticks out-of-hand. If you prefer smaller servings, grill 1 or 2 chicken drumsticks for each person.

PREP: 5 minutes **GRILL:** 45 minutes **MAKES:** 4 servings

- 4 turkey drumsticks (2 to 4 pounds total)
- 1 tablespoon cooking oil

  Salt

  Ground black pepper

one Brush drumsticks with cooking oil. Sprinkle with salt and pepper.

two For a charcoal grill, arrange medium-hot coals around a drip pan. Test for medium heat above the pan. Place turkey drumsticks on grill rack over drip pan. Cover and grill for 45 minutes to 1¼ hours or until turkey is tender and no longer pink (180°F). Add coals as necessary to maintain heat. (For a gas grill, preheat grill. Reduce heat to medium. Adjust for indirect cooking. Grill as above.)

NUTRITION FACTS PER SERVING: 283 cal., 16 g total fat (4 g sat. fat), 119 mg chol., 235 mg sodium, 0 g carbo., 0 g fiber, 32 g pro.

behemoth-style chicken drumsticks: Prepare as directed, except use 8 chicken drumsticks. Cover and grill for 50 to 60 minutes or until chicken is tender and no longer pink (180°F).

MAKES: 4 to 8 servings.

NUTRITION FACTS PER SERVING: 262 cal., 16 g total fat (4 g sat. fat), 118 mg chol., 242 mg sodium, 0 g carbo., 0 g fiber, 28 g pro.

best-ever turkey on the grill

Rubbing the seasoning under the turkey or chicken skin before cooking results in a moist, juicy bird that's sure to get rave reviews.

PREP: 20 minutes **GRILL:** 2½ hours **MAKES:** 8 to 10 servings

1	8- to 12-pound fresh or frozen whole turkey
2	teaspoons dried Italian seasoning, basil, or oregano, crushed
1	teaspoon poultry seasoning
½	teaspoon salt
½	teaspoon ground black pepper

one Thaw turkey, if frozen. Remove the neck and giblets. Rinse turkey; pat dry with paper towels. In a small bowl combine Italian seasoning, poultry seasoning, salt, and pepper.

two Starting at the neck on one side of the breast, slip your fingers between skin and meat, loosening the skin as you work toward the tail end. Once your entire hand is under the skin, free the skin around the top of the thigh and leg area up to, but not around, the tip of the drumstick. Repeat on the other side of the breast. Rub seasonings under the skin of turkey breast and legs. Skewer the neck skin to the back. Tie legs to tail. Twist wing tips under the back. Insert an oven-going meat thermometer into the center of an inside thigh muscle, making sure bulb does not touch bone.

three For a charcoal grill, arrange medium-hot coals around a drip pan. Test for medium heat above the pan. Place turkey, breast side up, on grill rack over drip pan. Cover and grill for 2½ to 3½ hours or until meat thermometer registers 180°F. Add coals as necessary to maintain the heat. (For a gas grill, preheat grill. Reduce heat to medium. Adjust for indirect cooking. Place the turkey on a rack in a roasting pan, place on grill rack, and grill as above.)

four Remove from grill; cover with foil. Let stand for 15 minutes before carving.

NUTRITION FACTS PER SERVING: 449 cal., 14 g total fat (4 g sat. fat), 275 mg chol., 221 mg sodium, 0 g carbo., 0 g fiber, 76 g pro.

cajun barbecue turkey

Look for Cajun seasoning in the spice section of the supermarket.

PREP: 30 minutes **STAND:** 1 hour + 15 minutes **GRILL:** 2½ hours
MAKES: 8 to 10 servings

1	8- to 10-pound fresh or frozen whole turkey
3	cups water
3	tablespoons Cajun seasoning
1	tablespoon poultry seasoning
½	teaspoon instant chicken bouillon granules
½	teaspoon garlic powder
¼	to ½ teaspoon cayenne pepper
2	tablespoons butter or margarine

one Thaw turkey, if frozen. Rinse turkey; pat dry with paper towels. Skewer the neck skin to the back. Tie legs to tail. Twist wing tips under the back.

two In a large saucepan combine the water, Cajun seasoning, poultry seasoning, bouillon granules, garlic powder, and cayenne pepper. Bring to boiling. Remove from heat. Stir in butter until melted. Cover; let stand for 1 hour. Strain through a fine-mesh sieve; discard spices.

three Using a flavor-injector syringe, inject the water-spice mixture deep into the meat of the turkey. (This may take up to 20 injections, so try to evenly distribute the seasoned broth in the turkey. If the syringe gets clogged with a bit of seasoning, flush it out with water and a toothpick.) Insert an oven-going meat thermometer into the center of an inside thigh muscle, making sure bulb does not touch bone.

four For charcoal grill, arrange medium-hot coals around a drip pan. Test for medium heat above pan. Place turkey, breast side up, on grill rack over drip pan. Cover and grill for 2½ to 3 hours or until meat thermometer registers 180°F. Add coals as necessary to maintain heat. (For gas grill, preheat grill. Reduce heat to medium. Adjust for indirect cooking. Place turkey on a rack in a roasting pan, place on grill rack, and grill as above.)

five Remove turkey from grill; cover with foil. Let stand for 15 minutes before carving.

NUTRITION FACTS PER SERVING: 487 cal., 17 g total fat (6 g sat. fat), 283 mg chol., 458 mg sodium, 3 g carbo., 1 g fiber, 77 g pro.

turkey tenderloins
with sweet pepper salsa

The roasted red sweet pepper and orange salsa is equally delicious with grilled or broiled chicken.

PREP: 15 minutes **MARINATE:** 2 to 4 hours **GRILL:** 12 minutes
MAKES: 6 servings

1½ pounds turkey breast tenderloins

⅓ cup olive oil

¼ cup lemon juice

1 teaspoon finely shredded orange peel

¼ cup orange juice

2 teaspoons bottled minced garlic (4 cloves)

¼ teaspoon salt

¼ teaspoon ground black pepper

1 recipe Sweet Pepper-Citrus Salsa

one Split each turkey breast tenderloin in half horizontally. Place turkey in a resealable plastic bag set in a shallow dish. For marinade, in a small bowl combine oil, lemon juice, orange peel, orange juice, garlic, salt, and pepper. Pour marinade over turkey. Seal bag; turn to coat turkey. Marinate in the refrigerator for at least 2 hours or up to 4 hours, turning bag occasionally.

two Drain turkey, reserving marinade. For a charcoal grill, grill turkey on the rack of an uncovered grill directly over medium coals for 12 to 15 minutes or until turkey is no longer pink (170°F), turning once and brushing once with reserved marinade halfway through grilling. (For a gas grill, preheat grill. Reduce heat to medium. Place turkey on grill rack over heat. Cover and grill as above.) Discard any remaining marinade. Serve with Sweet Pepper-Citrus Salsa.

NUTRITION FACTS PER SERVING: 206 cal., 10 g total fat (2 g sat. fat), 50 mg chol., 107 mg sodium, 6 g carbo., 1 g fiber, 22 g pro.

sweet pepper-citrus salsa: In a small bowl combine one 7-ounce jar roasted red sweet peppers, drained and chopped; 1 orange, peeled, seeded, and cut up; 2 green onions, sliced; 2 tablespoons balsamic vinegar; and 1 tablespoon snipped fresh basil or 1 teaspoon dried basil, crushed. Cover and refrigerate until serving time.

turkey tenderloins with cilantro pesto

Substituting cilantro for basil in pesto gives it a Southwestern flair. Another time, savor the pesto with chicken, fish, or shrimp.

PREP: 15 minutes **GRILL:** 12 minutes **MAKES:** 8 servings

2	pounds turkey breast tenderloins
	Salt
	Ground black pepper
1½	cups lightly packed fresh cilantro sprigs and/or fresh basil leaves
⅓	cup walnuts
3	tablespoons olive oil
2	tablespoons lime juice
1	teaspoon bottled minced garlic (2 cloves)
¼	teaspoon salt
	Lime wedges or lemon wedges (optional)

one Split each turkey breast tenderloin in half horizontally. Sprinkle turkey with salt and pepper; set aside.

two For cilantro pesto, in a food processor/bleder combine cilantro and/or basil, walnuts, oil, lime juice, garlic, and the ¼ teaspoon salt. Cover and process until nearly smooth. Divide pesto in half. Chill half of the pesto to serve with turkey.

three For a charcoal grill, grill turkey on the rack of an uncovered grill directly over medium coals for 7 minutes; turn. Brush lightly with the unchilled half of the cilantro pesto. Grill for 5 to 8 minutes more or until turkey is tender and no longer pink (170°F). (For gas grill, preheat grill. Reduce heat to medium. Place turkey on grill rack over heat. Cover and grill as above.) Discard remainder of cilantro pesto used as a brush-on.

four Serve turkey with remaining chilled pesto. If desired, serve with lime wedges to squeeze over turkey.

NUTRITION FACTS PER SERVING: 213 cal., 10 g total fat (2 g sat. fat), 68 mg chol., 134 mg sodium, 2 g carbo., 1 g fiber, 28 g pro.

border grilled turkey salad

Try a fresh new twist on taco salad. Chili-and-lime-flavored strips of grilled turkey are served over crisp greens and drizzled with a hot pepper-spiced, dried tomato vinaigrette. It's all topped off with crunchy crumbled tortilla chips.

PREP: 20 minutes **MARINATE:** 30 minutes to 3 hours **GRILL:** 12 minutes
MAKES: 4 servings

1	pound turkey breast tenderloins
¼	cup lime juice
1	teaspoon chili powder
1	teaspoon bottled minced garlic (2 cloves)
¾	cup bottled dried tomato vinaigrette*
1	medium fresh jalapeño chile pepper, seeded and finely chopped**
4	cups torn mixed salad greens
1	cup peeled, seeded, and chopped cucumber or peeled and chopped jicama
1	large tomato, coarsely chopped
8	baked tortilla chips, broken into bite-size pieces

one Split each turkey breast tenderloin in half horizontally. Place turkey in a resealable plastic bag set in a shallow dish. For marinade, in a small bowl combine lime juice, chili powder, and garlic. Pour marinade over turkey. Seal bag; turn to coat turkey. Marinate in refrigerator for at least 30 minutes or up to 3 hours, turning bag occasionally.

two Drain turkey, reserving marinade. For a charcoal grill, grill turkey on rack of an uncovered grill directly over medium coals for 12 to 15 minutes or until turkey is no longer pink (170°F), turning once and brushing with the reserved marinade during the first 5 minutes of grilling. (For a gas grill, preheat grill. Reduce heat to medium. Place turkey on grill rack over heat. Cover and grill as above.) Discard any remaining marinade. Cut turkey into bite-size strips.

three Meanwhile, for dressing, in a small bowl stir together tomato vinaigrette and jalapeño pepper. In a large bowl combine greens, cucumber or jicama, and tomato; toss to mix. Divide greens mixture among 4 dinner plates; arrange turkey on top of greens. Drizzle with dressing and sprinkle with tortilla chips.

NUTRITION FACTS PER SERVING: 363 cal., 19 g total fat (3 g sat. fat), 79 mg chol., 402 mg sodium, 13 g carbo., 2 g fiber, 36 g pro.

*NOTE: If you can't find dried tomato vinaigrette, substitute ⅔ cup bottled red wine vinaigrette and 2 tablespoons snipped, drained oil-packed dried tomatoes.

**NOTE: Because chile peppers contain volatile oils that can burn your skin and eyes, avoid direct contact with them as much as possible. When working with chile peppers, wear plastic or rubber gloves. If your bare hands do touch the chile peppers, wash your hands and nails well with soap and warm water.

glazed turkey burgers

A glaze of mustard and fruit preserves gives these burgers a sweet-sour flavor.

PREP: 20 minutes **GRILL:** 14 minutes **MAKES:** 4 servings

1	tablespoon yellow mustard
1	tablespoon cherry, apricot, peach, or pineapple preserves
1	beaten egg
¼	cup quick-cooking rolled oats
¼	cup finely chopped celery
3	tablespoons snipped dried tart cherries or dried apricots (optional)
¼	teaspoon salt
⅛	teaspoon ground black pepper
1	pound uncooked ground turkey or chicken
4	kaiser rolls or hamburger buns, split and toasted
	Desired accompaniments, such as mayonnaise or salad dressing, lettuce leaves, and/or tomato slices (optional)

one For glaze, in a small bowl stir together mustard and preserves; set aside. In a medium bowl combine egg, rolled oats, celery, dried cherries (if desired), salt, and pepper. Add ground turkey; mix well. Shape into four ¾-inch-thick patties.

two For a charcoal grill, grill patties on the greased rack of an uncovered grill directly over medium coals for 14 to 18 minutes or until no longer pink (165°F),* turning once halfway through grilling and brushing with glaze during the last minute of grilling. (For a gas grill, preheat grill. Reduce heat to medium. Place patties on greased grill rack over heat. Cover and grill as above.) Serve burgers on rolls or buns. Brush any remaining glaze over burgers. If desired, serve with your choice of accompaniments.

NUTRITION FACTS PER SERVING: 397 cal., 14 g total fat (3 g sat. fat), 143 mg chol., 599 mg sodium, 38 g carbo., 2 g fiber, 28 g pro.

*NOTE: The internal color of a burger is not a reliable doneness indicator. A turkey or chicken patty cooked to 165°F is safe, regardless of color. To measure the doneness of a patty, insert an instant-read thermometer through the side of the patty to a depth of 2 to 3 inches.

honey-bourbon salmon

Brown sugar, bourbon, soy sauce, and ginger combine to create an extraordinary marinade for salmon steaks.

PREP: 10 minutes **MARINATE:** 1 hour **GRILL:** 8 minutes **MAKES:** 4 servings

4	6- to 8-ounce fresh or frozen salmon steaks, cut 1 inch thick
¾	cup bourbon whiskey
½	cup packed brown sugar
2	tablespoons honey
2	teaspoons soy sauce
½	teaspoon ground ginger
¼	teaspoon ground black pepper

one Thaw salmon, if frozen; rinse and pat dry with paper towels. Place in a resealable plastic bag set in a shallow dish.

two For marinade, in a small bowl stir together the bourbon, brown sugar, honey, soy sauce, ginger, and pepper. Pour over fish in the bag. Seal bag; turn gently to coat fish. Marinate in refrigerator for 1 hour, turning bag occasionally.

three Drain fish, reserving marinade. For a charcoal grill, grill fish on the greased rack of an uncovered grill directly over medium coals for 8 to 12 minutes or until fish flakes easily when tested with a fork, gently turning once and brushing once with reserved marinade halfway through grilling. (For a gas grill, preheat grill. Reduce heat to medium. Place fish on greased grill rack over heat. Cover and grill as above.) Discard any remaining marinade.

NUTRITION FACTS PER SERVING: 322 cal., 6 g total fat (1 g sat. fat), 88 mg chol., 197 mg sodium, 19 g carbo., 0 g fiber, 34 g pro.

tuna with peanut sauce

Asian flavors—ginger, sesame, soy, and garlic—season this fast-cooking meal. You can make the sauce ahead and simply reheat at serving time. This sauce is also tasty on chicken.

PREP: 15 minutes **GRILL:** 8 minutes **MAKES:** 4 servings

4	4-ounce fresh or frozen tuna steaks (albacore or yellow fin), cut 1 inch thick
½	cup lightly salted peanuts
¼	cup water
1	green onion, cut into 1-inch pieces
2	tablespoons toasted sesame oil
1	tablespoon soy sauce
1	tablespoon rice vinegar
1	teaspoon sugar
1	teaspoon grated fresh ginger
½	teaspoon bottled minced garlic (1 clove)
2	to 3 tablespoons water
1	tablespoon bottled teriyaki sauce
1	tablespoon water
	Chopped peanuts (optional)
	Sliced green onion (optional)

one Thaw fish, if frozen; rinse and pat dry with paper towels. For peanut sauce, in a food processor/blender combine the ½ cup peanuts, the ¼ cup water, the green onion pieces, sesame oil, soy sauce, rice vinegar, sugar, ginger, and garlic. Cover and process until almost smooth; pour into a small saucepan. Stir in enough of the 2 to 3 tablespoons water to thin slightly; set aside.

two In a small bowl combine teriyaki sauce and the 1 tablespoon water. Brush both sides of each tuna steak with the teriyaki mixture.

three For charcoal grill, grill tuna on the greased rack of an uncovered grill directly over medium coals for 8 to 12 minutes or until fish flakes easily when tested with a fork, gently turning once halfway through grilling. (For gas grill, preheat grill. Reduce heat to medium. Place fish on greased grill rack over heat. Cover and grill as above.)

four Slowly warm peanut sauce over medium-low heat. (Sauce will thicken slightly as it is heated. Stir in additional water, if necessary.) Spoon sauce over tuna. If desired, garnish with chopped peanuts and sliced green onion.

NUTRITION FACTS PER SERVING: 301 cal., 17 g total fat (2 g sat. fat), 51 mg chol., 524 mg sodium, 6 g carbo., 2 g fiber, 32 g pro.

basil halibut steaks

Make the most of fresh basil—from your garden, the farmer's market, or the supermarket—in this savory dish.

PREP: 25 minutes **GRILL:** 8 minutes **MAKES:** 4 servings

2	fresh or frozen halibut steaks, cut 1 inch thick (about 1½ pounds total)
1	medium onion, chopped
½	teaspoon bottled minced garlic (1 clove)
2	tablespoons olive oil
2	to 3 cups chopped, peeled tomatoes
¼	teaspoon salt
¼	teaspoon ground black pepper
¼	cup snipped fresh basil
1	tablespoon butter or margarine, melted
	Salt
	Ground black pepper

one Thaw fish, if frozen; rinse and pat dry with paper towels. Set aside.

two In a medium skillet cook onion and garlic in hot oil until tender. Stir in tomatoes, the ¼ teaspoon salt, and the ¼ teaspoon pepper. Bring to boiling; reduce heat. Simmer, uncovered, for 15 minutes. Stir in 2 tablespoons of the basil.

three Meanwhile, in a small bowl combine melted butter and the remaining 2 tablespoons basil; brush over one side of each halibut steak.

four For a charcoal grill, grill fish on the greased rack of an uncovered grill directly over medium coals for 8 to 12 minutes or until fish flakes easily when tested with a fork, gently turning once halfway through grilling. (For a gas grill, preheat grill. Reduce heat to medium. Place fish on greased grill rack over heat. Cover and grill as above.)

five Season fish to taste with additional salt and pepper. Serve with tomato mixture.

NUTRITION FACTS PER SERVING: 302 cal., 14 g total fat (3 g sat. fat), 62 mg chol., 265 mg sodium, 7 g carbo., 2 g fiber, 37 g pro.

halibut with blueberry-pepper jam

If halibut isn't available, opt for sea bass or salmon fillets.

PREP: 25 minutes **GRILL:** 12 minutes **MAKES:** 4 servings

- 4   5- to 6-ounce fresh or frozen halibut steaks or fillets or sea bass or salmon fillets, about 1 inch thick
- 1   cup fresh blueberries, rinsed and drained
- 1   teaspoon snipped fresh sage
- ½   teaspoon freshly ground black pepper
- 1   cup purchased garlic croutons, coarsely crushed
- ¼   cup snipped fresh sage
- 1   teaspoon finely shredded orange peel
- ¼   teaspoon freshly ground black pepper
- 2   tablespoons orange juice
- 1   tablespoon olive oil
      Olive oil (optional)
      Fresh sage leaves (optional)

one Thaw fish, if frozen; rinse and pat dry with paper towels. Set aside.

two For blueberry-pepper jam, in a medium bowl mash ¾ cup of the blueberries with a potato masher or fork. Stir in the remaining ¼ cup blueberries, the 1 teaspoon sage, and the ½ teaspoon pepper. Cover and chill until ready to serve. In a small bowl combine crushed croutons, the ¼ cup sage, the orange peel, and the ¼ teaspoon pepper. Stir in orange juice and the 1 tablespoon olive oil until lightly moistened; set aside.

three For a charcoal grill, grill fish on the greased rack of an uncovered grill directly over medium coals for 5 minutes. Carefully turn fish; top evenly with crouton topping, pressing onto fish. Grill for 7 to 10 minutes more or until fish flakes easily when tested with a fork. (For a gas grill, preheat grill. Reduce heat to medium. Place fish on greased grill rack over heat. Cover and grill as above.)

four To serve, place fish on serving platter. Serve with blueberry-pepper jam. If desired, drizzle fish with additional olive oil and garnish with sage leaves.

NUTRITION FACTS PER SERVING: 222 cal., 7 g total fat (1 g sat. fat), 45 mg chol., 101 mg sodium, 8 g carbo., 1 g fiber, 30 g pro.

lime-marinated halibut

The lime juice in this marinade flavors and tenderizes the fish—but don't let the fish soak any longer than 20 minutes or the acidic juice will begin to affect its appearance, turning it white or opaque.

PREP: 8 minutes **MARINATE:** 20 minutes **GRILL:** 8 minutes
MAKES: 4 servings

4	5-ounce fresh or frozen halibut steaks, cut 1 inch thick
1	lime
2	teaspoons olive oil
¼	teaspoon salt
1¼	cups chicken broth
1	cup quick-cooking couscous
1	cup cherry tomatoes, halved
2	tablespoons snipped fresh cilantro
2	tablespoons snipped fresh mint

one Thaw fish, if frozen; rinse and pat dry with paper towels. Finely shred enough peel from the lime to make 1 teaspoon; set aside. For marinade, halve and squeeze enough juice from the lime to make 2 tablespoons. In a shallow dish combine the lime juice, olive oil, and salt. Add fish, turning to coat. Cover and marinate at room temperature for 20 minutes, turning fish once.

two Drain fish, discarding marinade. For a charcoal grill, grill fish on the greased rack of an uncovered grill directly over medium coals for 8 to 12 minutes or until fish flakes easily when tested with a fork, gently turning once halfway through grilling. (For a gas grill, preheat grill. Reduce heat to medium. Place fish on greased grill rack over heat. Cover and grill as above.)

three Meanwhile, for couscous, in a medium saucepan bring chicken broth to boiling. Stir in couscous. Remove from heat; cover and let stand for 5 minutes. Fluff with a fork. Stir in cherry tomatoes, cilantro, mint, and the reserved lime peel. Cover and let stand for 2 to 3 minutes more or until tomatoes are warm. Serve with grilled fish.

NUTRITION FACTS PER SERVING: 372 cal., 7 g total fat (1 g sat. fat), 45 mg chol., 545 mg sodium, 39 g carbo., 3 g fiber, 37 g pro.

swordfish with spicy tomato sauce

This vibrant and fresh fish entrée combines two popular Sicilian foods, swordfish and a spicy, fresh tomato sauce. Couscous, a North African favorite, makes a great serve-along.

PREP: 15 minutes **GRILL:** 8 minutes **MAKES:** 4 servings

4	fresh or frozen swordfish steaks, cut 1 inch thick (about 1¼ pounds total)
4	teaspoons cooking oil
½	teaspoon salt
¼	teaspoon ground black pepper
¼	cup chopped onion
1	small fresh serrano or jalapeño chile pepper, seeded and finely chopped*
½	teaspoon bottled minced garlic (1 clove)
½	teaspoon ground turmeric
¼	teaspoon ground coriander
1½	cups chopped plum tomatoes
1	tablespoon snipped fresh cilantro
	Hot cooked couscous (optional)

one Thaw fish, if frozen; rinse and pat dry with paper towels. Drizzle 2 teaspoons of the oil over swordfish. Sprinkle with ¼ teaspoon of the salt and the pepper.

two For a charcoal grill, grill fish steaks on the greased rack of an uncovered grill directly over medium coals for 8 to 12 minutes or until fish flakes easily when tested with a fork, gently turning once halfway through grilling. (For a gas grill, preheat grill. Reduce heat to medium. Place fish on greased grill rack over heat. Cover and grill as above.)

three Meanwhile, for the spicy tomato sauce, in a medium skillet heat the remaining 2 teaspoons oil over medium heat. Add onion, chile pepper, garlic, turmeric, and coriander; cook about 2 minutes or until onions are tender. Stir in tomatoes and the remaining ¼ teaspoon salt; cook for 2 to 3 minutes or just until tomatoes are tender. Remove from heat; stir in cilantro. Serve spicy tomato sauce over fish. If desired, serve with couscous.

NUTRITION FACTS PER SERVING: 237 cal., 11 g total fat (2 g sat. fat), 56 mg chol., 402 mg sodium, 5 g carbo., 1 g fiber, 29 g pro.

*NOTE: Because chile peppers contain volatile oils that can burn your skin and eyes, avoid direct contact with them as much as possible. When working with chile peppers, wear plastic or rubber gloves. If your bare hands do touch the chile peppers, wash your hands and nails well with soap and warm water.

dilly salmon fillets

A quick, dill-infused, Dijon-flavored mayonnaise caps off these Scandinavian-style salmon fillets. For a built-in salad and extra freshness, serve them on a bed of shredded cucumber.

PREP: 15 minutes **MARINATE:** 10 minutes
GRILL: 7 to 9 minutes per ½-inch thickness **MAKES:** 4 servings

4	6-ounce fresh or frozen skinless salmon fillets, ½ to ¾ inch thick
3	tablespoons lemon juice
2	tablespoons snipped fresh dill
2	tablespoons mayonnaise or salad dressing
2	teaspoons Dijon-style mustard
	Dash ground black pepper

one Thaw fish, if frozen; rinse and pat dry with paper towels. Measure thickness of fish. Place fish in a shallow dish. In a small bowl combine the lemon juice and 1 tablespoon of the dill; pour over fish. Marinate at room temperature for 10 minutes. Meanwhile, in a small bowl stir together the remaining 1 tablespoon dill, the mayonnaise, mustard, and pepper; set aside.

two For a charcoal grill, arrange medium-hot coals around a drip pan. Test for medium heat above the pan. Place fish on greased grill rack over drip pan. Cover and grill until fish flakes easily when tested with a fork, gently turning once and spreading with the mayonnaise mixture halfway through grilling. Allow 7 to 9 minutes per ½-inch thickness of fish. (For a gas grill, preheat grill. Reduce heat to medium. Adjust for indirect cooking. Grill as above.)

NUTRITION FACTS PER SERVING: 211 cal., 11 g total fat (2 g sat. fat), 35 mg chol., 204 mg sodium, 1 g carbo., 0 g fiber, 25 g pro.

fish & vegetable packets

The whole meal—except for the accompanying rice—is cooked on the grill in a foil packet. Served in its foil pouch, it makes an attractive, great-tasting dinner with few dishes to wash.

PREP: 40 minutes **GRILL:** 12 to 14 minutes per ½-inch thickness
MAKES: 4 servings

1	pound fresh or frozen skinless salmon, orange roughy, cod, or tilapia fillets, ½ to ¾ inch thick
	Nonstick cooking spray
2	cups carrots cut into thin bite-size strips
2	cups red sweet pepper cut into bite-size strips
12	fresh asparagus spears (about 12 ounces), trimmed
4	small yellow summer squash (about 1 pound), cut into ¼-inch slices
½	cup dry white wine or chicken broth
2	teaspoons snipped fresh rosemary or ½ teaspoon dried rosemary, crushed
1	teaspoon bottled minced garlic (2 cloves)
¼	teaspoon salt
¼	teaspoon ground black pepper
2	tablespoons butter or margarine, cut up
	Hot cooked white or brown rice

one Thaw fish, if frozen; rinse and pat dry with paper towels. Measure thickness of fish. Cut into 4 serving-size pieces. Set aside.

two Cut eight 18-inch squares heavy foil. Stack 2 squares together; repeat to form 4 stacks total. Coat 1 side of each stack with nonstick cooking spray. Divide carrots, sweet pepper, and asparagus among stacks of foil. Top with the fish and squash.

three For seasonings, in a small bowl combine wine, rosemary, garlic, salt, and black pepper. Drizzle over fish and vegetables; dot with butter. Bring up 2 opposite edges of each foil stack; seal with a double fold. Fold remaining ends to completely enclose the fish and vegetables, leaving space for steam to build.

four For a charcoal grill, place foil packets on the grill rack of an uncovered grill directly over medium coals. Grill until fish flakes easily when tested with a fork and vegetables are tender, carefully opening packets to check doneness. Allow 12 to 14 minutes per ½-inch thickness of fish. (For a gas grill, preheat grill. Reduce heat to medium. Place foil packets on grill rack over heat. Cover and grill as above.) Serve with hot cooked rice.

NUTRITION FACTS PER SERVING: 518 cal., 22 g total fat (8 g sat. fat), 91 mg chol., 294 mg sodium, 43 g carbo., 6 g fiber, 32 g pro.

sesame-ginger grilled salmon

Toasting sesame seeds is easy. Place them in a small, heavy skillet over low heat and cook, stirring frequently, for 5 to 7 minutes or until they're golden brown and fragrant.

PREP: 15 minutes **MARINATE:** 30 minutes or 2 hours
GRILL: 7 to 9 minutes per ½-inch thickness **MAKES:** 4 servings

4	5-ounce fresh or frozen skinless salmon fillets, ¾ to 1 inch thick
¼	cup light soy sauce
2	tablespoons lime juice
1	tablespoon grated fresh ginger
1	teaspoon brown sugar
½	teaspoon toasted sesame oil
2	tablespoons sesame seeds, toasted

one Thaw fish, if frozen; rinse and pat dry with paper towels. Measure thickness of fish. For marinade, in a shallow dish combine soy sauce, lime juice, ginger, brown sugar, and sesame oil. Add fish, turning to coat. Cover and marinate at room temperature for 30 minutes or in the refrigerator for 2 hours, turning fish occasionally.

two Drain fish, discarding marinade. For a charcoal grill, arrange medium-hot coals around a drip pan. Test for medium heat above the pan. Place fish on greased grill rack over drip pan, tucking under any thin edges. Sprinkle fish with sesame seeds. Cover and grill until fish flakes easily when tested with a fork. Allow 7 to 9 minutes per ½-inch thickness of fish. Do not turn fish. (For a gas grill, preheat grill. Reduce heat to medium. Adjust for indirect cooking. Grill as above.)

NUTRITION FACTS PER SERVING: 282 cal., 17 g total fat (4 g sat. fat), 93 mg chol., 130 mg sodium, 2 g carbo., 1 g fiber, 29 g pro.

red snapper with fresh herb-pecan crust

Butter, chopped pecans, fresh herbs, and a touch of lemon and garlic make a toasty crust on this meaty grilled red snapper. Instead of flat-leaf parsley, you can substitute your favorite herb. It's terrific on fresh walleye too!

PREP: 15 minutes **GRILL:** 4 to 6 minutes per ½-inch thickness
MAKES: 4 servings

4	5- or 6-ounce fresh or frozen red snapper fillets with skin, ½ to 1 inch thick
⅓	cup finely chopped pecans
2	tablespoons fine dry bread crumbs
2	tablespoons butter or margarine, softened
1	teaspoon finely shredded lemon peel
1	teaspoon bottled minced garlic (2 cloves)
1	tablespoon snipped fresh flat-leaf parsley
¼	teaspoon salt
⅛	teaspoon ground black pepper
	Dash cayenne pepper
	Snipped fresh flat-leaf parsley (optional)
	Lemon wedges (optional)

one Thaw fish, if frozen; rinse and pat dry with paper towels. Measure thickness of fish. In a small bowl combine pecans, bread crumbs, butter, lemon peel, garlic, the 1 tablespoon parsley, the salt, black pepper, and cayenne pepper.

two For a charcoal grill, place fish, skin side down, on the greased rack of an uncovered grill directly over medium coals. Spoon pecan mixture on top of fillets; spread slightly. Grill until fish flakes easily when tested with a fork. Allow 4 to 6 minutes per ½-inch thickness of fish. (For a gas grill, preheat grill. Reduce heat to medium. Place fish on greased grill rack over heat. Spoon pecan mixture on top of fillets; spread slightly. Cover and grill as above.) If desired, sprinkle fish with additional snipped parsley and serve with lemon wedges.

NUTRITION FACTS PER SERVING: 268 cal., 14 g total fat (4 g sat. fat), 67 mg chol., 287 mg sodium, 7 g carbo., 8 g fiber, 30 g pro.

snapper with cilantro pesto

Cilantro, used in a pesto, has a freshness that goes beautifully with fish. Try the pesto in other recipes. For a change of pace, stir it into angel hair pasta to create a side dish for grilled fish.

PREP: 15 minutes **GRILL:** 4 to 6 minutes per ½-inch thickness
MAKES: 4 servings

4	4- to 5-ounce fresh or frozen red snapper or halibut fillets, ½ to ¾ inch thick
1	cup loosely packed fresh parsley leaves
½	cup loosely packed fresh cilantro leaves
3	tablespoons grated Parmesan cheese
2	tablespoons pine nuts or slivered almonds
2	teaspoons lemon juice
1½	teaspoons bottled minced garlic (3 cloves)
⅛	teaspoon salt
2	tablespoons olive oil
1	tablespoon lemon juice
2	teaspoons olive oil
	Salt
	Ground black pepper
1	plum tomato, seeded and chopped

one Thaw fish, if frozen; rinse and pat dry with paper towels. Measure thickness of fish.

two For pesto, in a food processor/blender combine the parsley, cilantro, Parmesan cheese, nuts, the 2 teaspoons lemon juice, the garlic, and the ⅛ teaspoon salt. Cover and process with several on-off turns until nearly smooth, stopping the machine and scraping down sides as necessary. With the machine running slowly, gradually add the 2 tablespoons oil; blend until the consistency of softened butter, scraping sides as necessary. Transfer to a small bowl. Set aside.

three In a small bowl stir together the 1 tablespoon lemon juice and the 2 teaspoons oil. Brush fish with lemon mixture. Sprinkle fish with salt and pepper.

four Place fish in a greased grill basket, tucking under any thin edges. For a charcoal grill, grill fish in basket on the rack of an uncovered grill directly over medium coals until fish flakes easily when tested with a fork, turning basket once halfway through grilling. Allow 4 to 6 minutes per ½-inch thickness of fish. (For a gas grill, preheat grill. Reduce heat to medium. Place fish in basket on grill rack over heat. Cover and grill as above.)

five To serve, spoon pesto over fish and top with tomato.

NUTRITION FACTS PER SERVING: 254 cal., 15 g total fat (3 g sat. fat), 45 mg chol., 281 mg sodium, 4 g carbo., 0 g fiber, 27 g pro.

orange & dill sea bass

When it's time to give the fish-and-lemon combo a vacation, explore other citrus possibilities. Here, sea bass is perfumed orange by "baking" it on your grill on a bed of orange slices.

PREP: 15 minutes **GRILL:** 6 minutes **MAKES:** 4 servings

4	5- to 6-ounce fresh or frozen sea bass or orange roughy fillets, about ¾ inch thick
2	tablespoons snipped fresh dill
2	tablespoons olive oil
¼	teaspoon salt
¼	teaspoon ground white pepper
4	large oranges, cut into ¼-inch slices
1	orange, cut into wedges
	Fresh dill sprigs (optional)

one Thaw fish, if frozen; rinse and pat dry with paper towels. In a small bowl stir together the snipped dill, oil, salt, and white pepper. Brush both sides of fish with dill mixture.

two For a charcoal grill, place medium coals in bottom of a grill with a cover. Arrange a bed of orange slices on the greased grill rack directly over coals. Arrange fish on orange slices. Cover; grill for 6 to 9 minutes or until fish flakes easily when tested with a fork. Do not turn fish. (For a gas grill, preheat grill. Reduce heat to medium. Arrange orange slices and fish on greased grill rack over heat. Grill as above.)

three To serve, use a spatula to transfer fish and grilled orange slices to a serving platter or dinner plates. Squeeze the juice from orange wedges over fish. If desired, garnish with dill sprigs.

NUTRITION FACTS PER SERVING: 207 cal., 10 g total fat (2 g sat. fat), 59 mg chol., 230 mg sodium, 2 g carbo., 0 g fiber, 26 g pro.

mahi mahi with vegetable slaw

The cabbage, carrot, and jicama slaw gives this flavorful dish a pleasant crunch.

PREP: 15 minutes **MARINATE:** 30 minutes
GRILL: 4 to 6 minutes per ½-inch thickness **MAKES:** 4 servings

4	5- to 6-ounce fresh or frozen mahi mahi or pike fillets, ½ to ¾ inch thick
1	teaspoon finely shredded lime peel (set aside)
¼	cup lime juice
¼	cup snipped fresh cilantro
3	tablespoons olive oil
1	tablespoon honey
1	fresh jalapeño chile pepper, seeded and finely chopped*
1½	teaspoons bottled minced garlic (3 cloves)
⅛	teaspoon salt
1½	cups packaged shredded cabbage with carrot (coleslaw mix)
1	cup shredded jicama

one Thaw fish, if frozen; rinse and pat dry with paper towels. Measure thickness of fish. Place fish in a shallow dish. For dressing, in a small bowl combine lime juice, cilantro, oil, honey, jalapeño pepper, garlic, and salt; divide in half. Stir lime peel into 1 portion of the dressing. Pour dressing with lime peel over fish; turn fish to coat. Cover; marinate at room temperature for 30 minutes.

two For slaw, in a medium bowl combine cabbage mixture and jicama. Pour remaining dressing over slaw; toss to coat. Cover and chill until ready to serve.

three Drain fish, discarding marinade. Place fish in a well-greased wire grill basket, tucking under any thin edges. For a charcoal grill, grill fish in basket on the rack of an uncovered grill directly over medium coals until fish flakes easily when tested with a fork, turning basket once halfway through grilling. Allow 4 to 6 minutes per ½-inch thickness. (For a gas grill, preheat grill. Reduce heat to medium. Place fish in basket on grill rack over heat. Cover and grill as above.) Serve fish with slaw.

NUTRITION FACTS PER SERVING: 276 cal., 10 g total fat (1 g sat. fat), 67 mg chol., 130 mg sodium, 12 g carbo., 1 g fiber, 34 g pro.

*****NOTE:** Because chile peppers contain volatile oils that can burn your skin and eyes, avoid direct contact with them as much as possible. When working with chile peppers, wear plastic or rubber gloves. If your bare hands do touch the chile peppers, wash your hands and nails well with soap and warm water.

blackened catfish with roasted potatoes

Vegetables roasted in olive oil add color and variety to this version of a Cajun classic.

PREP: 20 minutes **GRILL:** 35 minutes **MAKES:** 4 servings

4	4- to 5-ounce fresh or frozen catfish or red snapper fillets, about ½ inch thick
1	tablespoon olive oil
¼	teaspoon salt
	Several dashes bottled hot pepper sauce
1½	pounds tiny new potatoes, thinly sliced
4	medium carrots, thinly sliced
1	medium green sweet pepper, cut into thin strips
1	medium onion, sliced
½	teaspoon Cajun seasoning
	Nonstick cooking spray
1	tablespoon snipped fresh chervil or parsley

one Thaw fish, if frozen; rinse and pat dry with paper towels. Fold a 48×18-inch piece of heavy foil in half to make a 24×18-inch rectangle. In a large bowl combine oil, salt, and hot pepper sauce. Add the potatoes, carrots, sweet pepper, and onion; toss to coat. Place in the center of foil. Bring up 2 opposite edges of foil; seal with a double fold. Fold remaining ends to completely enclose vegetables, leaving space for steam to build.

two For a charcoal grill, grill vegetable packet on the greased rack of an uncovered grill directly over medium coals for 35 to 40 minutes or until potatoes and carrots are tender.

three Sprinkle both sides of fish with Cajun seasoning and lightly coat with nonstick cooking spray. Place fish in a well-greased wire grill basket, tucking under any thin edges. Add grill basket to grill beside vegetable packet for the last 4 to 6 minutes of grilling. Grill until fish flakes easily with a fork, gently turning grill basket once halfway through grilling. (For a gas grill, preheat grill. Reduce heat to medium. Place vegetable packet, then fish in grill basket on grill rack over heat. Cover and grill as above.)

four To serve, sprinkle fish and vegetables with snipped chervil or parsley.

NUTRITION FACTS PER SERVING: 352 cal., 6 g total fat (1 g sat. fat), 42 mg chol., 266 mg sodium, 48 g carbo., 5 g fiber, 28 g pro.

trout with mushrooms

Whether you pull it from a stream or from the nearest supermarket, fresh trout needs few seasonings to complement its delicate flavor.

PREP: 15 minutes **GRILL:** 6 minutes **MAKES:** 4 servings

4	8-ounce fresh or frozen dressed whole trout (heads removed, if desired)
1	large lemon, halved
¼	cup olive oil
4	teaspoons snipped fresh thyme or 1 teaspoon dried thyme, crushed
¼	teaspoon salt
¼	teaspoon crushed red pepper
1½	cups sliced jumbo button mushrooms (4 ounces)
1	bunch green onions (8 to 10)
4	sprigs fresh thyme

one Thaw fish, if frozen; rinse and pat dry with paper towels. Strain juice from 1 lemon half into a small bowl. Set aside. Thinly slice remaining lemon half. Cut the slices in half. Set aside.

two In a small bowl stir together the lemon juice, olive oil, snipped or dried thyme, salt, and crushed red pepper. Set aside ¼ cup of the lemon juice mixture. Toss the sliced mushrooms with the remaining lemon juice mixture; cover and set aside.

three Trim off the root end and the first inch of the green tops of each green onion. Brush the onion pieces with some of the reserved ¼ cup lemon juice mixture.

four Place trout in a grill basket. Tuck 2 halved lemon slices and a thyme sprig inside the cavity of each trout. Brush skin and inside flesh of trout with the remainder of the ¼ cup lemon juice mixture.

five For a charcoal grill, grill fish on a greased rack of an uncovered grill directly over medium coals for 6 to 9 minutes or until fish flakes easily when tested with a fork. Grill green onions alongside fish for 4 to 6 minutes or until tender, turning once. (For a gas grill, preheat grill. Reduce heat to medium. Place fish, then green onions on greased grill rack over heat. Cover and grill as above.)

six To serve, arrange green onions on 4 dinner plates. Arrange fish on green onions. Spoon the marinated mushroom slices over fish.

NUTRITION FACTS PER SERVING: 454 cal., 26 g total fat (5 g sat. fat), 133 mg chol., 231 mg sodium, 4 g carbo., 1 g fiber, 49 g pro.

ginger tuna kabobs

A touch of honey added to the reserved marinade makes a delicious brush-on for these grilled tuna, pineapple, and vegetable kabobs.

PREP: 30 minutes **MARINATE:** 30 minutes **GRILL:** 8 minutes
MAKES: 4 servings

12	ounces fresh or frozen skinless tuna steaks, cut 1 inch thick
3	tablespoons reduced-sodium soy sauce
3	tablespoons water
1	tablespoon snipped green onion tops or snipped fresh chives
2	teaspoons grated fresh ginger
½	of a medium fresh pineapple, cored and cut into 1-inch cubes
1	medium red or green sweet pepper, cut into 1½-inch squares
6	green onions, cut into 2-inch pieces
¼	cup honey

one Thaw tuna, if frozen; rinse and pat dry with paper towels. Cut tuna into 1-inch cubes. Place in a resealable plastic bag set in a shallow dish. Add soy sauce, the water, snipped green onion tops, and ginger. Seal bag; turn gently to coat tuna. Marinate in the refrigerator for 30 minutes.

two Drain tuna, reserving marinade. On long metal skewers, alternately thread tuna, pineapple, sweet pepper, and green onion pieces, leaving ¼-inch space between pieces. For a charcoal grill, grill kabobs on the greased rack of an uncovered grill directly over medium coals for 8 to 12 minutes or until tuna flakes easily when tested with a fork, turning kabobs once halfway through grilling. (For a gas grill, preheat grill. Reduce heat to medium. Place kabobs on greased grill rack over heat. Cover and grill as above.)

three Meanwhile, bring reserved marinade to boiling; strain. Discard any solids. Stir honey into hot marinade. Brush tuna, pineapple, and vegetables generously with honey-soy mixture just before serving.

NUTRITION FACTS PER SERVING: 251 cal., 5 g total fat (1 g sat. fat), 32 mg chol., 446 mg sodium, 32 g carbo., 2 g fiber, 22 g pro.

salmon with cucumber kabobs

Cooked cucumbers provide a pleasant change of pace on these kabobs. Though their characteristic crispness disappears with cooking, their delicacy does not.

PREP: 15 minutes   **MARINATE:** 10 to 20 minutes
GRILL: 4 to 6 minutes per ½-inch thickness   **MAKES:** 4 servings

- 4   6- to 8-ounce fresh or frozen skinless salmon fillets, ½ to 1 inch thick
- ⅓   cup lemon juice
- 1   tablespoon olive oil or cooking oil
- 2   teaspoons snipped fresh tarragon
- 1   medium cucumber, halved lengthwise and cut into 1-inch-thick slices
- 1   medium red onion, cut into wedges
- 8   cherry tomatoes
    Hot cooked rice (optional)

one Thaw fish, if frozen; rinse and pat dry with paper towels. Measure thickness of fish. Place fish in a resealable plastic bag set in a shallow dish. For marinade, in a small bowl combine lemon juice, oil, and tarragon. For basting sauce, set aside half of the marinade. Pour the remaining marinade over fish. Seal bag; turn to coat fish. Marinate at room temperature for at least 10 minutes or up to 20 minutes. Meanwhile, on four 10-inch skewers, alternately thread cucumber and onion.

two Drain fish, discarding marinade. Place fish in a well-greased wire grill basket, tucking under any thin edges. For a charcoal grill, grill the fish and vegetable kabobs on the rack of an uncovered grill directly over medium coals until fish flakes easily when tested with a fork and vegetables are tender, gently turning once and brushing once with basting sauce halfway through grilling. Allow 4 to 6 minutes per ½-inch thickness of fish and 8 to 12 minutes for vegetables. (For a gas grill, preheat grill. Reduce heat to medium. Place fish in basket and vegetables on greased grill rack over heat. Cover and grill as above.) Add the tomatoes to the ends of the kabobs for the last 2 minutes of grilling.

three If desired, serve fish and vegetables with hot cooked rice.

NUTRITION FACTS PER SERVING: 201 cal., 8 g total fat (2 g sat. fat), 31 mg chol., 106 mg sodium, 6 g carbo., 1 g fiber, 25 g pro.

jambalaya on a stick

The combination of shrimp, smoked sausage, chicken, and vegetables is reminiscent of the Creole classic jambalaya.

PREP: 35 minutes **MARINATE:** 1 to 2 hours **SOAK:** 30 minutes
GRILL: 10 minutes **MAKES:** 6 servings

18	fresh or frozen large shrimp in shells (about 12 ounces)
12	ounces cooked smoked sausage links, cut into 12 pieces
8	ounces skinless, boneless chicken breast halves, cut into 1-inch pieces
1	medium green sweet pepper, cut into 1-inch pieces
1	medium onion, cut into 1-inch wedges
⅓	cup white wine vinegar
⅓	cup tomato sauce
2	tablespoons olive oil
2	teaspoons dried thyme, crushed
2	teaspoons bottled hot pepper sauce
¾	teaspoon dried minced garlic
24	8-inch wooden skewers
3	cups hot cooked rice
2	tablespoons snipped fresh parsley
6	cherry tomatoes

one Thaw shrimp, if frozen. Peel and devein shrimp. Rinse shrimp; pat dry with paper towels. Place shrimp, sausage, chicken, sweet pepper, and onion in a resealable plastic bag set in a shallow dish.

two In a small bowl combine vinegar, tomato sauce, oil, thyme, bottled hot pepper sauce, and garlic. Pour half of the tomato sauce mixture over meat and vegetables. Seal bag; turn to coat pieces. Marinate in the refrigerator for at least 1 hour or up to 2 hours, turning bag occasionally. Cover and chill remaining tomato sauce mixture.

three Meanwhile, soak wooden skewers in enough water to cover for 30 minutes; drain.

four Drain meat and vegetables, discarding marinade. On soaked skewers, alternately thread meat and vegetables (to secure pieces, use 2 skewers for each kabob—1 skewer through head end of shrimp and another skewer parallel to first skewer but through tail end of shrimp), leaving ¼ inch space between pieces.

five For a charcoal grill, grill skewers on the greased rack of an uncovered grill directly over medium coals for 10 to 12 minutes or until shrimp are opaque and chicken is no longer pink, turning occasionally. (For a gas grill, preheat grill. Reduce heat to medium. Place skewers on greased grill rack over heat. Cover and grill as above.)

six Meanwhile, in a small saucepan heat chilled tomato sauce mixture. Combine cooked rice and parsley. Serve rice mixture and cherry tomatoes with kabobs. Pass the warmed tomato sauce mixture.

NUTRITION FACTS PER SERVING: 451 cal., 23 g total fat (9 g sat. fat), 112 mg chol., 632 mg sodium, 30 g carbo., 2 g fiber, 27 g pro.

margarita kabobs

These shrimp kabobs with a brush-on sauce are based on the classic cocktail. The alcohol helps the flavors blend subtly, but you can omit it.

PREP: 30 minutes **GRILL:** 10 minutes **MAKES:** 6 servings

1¼	pounds fresh or frozen jumbo shrimp in shells or skinless, boneless chicken breast halves or thighs
1	large red or green sweet pepper, cut into bite-size pieces
1	medium red onion, cut into wedges
1	cup orange marmalade
⅓	cup lime juice
¼	cup tequila (optional)
2	tablespoons snipped fresh cilantro
2	tablespoons cooking oil
1	teaspoon bottled minced garlic (2 cloves)
6	½-inch-thick slices peeled fresh pineapple

one Thaw shrimp, if frozen. Peel and devein shrimp, leaving tails intact. Rinse shrimp; pat dry with paper towels. If using chicken, cut it into 1-inch chunks. On long metal skewers alternately thread shrimp and/or chicken, sweet pepper, and onion, leaving ¼ inch space between pieces.

two For sauce, in a small saucepan stir together orange marmalade, lime juice, tequila (if desired), cilantro, oil, and garlic. Cook and stir just until marmalade is melted.

three For a charcoal grill, grill kabobs on the greased rack of an uncovered grill directly over medium coals for 10 to 12 minutes or until shrimp are opaque and chicken is no longer pink, turning once halfway through grilling. After 5 minutes of grilling, add pineapple to grill rack. Turn pineapple once and brush pineapple and shrimp once with sauce during the last 3 minutes of grilling. (For a gas grill, preheat grill. Reduce heat to medium. Place skewers, then pineapple on greased grill rack over heat. Cover and grill as above.)

four To serve, reheat sauce until bubbly; pass warm sauce with kabobs and pineapple.

NUTRITION FACTS PER SERVING: 314 cal., 6 g total fat (1 g sat. fat), 108 mg chol., 141 mg sodium, 52 g carbo., 2 g fiber, 16 g pro.

rosemary-orange shrimp kabobs

With shrimp, turkey bacon, and a special orange-flavored couscous and sweet pepper combo, this dish is definitely company fare.

PREP: 30 minutes **GRILL:** 8 minutes **MAKES:** 4 servings

16	fresh or frozen jumbo shrimp in shells (about 1 pound total)
8	slices turkey bacon, halved crosswise
2	red and/or yellow sweet peppers, cut into 1-inch pieces
2	teaspoons finely shredded orange or blood orange peel
2	tablespoons orange or blood orange juice
2	teaspoons snipped fresh rosemary
2	cups hot cooked couscous
1	cup cooked or canned black beans, rinsed and drained

one Thaw shrimp, if frozen. Peel and devein shrimp, leaving tails intact. Rinse shrimp; pat dry with paper towels.

two Wrap each shrimp in a half slice of the bacon. On long metal skewers, alternately thread bacon-wrapped shrimp and sweet pepper pieces, leaving ¼ inch space between pieces. In a small bowl combine 1 teaspoon of the orange peel, the orange juice, and rosemary. Brush over kabobs.

three For a charcoal grill, grill kabobs on the greased rack of an uncovered grill directly over medium coals for 8 to 10 minutes or until shrimp are opaque and bacon is crisp, turning once halfway through grilling. (For a gas grill, preheat grill. Reduce heat to medium. Place kabobs on greased grill rack over heat. Cover and grill as above.)

four Meanwhile, in a medium saucepan stir together the remaining 1 teaspoon orange peel, the couscous, and black beans; heat through. Serve with shrimp and peppers.

NUTRITION FACTS PER SERVING: 310 cal., 7 g total fat (2 g sat. fat), 149 mg chol., 563 mg sodium, 36 g carbo., 2 g fiber, 26 g pro.

bbq shrimp on pineapple planks

Jumbo shrimp are more impressive, but medium shrimp also work well for these skewers. Use 24 medium shrimp and grill them for 5 to 8 minutes or until they turn opaque.

PREP: 40 minutes **MARINATE:** 30 minutes **SOAK:** 30 minutes
GRILL: 7 minutes **MAKES:** 8 servings

16	fresh or frozen jumbo shrimp in shells (about 1 pound)
¼	cup bottled barbecue sauce
1	to 2 tablespoons chopped canned chipotle chile peppers in adobo sauce*
3	tablespoons butter or margarine, melted
1	teaspoon bottled minced garlic (2 cloves)
8	6- to 8-inch wooden skewers
1	fresh medium pineapple, crown removed and peeled
½	cup chopped seeded cucumber
½	cup chopped peeled jicama
1	tablespoon lime juice or lemon juice
¼	teaspoon salt
	Bottled barbecue sauce
¼	cup snipped fresh cilantro

one Thaw shrimp, if frozen. Peel and devein shrimp, leaving tails intact. Rinse shrimp; pat dry with paper towels.

two In a medium bowl combine the ¼ cup barbecue sauce, the chipotle peppers, 2 tablespoons of the melted butter, and the garlic. Stir in shrimp. Cover and marinate in the refrigerator for 30 minutes, stirring occasionally.

three Meanwhile, soak wooden skewers in enough water to cover for 30 minutes; drain. Cut pineapple lengthwise into ½-inch slices. Chop 1 of the slices to measure ½ cup; set aside for relish. Halve each pineapple slice crosswise (you should have 8 planks of pineapple). Using remaining 1 tablespoon melted butter, brush both sides of each pineapple plank; set aside.

four For relish, in a bowl combine the chopped pineapple, the chopped cucumber, jicama, lime juice, and salt. Cover and set aside until serving time.

five Remove shrimp from marinade; discard marinade. Thread 2 jumbo shrimp onto each soaked skewer, leaving ¼ inch space between shrimp. For a charcoal grill, grill skewers and pineapple planks on the greased rack of an uncovered grill directly over medium coals until shrimp are opaque and pineapple is heated through, turning once halfway through grilling and brushing with additional bottled barbecue sauce during the last 1 minute of grilling. Allow 7 to 9 minutes for shrimp and 6 to 8 minutes for pineapple planks. (For a gas grill, preheat grill. Reduce heat to medium. Place skewers and pineapple planks on greased grill rack over heat. Cover and grill as above.)

six To serve, stir snipped cilantro into the relish. Place pineapple planks on a serving platter. Spoon some of the relish over the pineapple planks; top each pineapple plank with a shrimp skewer.

NUTRITION FACTS PER SERVING: 135 cal., 6 g total fat (5 g sat. fat), 110 mg chol., 228 mg sodium, 8 g carbo., 1 g fiber, 12 g pro.

*NOTE: Because chile peppers contain volatile oils that can burn your skin and eyes, avoid direct contact with them as much as possible. When working with chile peppers, wear plastic or rubber gloves. If your bare hands do touch the chile peppers, wash your hands and nails well with soap and warm water.

garlic & shrimp pasta toss

As any Italian cook knows, garlic, butter, shrimp, and pasta were made for each other. Using roasted garlic can make the best even better.

PREP: 25 minutes **GRILL:** 30 minutes + 8 minutes **MAKES:** 4 servings

1	pound fresh or frozen large shrimp in shells
1	large garlic bulb
1	tablespoon olive oil
2	tablespoons lemon juice
1	red or yellow sweet pepper, quartered lengthwise
1	onion, cut into ½-inch slices
3	cups dried cavatelli (curled shells) or bow tie pasta (farfalle) (about 8 ounces)
2	tablespoons butter, softened
½	teaspoon salt
½	teaspoon ground black pepper
⅓	cup shredded Asiago or Parmesan cheese

one Thaw shrimp, if frozen. Peel and devein shrimp, leaving tails intact. Rinse shrimp; pat dry with paper towels. Cover and refrigerate until ready to grill.

two Using a sharp knife, cut off the top ½ inch from garlic bulb to expose the ends of the individual cloves. Leaving garlic bulb whole, remove any loose, papery outer layers.

three Fold an 18×9-inch piece of heavy foil in half to make a 9-inch square. Place garlic bulb, cut side up, in center of foil. Drizzle bulb with 1½ teaspoons of the oil. Bring up opposite edges of foil and seal with a double fold. Fold remaining edges together to completely enclose garlic, leaving room for steam to build.

four For a charcoal grill, arrange medium-hot coals around a drip pan. Test for medium heat above the pan. Place garlic on greased grill rack over drip pan. Cover and grill for 30 minutes.

five Meanwhile, thread shrimp onto long metal skewers, leaving ¼ inch space between pieces. In a small bowl combine the remaining 1½ teaspoons oil and 1 tablespoon of the lemon juice; brush over shrimp, sweet pepper, and onion. Discard any remaining oil-lemon juice mixture.

six Add skewers to grill rack over drip pan; add sweet pepper and onion to grill rack directly over coals. Cover and grill for 8 to 10 minutes more or until garlic is soft, shrimp are opaque, and vegetables are tender, turning shrimp and vegetables once halfway through grilling. (For a gas grill, preheat grill. Reduce heat to medium. Adjust for indirect cooking. Grill as above.) Remove from grill. Cool garlic and vegetables slightly. Coarsely chop vegetables.

seven While shrimp and vegetables are grilling, cook pasta according to package directions; drain. Return drained pasta to hot pan.

eight Squeeze garlic pulp into a small bowl. Thoroughly mash garlic pulp. Add butter, salt, and black pepper; mix well. In a large bowl combine pasta and garlic mixture; toss to coat. Add shrimp, vegetables, remaining 1 tablespoon lemon juice, and the cheese; toss gently to mix. Serve immediately.

NUTRITION FACTS PER SERVING: 404 cal., 16 g total fat (7 g sat. fat), 174 mg chol., 567 mg sodium, 44 g carbo., 3 g fiber, 21 g pro.

pepper shrimp in peanut sauce

Enjoy grilled shrimp at their best in this colorful pasta dish.

PREP: 30 minutes **GRILL:** 5 minutes **MAKES:** 4 servings

1	pound fresh or frozen medium shrimp in shells
8	ounces dried bow tie pasta or linguine
½	cup water
¼	cup orange marmalade
2	tablespoons peanut butter
2	tablespoons soy sauce
2	teaspoons cornstarch
¼	teaspoon crushed red pepper
2	medium red, yellow, and/or green sweet peppers, cut into 1-inch pieces
	Chopped peanuts (optional)

one Thaw shrimp, if frozen. Peel and devein shrimp, leaving tails intact. Rinse shrimp; pat dry with paper towels. Set aside. Cook pasta according to package directions; drain. Return pasta to pan; keep warm.

two For sauce, in a small saucepan stir together the water, orange marmalade, peanut butter, soy sauce, cornstarch, and crushed red pepper. Bring to boiling; reduce heat. Cook and stir, uncovered, for 2 minutes. Remove from heat and keep warm.

three On long metal skewers, alternately thread shrimp and sweet peppers, leaving ¼ inch space between pieces. For a charcoal grill, grill kabobs on the greased rack of an uncovered grill directly over medium coals for 5 to 8 minutes or until shrimp are opaque, turning once halfway through grilling. (For a gas grill, preheat grill. Reduce heat to medium. Place skewers on greased grill rack over heat. Cover and grill as above.)

four To serve, add shrimp and peppers to the cooked pasta. Add the sauce; toss gently to coat. If desired, sprinkle servings with chopped peanuts.

NUTRITION FACTS PER SERVING: 382 cal., 7 g total fat (1 g sat. fat), 180 mg chol., 718 mg sodium, 57 g carbo., 3 g fiber, 24 g pro.

lobster tails with basil-walnut butter

As with many things so easy, this is sinfully delicious. Combine melted butter, garlic, walnuts, and fresh basil and serve it over sweet lobster meat.

PREP: 15 minutes **GRILL:** 12 minutes **MAKES:** 4 servings

4	8-ounce frozen lobster tails
2	teaspoons olive oil
⅓	cup butter
2	tablespoons snipped fresh basil
2	tablespoons finely chopped walnuts, toasted*
½	teaspoon bottled minced garlic (1 clove)

one Thaw lobster. Rinse and pat dry with paper towels. Place lobster tails, shell sides down, on a cutting board. To butterfly, with kitchen scissors, cut each lobster tail in half lengthwise, cutting to but not through the back shell. Bend backward to crack back shell and expose the meat. Brush lobster meat with oil.

two For a charcoal grill, grill lobster tails, shell sides down, on the greased rack of an uncovered grill directly over medium coals for 12 to 15 minutes or until lobster meat is opaque in the center and shells are bright red, turning once halfway through grilling. Do not overcook. (For a gas grill, preheat grill. Reduce heat to medium. Place lobster tails, shell sides down, on greased grill rack over heat. Cover and grill as above.)

three While lobster is grilling, in a small saucepan melt butter over low heat without stirring; cool slightly. Pour off and reserve clear top layer; discard milky bottom layer. In a small bowl combine butter, basil, walnuts, and garlic. To serve, spoon butter mixture over lobster meat.

NUTRITION FACTS PER SERVING: 321 cal., 21 g total fat (10 g sat. fat), 145 mg chol., 706 mg sodium, 3 g carbo., 0 g fiber, 30 g pro.

*NOTE: To toast walnuts, spread them in a single layer in a pie plate. Bake in a 350°F oven for 5 to 10 minutes or until light golden brown, watching carefully and stirring once or twice so nuts don't burn.

zucchini crab cakes

You'll need to start with about 1¼ pounds of crab legs to end up with 8 ounces of crabmeat. Be sure to discard any small pieces of shell or cartilage from the crabmeat.

PREP: 20 minutes **GRILL:** 6 minutes **MAKES:** 4 servings

1	cup coarsely shredded zucchini (about 5 ounces)
¼	cup thinly sliced green onions
6	teaspoons cooking oil
1	beaten egg
½	cup seasoned fine dry bread crumbs
1	tablespoon Dijon-style mustard
½	teaspoon snipped fresh lemon thyme or snipped fresh thyme
⅛	to ¼ teaspoon cayenne pepper (optional)
8	ounces cooked crabmeat, chopped (1½ cups)
2	red and/or yellow tomatoes, cut into ¼-inch slices
	Red and/or yellow cherry tomatoes (optional)
1	large lemon or lime, cut into wedges (optional)
1	recipe Tomato-Sour Cream Dipping Sauce

one In a large skillet cook and stir the zucchini and green onions in 2 teaspoons of the hot oil about 3 minutes or just until the vegetables are tender and the liquid is evaporated. Cool slightly.

two In a large bowl combine the egg, bread crumbs, mustard, thyme, and, if desired, cayenne pepper. Add the zucchini mixture and crabmeat; mix well. Using about ¼ cup of the mixture for each crab cake, shape into 8 patties, each about 2½ inches in diameter. Brush both sides of each patty lightly with the remaining 4 teaspoons oil.

three For a charcoal grill, grill crab cakes on the greased rack of an uncovered grill or on a grilling tray placed on the rack directly over medium-hot coals for 6 to 8 minutes or until golden brown, gently turning once halfway through grilling. (For a gas grill, preheat grill. Reduce heat to medium. Place crab cakes on greased grill rack or on a grilling tray placed on the rack over heat. Cover and grill as above.)

four For each serving, overlap 2 patties on a dinner plate along with sliced tomatoes. If desired, garnish with cherry tomatoes and lemon wedges. Serve with Tomato-Sour Cream Dipping Sauce.

tomato-sour cream dipping sauce: In a small bowl stir together ½ cup dairy sour cream, 3 tablespoons finely chopped yellow and/or red tomatoes, 1 to 2 tablespoons lemon juice or lime juice, and ⅛ teaspoon seasoned salt. Cover and chill in the refrigerator until serving time (up to 2 hours).

NUTRITION FACTS PER SERVING, WITH 2 TABLESPOONS DIPPING SAUCE: 277 cal., 16 g total fat (5 g sat. fat), 123 mg chol., 424 mg sodium, 16 g carbo., 2 g fiber, 17 g pro.

skillet-grilled mussels

The mussels cook beautifully in a skillet, and the sauce that develops is perfect for dipping crusty pieces of bread.

PREP: 20 minutes **SOAK:** 15 minutes + 15 minutes + 15 minutes
GRILL: 6 minutes **MAKES:** 6 to 8 appetizer servings

24	fresh mussels in shells
1	cup salt
1/3	cup butter, cut into small pieces
2	tablespoons olive oil
1	tablespoon lemon juice
1/8	teaspoon bottled hot pepper sauce
	French bread or sourdough bread (optional)

one Scrub mussels under cold running water. Using your fingers, pull out the beards that are visible between the shells. In an 8-quart kettle or Dutch oven combine 4 quarts cold water and 1/3 cup of the salt; add mussels. Soak for 15 minutes; drain and rinse. Discard water. Repeat soaking, draining, and rinsing twice, using new water and salt each time.

two Evenly distribute the butter pieces in a large cast-iron skillet or a 9×9×2-inch baking pan. Drizzle with olive oil, lemon juice, and hot pepper sauce. Place mussels on top of butter mixture.

three For a charcoal grill, in a grill with a cover place mussels in skillet on grill rack directly over medium coals. Cover and grill for 6 to 10 minutes or until the mussels have opened. Discard any mussels that do not open. (For a gas grill, preheat grill. Reduce heat to medium. Grill as above.)

four If desired, serve mussels with French or sourdough bread, dipping bread into pan juices.

NUTRITION FACTS PER SERVING: 227 cal., 17 g total fat (7 g sat. fat), 59 mg chol., 312 mg sodium, 4 g carbo., 0 g fiber, 14 g pro.

barbecue sauce

There's enough of this sweet, tangy sauce to slather on during grilling plus pass at the table.

PREP: 10 minutes **COOK:** 30 minutes **MAKES:** 3 cups

1	15-ounce can tomato sauce
½	cup cider vinegar
½	cup packed brown sugar
2	tablespoons finely chopped onion
2	tablespoons liquid smoke
1	tablespoon Worcestershire sauce
1	teaspoon chili powder
½	teaspoon bottled minced garlic (1 clove)
¼	teaspoon celery salt
⅛	to ¼ teaspoon cayenne pepper
⅛	teaspoon ground allspice
3	drops bottled hot pepper sauce

one In a medium saucepan combine tomato sauce, vinegar, brown sugar, onion, liquid smoke, Worcestershire sauce, chili powder, garlic, celery salt, cayenne pepper, allspice, and hot pepper sauce. Bring to boiling; reduce heat. Simmer, uncovered, about 30 minutes or until desired consistency.

two Use warm to brush on beef, pork, or poultry during the last 5 to 10 minutes of grilling. Reheat any remaining sauce until bubbly; pass with grilled meat. Cover and store unused sauce in refrigerator for up to 3 days.

NUTRITION FACTS PER 2-TABLESPOON SERVING: 24 cal., 0 g total fat, 0 mg chol., 108 mg sodium, 6 g carbo., 0 g fiber, 0 g pro.

basic moppin' sauce

Use a pastry or basting brush as a mop for brushing on this coffee-accented sauce.

PREP: 15 minutes **COOK:** 30 minutes **MAKES:** 2 cups

1	cup strong coffee
1	cup ketchup
½	cup Worcestershire sauce
¼	cup butter or margarine
1	tablespoon sugar
1	to 2 teaspoons freshly ground black pepper
½	teaspoon salt (optional)

one In a medium saucepan combine coffee, ketchup, Worcestershire sauce, butter, sugar, pepper, and, if desired, salt. Bring to boiling, stirring occasionally; reduce heat. Simmer, uncovered, for 30 minutes, stirring frequently.

two Use warm to brush on beef, pork, or poultry during the last 5 to 10 minutes of grilling. Reheat any remaining sauce until bubbly; pass with grilled meat. Cover and store unused sauce in refrigerator for up to 3 days.

NUTRITION FACTS PER 2-TABLESPOON SERVING: 52 cal., 4 g total fat (2 g sat. fat), 7 mg chol., 292 mg sodium, 6 g carbo., 0 g fiber, 0 g pro.

latino barbecue ketchup

Chipotle and jalapeño chile peppers add spark to this burger topper.

START TO FINISH: 15 minutes **MAKES:** 1⅔ cups

1	cup chopped green onions
¼	to ½ cup canned chipotle chile peppers in adobo sauce
1	fresh jalapeño chile pepper, chopped*
1	tablespoon snipped fresh oregano
1	teaspoon bottled minced garlic (2 cloves)
½	teaspoon salt
1	cup ketchup
¼	cup red wine vinegar
2	tablespoons olive oil

one In a food processor bowl combine green onions, chipotle peppers, jalapeño pepper, oregano, garlic, and salt. Cover; process until combined. Add ketchup, red wine vinegar, and olive oil; process until smooth. Serve with grilled burgers. Cover and store unused ketchup in refrigerator for up to 3 days.

NUTRITION FACTS PER 2-TABLESPOON SERVING: 45 cal., 2 g total fat (0 g sat. fat), 0 mg chol., 332 mg sodium, 6 g carbo., 1 g fiber, 0 g pro.

*NOTE: Because chile peppers contain volatile oils that can burn your skin and eyes, avoid direct contact with them as much as possible. When working with chile peppers, wear plastic or rubber gloves. If your bare hands do touch the chile peppers, wash your hands and nails well with soap and warm water.

kansas city barbecue sauce

Kansas City is a notoriously competitive barbecue town—so much so that some sauce recipes are secrets taken to the grave.

PREP: 10 minutes **COOK:** 30 minutes **MAKES:** about 1⅓ cups

½   cup finely chopped onion

1   teaspoon bottled minced garlic (2 cloves)

1   tablespoon olive oil or cooking oil

¾   cup apple juice or apple cider

½   of a 6-ounce can tomato paste (⅓ cup)

¼   cup cider vinegar

2   tablespoons brown sugar

2   tablespoons molasses

1   tablespoon paprika

1   tablespoon prepared horseradish

1   tablespoon Worcestershire sauce

1   teaspoon salt

½   teaspoon ground black pepper

one In a medium saucepan cook onion and garlic in hot oil until onion is tender. Stir in apple juice, tomato paste, vinegar, brown sugar, molasses, paprika, horseradish, Worcestershire sauce, salt, and pepper. Bring to boiling; reduce heat. Simmer, uncovered, about 30 minutes or until desired consistency, stirring occasionally.

two Use warm to brush on beef, pork, or poultry during the last 5 to 10 minutes of grilling. Reheat any remaining sauce until bubbly; pass with grilled meat. Cover and store unused sauce in refrigerator for up to 3 days.

NUTRITION FACTS PER 2-TABLESPOON SERVING: 52 cal., 2 g total fat (0 g sat. fat), 0 mg chol., 300 mg sodium, 10 g carbo., 0 g fiber, 0 g pro.

mango & pepper bbq sauce

What starts out as a chunky fresh-fruit-and-vegetable salsa you could serve alongside your grilled food winds up being pureed into a terrific barbecue sauce for the top of it.

START TO FINISH: 20 minutes   **MAKES:** about 2½ cups

2	cups chopped red sweet pepper
½	cup chopped onion
2	tablespoons cooking oil
2	medium mangoes, seeded, peeled, and chopped (2 cups)
¼	cup packed brown sugar
2	tablespoons rice vinegar
½	teaspoon crushed red pepper
¼	teaspoon salt
2	tablespoons finely chopped green onion

one In a large skillet cook the sweet pepper and onion in hot oil just until tender. Stir in the mangoes, brown sugar, vinegar, crushed red pepper, and salt. Bring to boiling; reduce heat. Simmer, uncovered, about 10 minutes or until mangoes are tender. Cool mixture slightly. Transfer mixture to a food processor /blender bowl. Cover and blend until nearly smooth. Stir in green onion.

two Use warm to brush on pork, chicken, fish, or shrimp during the last 5 to 10 minutes of grilling. Reheat any remaining sauce until bubbly; pass with grilled meat. Cover and store unused sauce in refrigerator for up to 3 days.

NUTRITION FACTS PER 2-TABLESPOON SERVING: 38 cal., 2 g total fat (0 g sat. fat), 0 mg chol., 28 mg sodium, 6 g carbo., 0 g fiber, 0 g pro.

pacific rim bbq sauce

This spunky barbecue brush-on is great for everything from chicken and ribs to steak and burgers.

PREP: 10 minutes **COOK:** 25 minutes **MAKES:** 1 cup

1	teaspoon bottled minced garlic (2 cloves)
1	teaspoon grated fresh ginger
2	teaspoons cooking oil
½	cup packed brown sugar
½	cup whiskey
¼	cup bottled hoisin sauce
¼	cup soy sauce
¼	cup frozen pineapple juice concentrate, thawed
¼	cup rice vinegar

one In a medium saucepan cook and stir garlic and ginger in hot oil for 1 minute. Stir in brown sugar, whiskey, hoisin sauce, soy sauce, pineapple juice concentrate, and rice vinegar. Bring to boiling; reduce heat. Simmer, uncovered, for 25 to 30 minutes or until reduced to 1 cup, stirring occasionally.

two Use warm to brush on steaks, ribs, poultry, or burgers during the last 5 to 10 minutes of grilling. Reheat any remaining sauce until bubbly; pass with grilled meat. Cover and store unused sauce in refrigerator for up to 3 days.

NUTRITION FACTS PER 2-TABLESPOON SERVING: 140 cal., 2 g total fat (0 g sat. fat), 0 mg chol., 555 mg sodium, 21 g carbo., 0 g fiber, 1 g pro.

mutha sauce

This zippy sauce is great on beef or pork.

PREP: 20 minutes **COOK:** 20 minutes **MAKES:** about 2 cups

⅓	cup finely chopped onion
2	tablespoons finely chopped green onion
1	small fresh jalapeño chile pepper, seeded and finely chopped*
1	tablespoon cooking oil
2	teaspoons bottled minced garlic (4 cloves)
1	8-ounce can tomato sauce
½	cup ketchup
¼	cup packed brown sugar
3	tablespoons Worcestershire sauce
2	tablespoons vinegar
1	tablespoon lemon juice
1	tablespoon bottled hot pepper sauce
1	tablespoon spicy brown mustard
1	tablespoon molasses
1	teaspoon chili powder
½	teaspoon coarsely ground black pepper
⅛	teaspoon ground allspice
1	teaspoon liquid smoke

one In large saucepan cook onion, green onion, and jalapeño pepper in hot oil until onion is tender, stirring occasionally. Add garlic; cook for 1 minute more. Add tomato sauce, ketchup, brown sugar, Worcestershire, vinegar, lemon juice, pepper sauce, mustard, molasses, chili powder, black pepper, and allspice. Stir in ¼ cup water. Bring to boiling; reduce heat. Cover; simmer 20 minutes. Stir in liquid smoke.

two Use warm to brush on beef or pork during last 5 to 10 minutes of grilling. Reheat any remaining sauce until bubbly; pass with grilled meat. Cover and store unused sauce in refrigerator for up to 3 days.

NUTRITION FACTS PER 2-TABLESPOON SERVING: 44 cal., 1 g total fat (0 g sat. fat), 0 mg chol., 215 mg sodium, 9 g carbo., 0 g fiber, 0 g pro.

*NOTE: Because chile peppers contain volatile oils that can burn your skin and eyes, avoid direct contact with them as much as possible. When working with chile peppers, wear plastic or rubber gloves. If your bare hands do touch the chile peppers, wash your hands and nails well with soap and warm water.

five-alarm sauce

If you can't get to Kansas City, Houston, or some other smoke-and-fire-hub, turn your backyard into BBQ central with this multi-spiced sauce.

START TO FINISH: 20 minutes **MAKES:** 2½ cups

1	cup ketchup
1	large tomato, peeled, seeded, and chopped
1	small green sweet pepper, chopped
2	tablespoons chopped onion
2	tablespoons brown sugar
1	to 2 tablespoons bottled steak sauce
1	to 2 tablespoons Worcestershire sauce
½	teaspoon garlic powder
¼	teaspoon ground nutmeg
¼	teaspoon ground cinnamon
¼	teaspoon ground cloves
⅛	teaspoon ground ginger
⅛	teaspoon ground black pepper

one In a small saucepan stir together ketchup, tomato, sweet pepper, onion, brown sugar, steak sauce, Worcestershire sauce, garlic powder, nutmeg, cinnamon, cloves, ginger, and black pepper. Bring to boiling; reduce heat. Cover and simmer about 5 minutes or until sweet pepper is crisp-tender.

two Use warm to brush on beef or chicken during the last 5 to 10 minutes of grilling. Reheat any remaining sauce until bubbly; pass with grilled meat. Cover and store unused sauce in refrigerator for up to 3 days.

NUTRITION FACTS PER 2-TABLESPOON SERVING: 22 cal., 0 g total fat, 0 mg chol., 165 mg sodium, 6 g carbo., 0 g fiber, 0 g pro.

honey-peach sauce

This sweet sauce is the taste of summer boiled down to the basics: juicy peaches, honey, zingy cracked black pepper, and fresh thyme.

PREP: 10 minutes **COOK:** 15 minutes **MAKES:** about 1¾ cups

4	medium peaches (about 1⅓ pounds total)
2	tablespoons lemon juice
2	tablespoons honey
½	teaspoon cracked black pepper
1	to 2 teaspoons snipped fresh thyme

one Peel and cut up 3 of the peaches. Place cut up peaches in a food processor/blender bowl. Add lemon juice, honey, and pepper. Cover and blend until smooth. Transfer to a medium saucepan.

two Bring to boiling; reduce heat. Simmer, uncovered, about 15 minutes or until sauce is slightly thickened, stirring occasionally. Remove from heat. Peel and finely chop the remaining peach; stir into the sauce. Stir in thyme.

three Use warm to brush on beef, lamb, pork, poultry, or fish during the last 5 to 10 minutes of grilling. Reheat any remaining sauce until bubbly; pass with grilled meat. Cover and store unused sauce in refrigerator for up to 24 hours.

NUTRITION FACTS PER 2-TABLESPOON SERVING: 31 cal., 0 g total fat, 0 mg chol., 0 mg sodium, 8 g carbo., 1 g fiber, 0 g pro.

mushroom-garlic sauce

Serve this first-rate sauce with meat, poultry, or fish.

START TO FINISH: 25 minutes **MAKES:** 2½ cups

2	8-ounce packages fresh mushrooms, quartered
¼	cup finely chopped shallots
1	tablespoon bottled minced garlic (6 cloves)
½	teaspoon curry powder
⅛	to ¼ teaspoon crushed red pepper
2	tablespoons olive oil
¾	cup chicken broth
2	teaspoons soy sauce
¼	teaspoon ground nutmeg
¼	cup dry white wine or chicken broth
1	tablespoon cornstarch

one In large saucepan cook mushrooms, shallots, garlic, curry powder, and crushed red pepper in hot oil until mushrooms are tender. Add the ¾ cup chicken broth, the soy sauce, and nutmeg; bring to boiling. In a small bowl stir together wine or additional chicken broth and cornstarch; add to saucepan. Cook and stir until thickened and bubbly; cook and stir for 2 minutes more. Serve with grilled beef, pork, lamb, poultry, or fish.

NUTRITION FACTS PER ¼-CUP SERVING: 52 cal., 4 g total fat (1 g sat. fat), 0 mg chol., 139 mg sodium, 3 g carbo., 0 g fiber, 2 g pro.

cucumber-dill sauce

Dress up grilled fish steaks or fillets with this fresh-tasting sauce.

START TO FINISH: 10 minutes **MAKES:** ⅔ cup

⅓	cup finely chopped seeded cucumber
3	tablespoons plain yogurt
2	tablespoons mayonnaise or salad dressing
2	teaspoons snipped fresh dill
2	teaspoons prepared horseradish

one In a small bowl combine cucumber, yogurt, mayonnaise, dill, and horseradish. Serve immediately or cover and chill up to 4 hours. Serve with grilled fish.

NUTRITION FACTS PER 2-TABLESPOON SERVING: 59 cal., 6 g total fat (1 g sat. fat), 3 mg chol., 50 mg sodium, 1 g carbo., 0 g fiber, 1 g pro.

double-pepper barbecue rub

To get maximum flavor, sprinkle about 2 tablespoons of the spice mixture on each pound of meat or poultry.

START TO FINISH: 15 minutes
MAKES: about ⅔ cup rub (enough for 4 to 6 pounds meat or poultry)

¼	cup paprika
1	tablespoon salt
1	tablespoon ground cumin
1	tablespoon brown sugar
1	tablespoon chili powder
1	tablespoon ground black pepper
1½	teaspoons cayenne pepper
¼	teaspoon ground cloves

one In a small bowl stir together paprika, salt, cumin, brown sugar, chili powder, black pepper, cayenne pepper, and cloves.

two To use, generously sprinkle spice mixture evenly over beef, pork, or chicken about 10 minutes before grilling; rub in with your fingers. Grill meat or poultry. Cover and store unused spice mixture in a screw-top jar or resealable plastic bag for up to 1 month.

NUTRITION FACTS PER TEASPOON RUB: 7 cal., 0 g total fat, 0 mg chol., 203 mg sodium, 1 g carbo., 0 g fiber, 0 g pro.

best beef marinade

Fresh thyme flavors this very simple, very tasty marinade.

PREP: 10 minutes **MARINATE:** 30 minutes or 3 to 24 hours
MAKES: about ½ cup marinade (enough for 1 to 1½ pounds beef)

¼	cup chopped shallots
3	tablespoons soy sauce
2	tablespoons olive oil
2	tablespoons balsamic vinegar or cider vinegar
4	teaspoons snipped fresh thyme
½	teaspoon bottled minced garlic (1 clove)
½	teaspoon cracked black pepper

one In a small bowl combine shallots, soy sauce, olive oil, vinegar, thyme, garlic, and cracked pepper.

two To use, pour marinade over beef in a resealable plastic bag set in a shallow dish. Seal bag; turn to coat meat. Marinate in the refrigerator about 30 minutes for tender cuts (such as tenderloin or sirloin) or at least 3 hours or up to 24 hours for tougher cuts (such as flank steak), turning bag occasionally. Drain, reserving marinade. Grill beef until done, brushing occasionally with reserved marinade up to the last 5 minutes of grilling. Discard any remaining marinade.

NUTRITION FACTS PER TABLESPOON MARINADE: 42 cal., 3 g total fat (0 g sat. fat), 0 mg chol., 387 mg sodium, 3 g carbo., 0 g fiber, 1 g pro.

pineapple-ginger marinade

Five-spice powder is a blend of cinnamon, cloves, fennel seeds, star anise, and Szechwan peppercorns.

PREP: 10 minutes **MARINATE:** 30 minutes or 2 to 4 hours
MAKES: about ¾ cup (enough for 1½ pounds poultry, fish, or seafood)

- ½ cup unsweetened pineapple juice
- 2 tablespoons cooking oil
- 2 tablespoons finely chopped green sweet pepper
- 1 tablespoon finely chopped fresh ginger
- 1 teaspoon honey
- ¼ teaspoon five-spice powder

one In a small bowl combine pineapple juice, oil, sweet pepper, ginger, honey, and five-spice powder. To use, pour marinade over poultry, fish, or seafood in a resealable plastic bag set in a shallow dish. Seal bag; turn to coat poultry, fish, or seafood.

two Marinate in the refrigerator for at least 2 hours or up to 4 hours for poultry or at room temperature for 30 minutes for fish or seafood, turning bag occasionally. Drain, reserving marinade. Grill poultry, fish, or seafood until done, brushing often with reserved marinade up to the last 5 minutes of grilling. Discard any remaining marinade.

NUTRITION FACTS PER TABLESPOON MARINADE: 28 cal., 3 g total fat (0 g sat. fat), 0 mg chol., 0 mg sodium, 2 g carbo., 0 g fiber, 0 g pro.

savory stuffed breadsticks

After you taste this, you may never again be satisfied with plain breadsticks. The soft bread, crisp bacon, melted cheeses, green onions, and fresh thyme make for a satisfying side dish.

PREP: 25 minutes **GRILL:** 8 minutes **MAKES:** 6 breadsticks

4	slices bacon, cut up
½	cup chopped onion
¼	cup finely shredded Parmesan cheese (1 ounce)
¼	cup shredded sharp cheddar cheese (1 ounce)
2	tablespoons sliced green onion
1	tablespoon snipped fresh thyme
6	soft breadsticks or dinner rolls

one In a medium skillet cook bacon until crisp. Remove bacon; drain on paper towels. Drain off fat, reserving 1 tablespoon drippings in skillet. Add chopped onion to drippings. Cook over medium heat until tender, stirring occasionally. Cool slightly. Stir in bacon, cheeses, green onion, and thyme.

two Cut each breadstick in half lengthwise, cutting to but not through opposite side. Spread cut surfaces with bacon mixture.

three Fold six 24×18-inch pieces of heavy foil in half to make 18×12-inch rectangles. Place each breadstick in center of a foil rectangle. Bring up 2 opposite edges of each foil rectangle and seal with a double fold. Fold remaining edges to completely enclose each breadstick, leaving space for steam to build. If desired, chill for up to 8 hours.

four For a charcoal grill, grill breadstick packets on the rack of an uncovered grill directly over medium coals for 8 to 10 minutes or until cheddar cheese begins to melt, turning packets occasionally. (For a gas grill, preheat grill. Reduce heat to medium. Place breadstick packets on grill rack over heat. Cover and grill as above.)

NUTRITION FACTS PER BREADSTICK: 81 cal., 5 g total fat (2 g sat. fat), 12 mg chol., 165 mg sodium, 4 g carbo., 0 g fiber, 5 g pro.

asparagus with parmesan curls

Cheese curl garnishes are easy to make–even without new equipment or split-second timing. A vegetable peeler is all it takes to create a pile of Parmesan shavings. Simply scatter them over grilled asparagus like flower petals to create a stunning dish.

PREP: 15 minutes **MARINATE:** 30 minutes **GRILL:** 3 minutes
MAKES: 6 servings

1½	pounds fresh asparagus spears, trimmed
2	tablespoons olive oil
2	tablespoons lemon juice
½	teaspoon salt
¼	teaspoon ground black pepper
1	2-ounce block Parmesan cheese

one In a large skillet cook the asparagus spears in a small amount of boiling water for 3 minutes. Drain well. Meanwhile, for marinade, in a 2-quart rectangular baking dish stir together olive oil, lemon juice, salt, and pepper. Add drained asparagus, turning to coat. Cover and marinate at room temperature for 30 minutes. Drain asparagus, discarding marinade. Place asparagus on a grilling tray or in a grill basket.

two For a charcoal grill, grill asparagus on grilling tray or in grill basket on the rack of an uncovered grill directly over medium coals for 3 to 5 minutes or until asparagus is tender and begins to brown, turning once halfway through grilling. (For a gas grill, preheat grill. Reduce heat to medium. Place asparagus on grill rack over heat. Cover and grill as above.)

three To serve, arrange asparagus on a serving platter. Working over asparagus, use a vegetable peeler or cheese plane to cut thin, wide strips from the side of the block of Parmesan cheese.

NUTRITION FACTS PER SERVING: 95 cal., 7 g total fat (1 g sat. fat), 7 mg chol., 287 mg sodium, 4 g carbo., 1 g fiber, 6 g pro.

cast-iron skillet cowboy beans

Cowboy cooking is back. And it's good! Whether you make this over a charcoal grill on a camping trip or on the latest state-of-the-art grill in your backyard, the bubbling satisfaction of a skillet full of beans can't be beat.

PREP: 15 minutes **GRILL:** 15 minutes + 15 minutes **MAKES:** 6 servings

2	15-ounce cans pinto beans, rinsed and drained
½	cup chopped onion
½	cup ketchup
½	cup hot strong coffee
6	slices bacon, crisp-cooked, drained, and crumbled
2	tablespoons Worcestershire sauce
1	tablespoon brown sugar

one In a 9-inch cast-iron skillet combine pinto beans, onion, ketchup, coffee, bacon, Worcestershire sauce, and brown sugar.

two For a charcoal grill, grill beans in skillet on the rack of an uncovered grill directly over medium coals about 15 minutes or until bubbly. Grill for 15 to 20 minutes more or until beans are desired consistency, stirring occasionally. (For a gas grill, preheat grill. Reduce heat to medium. Place beans in skillet on grill rack over heat. Cover and grill as above.)

NUTRITION FACTS PER SERVING: 184 cal., 4 g total fat (1 g sat. fat), 5 mg chol., 1,003 mg sodium, 30 g carbo., 8 g fiber, 9 g pro.

grilled corn

Whether you're cooking burgers, steak, or chicken, this recipe for fresh summertime sweet corn makes a mouthwatering side dish grilled alongside the meat.

PREP: 10 minutes **SOAK:** 2 to 4 hours **GRILL:** 25 minutes **MAKES:** 4 servings

4	fresh ears of corn
¼	cup butter or margarine, softened
2	tablespoons snipped fresh chives, parsley, cilantro, or tarragon
¼	teaspoon salt
¼	teaspoon ground black pepper

one Peel back corn husks, but don't remove. Remove the corn silk; discard. Gently rinse the ears of corn. Pull the husks back up around the corn. Using 100 percent-cotton kitchen string, tie the husks shut. Cover corn with water. Soak for at least 2 hours or up to 4 hours.

two Drain corn. For a charcoal grill, grill corn on the rack of an uncovered grill directly over medium coals for 25 to 30 minutes or until the kernels are tender, turning once halfway through grilling. (For a gas grill, preheat grill. Reduce heat to medium. Place corn on grill rack over heat. Cover and grill as above.)

three In a small bowl stir together the butter, fresh herb, salt, and pepper. Remove string from the corn. Serve immediately with butter mixture.

NUTRITION FACTS PER SERVING: 186 cal., 13 g total fat (8 g sat. fat), 33 mg chol., 283 mg sodium, 17 g carbo., 3 g fiber, 3 g pro.

garlicky mushrooms

Ingredients, like people, are sometimes just meant for each other. That's certainly the case with garlic, butter, and mushrooms. Portobellos, with their rich, meaty flavor, put butter and garlic to especially good use.

PREP: 15 minutes **GRILL:** 6 minutes **MAKES:** 4 servings

1	pound fresh portobello mushrooms
¼	cup butter, melted
1½	teaspoons bottled minced garlic (3 cloves)
¼	teaspoon salt
⅛	teaspoon ground black pepper
1	tablespoon snipped fresh chives

one Cut the mushroom stems even with the caps; discard stems. Rinse mushroom caps; pat dry with paper towels.

two In a small bowl stir together melted butter, garlic, salt, and pepper; brush over mushrooms.

three For a charcoal grill, grill mushrooms on the rack of an uncovered grill directly over medium coals for 6 to 8 minutes or just until mushrooms are tender, turning once halfway through grilling. (For a gas grill, preheat grill. Reduce heat to medium. Place mushrooms on grill rack over heat. Cover and grill as above.)

four To serve, sprinkle mushrooms with chives.

NUTRITION FACTS PER SERVING: 133 cal., 12 g total fat (7 g sat. fat), 31 mg chol., 252 mg sodium, 6 g carbo., 2 g fiber, 3 g pro.

hearty grilled vegetables

Fresh herbs star in this colorful side dish. For top flavor, use a mixture of two or three herbs.

PREP: 15 minutes **GRILL:** 6 minutes **MAKES:** 4 servings

¼   cup olive oil

¼   cup snipped fresh thyme, basil, oregano, and/or chives

2   fresh portobello mushrooms
    (about 4 inches in diameter), halved

8   green onions

2   medium red and/or yellow sweet peppers,
    seeded and quartered lengthwise

1   medium zucchini, quartered lengthwise

    Salt

    Ground black pepper

    Fresh herbs (optional)

one In a large bowl stir together olive oil and the ¼ cup fresh herbs. Add mushrooms, green onions, sweet peppers, and zucchini. Toss gently to evenly coat vegetables.

two If desired, place the vegetables on a grilling tray. For a charcoal grill, grill vegetables on the rack of an uncovered grill directly over medium coals for 6 to 10 minutes or until tender, turning occasionally. (For a gas grill, preheat grill. Reduce heat to medium. Place vegetables on grill rack over heat. Cover and grill as above.)

three Season with salt and pepper. If desired, garnish with additional fresh herbs.

NUTRITION FACTS PER SERVING: 168 cal., 15 g total fat (2 g sat. fat), 0 mg chol., 45 mg sodium, 9 g carbo., 3 g fiber, 3 g pro.

grillside potato chips

For the best results, use Idaho russet potatoes. They have a low water content and will make a crisper chip.

PREP: 10 minutes **GRILL:** 15 minutes **STAND:** 8 minutes **MAKES:** 4 servings

1	pound baking potatoes (such as russet or long white), scrubbed and bias-cut into 1/16-inch slices
3	tablespoons cooking oil
1/2	teaspoon dried thyme, crushed
1/2	teaspoon coarse salt or seasoned salt

one Place potato slices in a Dutch oven. Add enough water to cover. Bring just to boiling. Cook for 2 to 3 minutes or until crisp-tender. Drain; place in a single layer on paper towels. Carefully brush both sides of each potato slice with cooking oil. Sprinkle with thyme and salt.

two For a charcoal grill, grill potato slices on the rack of an uncovered grill directly over medium-hot coals for 15 to 20 minutes or until browned and crisp, turning occasionally. (For a gas grill, preheat grill. Reduce heat. Place potatoes on grill rack over heat. Cover and grill as above.)

three Meanwhile, line a baking sheet with several layers of paper towels; set aside. Remove potato slices from grill; let stand for 8 to 10 minutes on prepared baking sheet. (Chips will crisp as they stand.)

NUTRITION FACTS PER SERVING: 209 cal., 10 g total fat (1 g sat. fat), 0 mg chol., 276 mg sodium, 27 g carbo., 1 g fiber, 3 g pro.

hot-off-the-grill potatoes

Dinner is easy when you tuck the vegetable packets alongside meat or poultry on the grill.

PREP: 20 minutes **GRILL:** 30 minutes **MAKES:** 4 servings

3	tablespoons butter
5	medium potatoes, scrubbed and thinly sliced
¼	cup chopped green onions
2	tablespoons coarsely snipped fresh parsley
2	tablespoons snipped fresh dill
2	tablespoons snipped fresh chives
2	tablespoons grated Parmesan cheese
¼	teaspoon salt
¼	teaspoon paprika
¼	teaspoon ground black pepper
3	slices bacon, crisp-cooked, drained, and crumbled

one Fold a 48×18-inch piece of heavy foil in half to make a 24×18-inch rectangle. Grease the foil with about 1 tablespoon of the butter.

two Place potatoes in the center of the foil. Sprinkle with green onions, parsley, dill, chives, Parmesan cheese, salt, paprika, and pepper. Top with bacon. (If desired, add the parsley and bacon just before serving instead of adding them to the packet.) Dot with remaining 2 tablespoons butter. Bring up 2 opposite edges of foil and seal with double fold. Fold remaining ends to completely enclose the potatoes, leaving space for steam to build.

three For a charcoal grill, grill foil packet on the rack of an uncovered grill directly over medium coals for 30 to 40 minutes or until potatoes are tender, turning packet every 10 minutes. (For a gas grill, preheat grill. Reduce heat to medium. Place foil packet on grill rack over heat. Cover and grill as above.)

NUTRITION FACTS PER SERVING: 236 cal., 13 g total fat (7 g sat. fat), 32 mg chol., 393 mg sodium, 24 g carbo., 3 g fiber, 6 g pro.

south-of-the-border potato skins

Grilling gives an old favorite a slightly new twist.

PREP: 15 minutes **GRILL:** 20 minutes + 5 minutes
MAKES: 12 appetizer servings

6	4- to 6-ounce baking potatoes (such as russet or long white)
1	tablespoon cooking oil
½	teaspoon bottled minced garlic (1 clove)
⅛	to ¼ teaspoon cayenne pepper
1	cup shredded taco cheese (4 ounces)
1	6-ounce container frozen avocado dip, thawed
¾	cup thick-and-chunky salsa
¾	cup dairy sour cream

one Scrub potatoes; cut each potato in half lengthwise. In a small bowl combine the oil, garlic, and cayenne pepper. Brush cut surfaces of potato halves with some of the oil mixture.

two For a charcoal grill, grill potatoes, cut sides down, on the rack of an uncovered grill directly over medium coals for 20 to 25 minutes or until tender, turning once halfway through grilling. (For a gas grill, preheat grill. Reduce heat to medium. Place potatoes, cut sides down, on grill rack over heat. Cover and grill as above.)

three Carefully scoop out the inside of each potato half, leaving a ½-inch-thick shell. Brush the insides of the potato shells with the remaining oil mixture. Sprinkle potatoes with cheese. Return potatoes to grill, cut sides up. Grill for 5 to 7 minutes more or until cheese is melted. Transfer to a serving platter.

four To serve, top potato shells with avocado dip, salsa, and sour cream.

NUTRITION FACTS PER SERVING: 148 cal., 10 g total fat (4 g sat. fat), 15 mg chol., 255 mg sodium, 13 g carbo., 0 g fiber, 4 g pro.

two-potato packet

Sweet potatoes were designed for more than marshmallows and Thanksgiving. You'll find sweet potatoes are great on the grill year-round.

PREP: 15 minutes **GRILL:** 30 minutes **STAND:** 1 minute **MAKES:** 4 servings

2   medium sweet potatoes, peeled and thinly sliced (about 12 ounces total)

4   small red potatoes, thinly sliced (about 8 ounces total)

4   onion slices, separated into rings

2   tablespoons butter or margarine, cut into small pieces

4   small fresh rosemary, basil, or oregano sprigs

⅛   teaspoon salt

⅛   teaspoon ground black pepper

½   cup shredded smoked provolone or Gouda cheese (2 ounces)

one Fold four 24×18-inch pieces of heavy foil in half to make 18×12-inch rectangles. Divide sweet potatoes and red potatoes among foil rectangles, alternating and overlapping slices. Top with onion, butter, herbs, salt, and pepper. Bring up 2 opposite edges of foil and seal with a double fold. Fold remaining edges together to completely enclose vegetables, leaving space for steam to build.

two For a charcoal grill, arrange medium-hot coals around edge of a grill with a cover. Test for medium heat above center of grill (not over coals). Place vegetable packets on grill rack over center of grill (not over coals). Cover and grill about 30 minutes or until potatoes are tender. (For a gas grill, preheat grill. Reduce heat to medium. Adjust for indirect cooking. Grill as above.)

three Remove packets from grill. Carefully open packets; sprinkle vegetables with cheese. Let stand for 1 to 2 minutes or until cheese is melted.

NUTRITION FACTS PER SERVING: 234 cal., 10 g total fat (6 g sat. fat), 25 mg chol., 260 mg sodium, 32 g carbo., 3 g fiber, 6 g pro.

warm tarragon potato salad

A picnic favorite has been lightened and brightened up with a tangy fresh herb and Dijon vinaigrette dressing, crunchy bok choy, and peppery radishes.

PREP: 10 minutes **GRILL:** 25 minutes **MAKES:** 8 servings

¼	cup salad oil
¼	cup vinegar
1	tablespoon sugar (optional)
1	teaspoon snipped fresh tarragon or dill or ¼ teaspoon dried tarragon, crushed, or dried dillweed
½	teaspoon Dijon-style mustard
1	pound tiny new potatoes and/or small yellow potatoes, cut into bite-size pieces
2	teaspoons salad oil
1	cup chopped bok choy
½	cup chopped red radishes
½	cup thinly sliced green onions
2	thin slices Canadian-style bacon, chopped (1 ounce total)
⅛	teaspoon ground black pepper
4	artichokes, cooked, halved lengthwise, and chokes removed (optional)

one For dressing, in a small bowl whisk together the ¼ cup oil, the vinegar, sugar (if desired), tarragon or dill, and mustard. Set aside.

two Lightly grease a 2-quart square disposable foil pan. Combine potatoes and the 2 teaspoons oil in prepared pan; toss to coat.

three For a charcoal grill, arrange medium-hot coals around the edge of a grill with a cover. Test for medium-hot heat above the center of grill (not over coals). Place potatoes in pan on grill rack over center of grill (not over coals). Cover and grill about 25 minutes or until potatoes are tender. (For a gas grill, preheat grill. Reduce heat to medium. Adjust for indirect cooking. Grill as above.) Cool potatoes slightly.

four In a large bowl combine potatoes, bok choy, radishes, green onions, Canadian-style bacon, and pepper. Add the dressing; toss gently to coat. If desired, spoon the salad into artichoke halves.

NUTRITION FACTS PER SERVING: 135 cal., 8 g total fat (1 g sat. fat), 2 mg chol., 68 mg sodium, 14 g carbo., 1 g fiber, 2 g pro.

fire-roasted acorn squash

Falling leaves and chilly evenings set the stage for winter squash. But rather than the usual brown sugar and butter treatment, try basting rings of squash with tarragon butter, then grilling them. They're delicious with grilled pork and a dry white wine.

PREP: 10 minutes **GRILL:** 45 minutes **MAKES:** 4 servings

1	tablespoon olive oil
½	teaspoon salt
¼	teaspoon ground black pepper
2	small acorn squash, cut crosswise into 1-inch-thick rings and seeded
2	tablespoons butter or margarine, melted
2	teaspoons snipped fresh tarragon or ½ teaspoon dried tarragon, crushed

one In a small bowl combine oil, salt, and pepper; brush over squash rings. In another small bowl stir together melted butter and tarragon; set aside.

two For a charcoal grill, arrange medium-hot coals around a drip pan. Test for medium heat above the pan. Place squash rings on grill rack over drip pan. Cover and grill about 45 minutes or until squash is tender, turning squash occasionally and brushing with butter mixture after 30 minutes of grilling. (For a gas grill, preheat grill. Reduce heat to medium. Adjust for indirect cooking. Grill as above.)

NUTRITION FACTS PER SERVING: 156 cal., 9 g total fat (4 g sat. fat), 15 mg chol., 332 mg sodium, 20 g carbo., 4 g fiber, 2 g pro.

shades of green kabobs

Create multicolor skewers with the baby veggies of your choice.

PREP: 20 minutes **MARINATE:** 1 to 24 hours **GRILL:** 8 minutes
MAKES: 6 servings

8	green onions
12	baby green pattypan squash
12	baby zucchini
1	cup sugar snap peas
⅓	cup olive oil
⅓	cup grated Parmesan cheese
3	tablespoons red wine vinegar
3	tablespoons snipped fresh oregano or 1½ teaspoons dried oregano, crushed
¼	teaspoon salt
¼	teaspoon ground black pepper

one Rinse and trim vegetables. Cut a 3-inch portion from the bottom of each of 6 of the green onions. Place pattypan squash, zucchini, sugar snap peas, and the 3-inch green onion portions in a resealable plastic bag set in a shallow dish.

two Finely chop remaining 2 green onions. For marinade, in a screw-top jar combine finely chopped green onion, oil, Parmesan cheese, vinegar, oregano, salt, and pepper. Cover and shake well. Pour over vegetables in bag. Seal bag; turn to coat vegetables. Marinate vegetables in the refrigerator for at least 1 hour or up to 24 hours, turning bag occasionally.

three Drain vegetables, reserving marinade. On long metal skewers, alternately thread pattypan squash, zucchini, sugar snap peas, and green onion portions. For a charcoal grill, grill kabobs on the rack of an uncovered grill directly over medium coals for 8 to 10 minutes or until vegetables are browned and tender, turning and brushing occasionally with reserved marinade. (For a gas grill, preheat grill. Reduce heat to medium. Place kabobs on grill rack over heat. Cover and grill as above.)

NUTRITION FACTS PER SERVING: 156 cal., 14 g total fat (3 g sat. fat), 4 mg chol., 194 mg sodium, 6 g carbo., 2 g fiber, 4 g pro.

apples with caramel crème fraîche

When the air cools and the leaves begin to turn, there's nothing sweeter than this elegant take on the caramel apple. Try the sauce on grilled bananas, pineapple, or pound cake.

PREP: 15 minutes **GRILL:** 2 minutes + 2 minutes + 2 Minutes + 2 minutes
MAKES: 6 servings

4	Granny Smith apples, cored
4	cups water
3	tablespoons lemon juice
½	cup whipping cream
½	cup dairy sour cream
⅓	cup caramel ice cream topping
3	tablespoons butter, melted

one Cut apples crosswise into ½-inch slices. In a large bowl combine the water and lemon juice. Soak apple slices in water mixture to prevent browning.

two For caramel crème fraîche, in a food processor/blender container combine whipping cream, sour cream, and caramel ice cream topping. Cover and blend for 1 to 2 minutes or until slightly thickened. (Or beat with an electric mixer on high speed about 2 minutes or until slightly thickened.) Set aside.

three Drain apple slices; pat dry with paper towels. Brush both sides of each apple slice with melted butter. For a charcoal grill, place apple slices on the grill rack of a grill with a cover directly over medium-hot coals. Cover and grill for 2 minutes. Rotate apple slices a half-turn to create a checkerboard grill pattern. Cover and grill for 2 minutes more. Turn apples over and repeat on other side. (For a gas grill, preheat grill. Reduce heat to medium-hot. Place apples on grill rack over heat. Cover and grill as above.)

four To serve, arrange 3 or 4 apple slices on each dessert plate and top with caramel crème fraîche.

NUTRITION FACTS PER SERVING: 265 cal., 17 g total fat (11 g sat. fat), 51 mg chol., 118 mg sodium, 28 g carbo., 2 g fiber, 2 g pro.

stuffed autumn apples & pears

Crushed gingersnaps and shredded orange peel enhance the nut filling.

PREP: 20 minutes **GRILL:** 20 minutes + 5 minutes **MAKES:** 4 servings

2	medium cooking apples (such as Rome Beauty, Granny Smith, or Golden Delicious)
2	medium ripe, yet firm, pears (such as Bosc, Anjou, or Bartlett)
2	tablespoons brown sugar
2	tablespoons butter or margarine, melted
¼	cup coarsely chopped walnuts
¼	cup raisins
4	gingersnaps, finely crushed
1	teaspoon finely shredded orange peel

one Peel the apples and pears. Cut the apples and pears in half lengthwise. Core the apples and pears, hollowing out the centers of each half.

two In a large bowl combine the fruit halves, 1 tablespoon of the brown sugar, and 1 tablespoon of the melted butter; toss gently to coat. Set aside. For nut filling, in a small bowl combine the remaining 1 tablespoon brown sugar, remaining 1 tablespoon butter, the walnuts, raisins, finely crushed gingersnaps, and orange peel; set aside.

three For charcoal grill, arrange medium-hot coals around a drip pan. Test for medium heat above the pan. Place fruit, cut sides down, on grill rack over drip pan. Cover and grill for 20 minutes. Turn fruit; spoon the nut filling into hollowed-out centers. Cover and grill about 5 minutes more or until fruit is tender. (For a gas grill, preheat grill. Reduce heat to medium. Adjust for indirect cooking. Grill as above.) Serve warm.

NUTRITION FACTS PER SERVING: 258 cal., 11 g total fat (4 g sat. fat), 15 mg chol., 102 mg sodium, 41 g carbo., 4 g fiber, 2 g pro.

peanut butter s'mores

Though you may not own up to it, this variation on the s'mores theme could become one of those private pleasures. No one will ever have to know your secret obsession.

PREP: 15 minutes **GRILL:** 7 minutes **MAKES:** 8 servings

- ¾ cup peanut butter
- 4 9- to 10-inch flour tortillas (burrito size)
- 1 cup tiny marshmallows
- ½ cup miniature semisweet chocolate pieces
- 1 medium ripe, yet firm, banana, thinly sliced

one Spread about 3 tablespoons of the peanut butter over one half of each tortilla. Top each with some of the marshmallows, chocolate pieces, and banana slices. Fold tortillas in half, pressing gently to flatten and seal slightly.

two For a charcoal grill, grill filled tortillas on the rack of an uncovered grill directly over medium coals for 7 to 9 minutes or until tortillas are golden and chocolate is melted, turning once halfway through grilling. (For a gas grill, preheat grill. Reduce heat to medium. Place filled tortillas on grill rack over heat. Cover and grill as above.)

three To serve, cut each filled tortilla into 4 wedges.

NUTRITION FACTS PER SERVING: 290 cal., 17 g total fat (3 g sat. fat), 0 mg chol., 207 mg sodium, 31 g carbo., 2 g fiber, 8 g pro.

mango blossoms

A mango is ripe when the skin is bright in color and the fruit yields very slightly to touch and has a strong floral aroma.

PREP: 30 minutes **GRILL:** 2 minutes + 4 minutes **MAKES:** 8 servings

4	mangoes
4	kiwifruit, peeled
½	of a 15-ounce purchased angel food cake
¼	cup butter or margarine, melted
3	tablespoons mild-flavored molasses or honey
	Vanilla ice cream (optional)

one Using a sharp knife, cut each mango lengthwise down both flat sides, keeping the blade about ¼ inch from the seed. Score mango pieces, making cuts through the fruit just to the peel in a crosshatch fashion. Set aside.

two Carefully remove and discard the peel remaining around the mango seeds. Cut away as much of the fruit remaining around each mango seed as you can; discard seeds. Place the removed fruit portion in a food processor/ blender container. Cover and blend fruit pieces until smooth. Transfer pureed fruit to a small covered container or a clean squeeze bottle. Chill until ready to use.

three Rinse the food processo/blender container. Place peeled kiwifruit in bowl or container. Cover and process or blend until smooth. If desired, strain the kiwifruit puree through a sieve to remove seeds. Transfer to a small covered container or squeeze bottle. Chill until ready to use.

four Cut angel food cake in half horizontally (forming 2 half-rings). Brush all sides of the cake with half of the melted butter. For a charcoal grill, grill cake on rack of an uncovered grill directly over medium coals for 2 to 3 minutes or until lightly browned, turning once. Cut angel food cake into large, irregular-shape croutons.

five Brush fruit side of reserved mango pieces with molasses and remaining melted butter. Grill mangoes, cut sides down, over medium coals for 4 to 6 minutes or until brown around the edges and heated through. (For a gas grill, preheat grill. Reduce heat to medium. Place cake, then mangoes on grill rack over heat. Cover and grill as above.)

six To serve, spoon or drizzle mango and kiwifruit sauces on the bottom of 8 chilled, shallow dessert bowls. Carefully bend the peel back on each mango half, pushing the inside up and out until the mango cubes pop up and separate. Place each mango "blossom" on sauces in dessert bowl. Surround with several cake croutons. If desired, serve with vanilla ice cream.

NUTRITION FACTS PER SERVING: 215 cal., 4 g total fat (3 g sat. fat), 15 mg chol., 249 mg sodium, 45 g carbo., 2 g fiber, 3 g pro.

hot-off-the-grill tropical treat

Looking for an informal yet special summer dish? You'll surprise your guests when you serve this sweet grilled fruit. Fresh pineapple slices get brushed with a nicely spiced lime and honey sauce while they grill to perfection.

PREP: 20 minutes **GRILL:** 8 minutes **MAKES:** 6 servings

1	large fresh pineapple, peeled and cored
¼	cup butter or margarine
1	teaspoon finely shredded lime peel
2	tablespoons lime juice
2	tablespoons honey
1	tablespoon cornstarch
¼	teaspoon ground ginger

one Cut pineapple crosswise into 6 slices. In a small saucepan melt butter over medium heat. In a small bowl stir together lime peel, lime juice, honey, cornstarch, and ginger. Stir into the melted butter. Cook and stir until mixture is thickened and bubbly. Cook and stir for 2 minutes more. Remove from heat.

two For a charcoal grill, grill pineapple slices on the rack of an uncovered grill directly over medium coals for 8 to 10 minutes or until heated through, turning once halfway through grilling and brushing frequently with lime-butter mixture. (For a gas grill, preheat grill. Reduce heat to medium. Place pineapple slices on grill rack over heat. Cover and grill as above.)

NUTRITION FACTS PER SERVING: 190 cal., 8 g total fat (5 g sat. fat), 22 mg chol., 91 mg sodium, 29 g carbo., 2 g fiber, 1 g pro.

30-minute
recipes

speed matters!

MASTER YOUR LISTS

Part of getting a meal on the table quickly is always having what you need. Use your computer to make a master shopping list, including blank lines on which to add specialty ingredients.

- Keep shopping list copies in the kitchen and stash some in your car to help spur your memory when stopping for groceries on the way home.
- Arrange the shopping list by department or by your favorite store's layout.
- Carry copies of your favorite quick recipes with you (in your purse, PDA, or glove compartment) so you can pick up ingredients on a whim.

SHOPPING SAVVY

- Stick with "your" grocery store. Whether you routinely shop at one or two, knowing where to find what you're after speeds the effort.
- No time to shop? Find a shopping and delivery service to bring groceries to your door. Check the phone book and Internet to find services—with many, you can order online. Your grocery store may even offer such services.

HELPFUL TIP

Turn over shopping tasks to a teenager. It's a great way for the teen to contribute to the family and develop shopping skills.

WHEN TIME IS OF THE ESSENCE SETUP MATTERS

- Empty the dishwasher before beginning meal preparation so it's ready to fill as you work.
- Store dishes near the dishwasher for fast, easy unloading. Put them on lower shelves so a youngster can handle the task.
- Get a good-looking swing-top or foot-operated pop-top trash can in a size bigger than you think you need. A too-small trash can that is stowed behind a door fills too quickly and gets marred with spills—as do doors and door pulls nearby.
- Store pots, pans, cutting boards, and utensils within easy reach of where you cook.
- Keep hand towels and paper towels near every location in the kitchen where you'll use them.
- Stash frequently used seasonings and oils near the counter where you use them.

set the table...

Set the table before you leave home in the morning, or have a family member do it. Seeing a set table when you come home and knowing dinner is just 30 minutes or less away is a welcome thought.

NOW YOU'RE COOKING! AND QUICKLY...

When time's short, try these quick ideas:

- Cut up leftover chicken, beef, pork, or seafood from last night's dinner and sprinkle it on cheese-topped tortillas to make quesadillas for tonight's meal. If you like, add chopped olives, roasted red peppers, and/or chili seasoning.
- Making French toast? Slice peaches, strawberries, or bananas and sear them in a hot skillet to serve as a juicy accompaniment.
- Leftover French toast? Cool the extra slices and slip them into resealable bags to stash in the fridge. Reheat for quick weekday breakfasts.
- Make breakfast for dinner. Scramble eggs or make an omelet. If you like, heat slices of ham or sausage links. They're quick and tasty. Add toast and fruit salad.
- Make a quiche—or two. Slices reheat quickly in the microwave and make a delicious meal with a salad or fruit.
- Stretch leftover chili or stew by ladling hot leftovers over baked potatoes, quick-cooking couscous, or corn bread.
- When you're relying on leftovers for the main dish, have dessert! Make it or buy it, but let the focus fall to this guilty pleasure.
- Stock the fridge with sandwich makings. Then use them for a meal. Make it fun and encourage creative sandwich-making. Serve a soup or dessert to round out the menu.
- Impromptu guests? Thaw some frozen raspberries to sprinkle over lemon sherbet or pool alongside a bakery brownie drizzled with chocolate sauce.

STOCK YOUR PANTRY, REFRIGERATOR, AND FREEZER

Use this list as a starter, adding or deleting items to suit your needs and preferences. Getting a feel for how fast you and your family consume various items also will help you keep your kitchen stocked.

Produce, Fruit

Tip: Slice fruits to serve with a meal, then for best appearance, toss apple or pear slices with a little lemon or lime juice diluted with water so the slices won't turn brown.

- Apples and pears
- Berries
- Grapes
- Lemons and limes (fresh or bottled juice)
- Oranges and grapefruit
- Peaches and Plums
- Pineapple

Produce, Vegetables

Tip: Steam fresh vegetables and serve them with a squeeze of lemon and pat of butter.

- Asparagus
- Beans
- Broccoli
- Carrots
- Cauliflower
- Garlic (fresh or bottled minced)
- Ginger (fresh or bottled minced)
- Onions
- Peas
- Potatoes (white or sweet)
- Salad greens
- Zucchini or summer squash

Meat Department

Tip: Ask your butcher to lend a hand. Most are more than happy to remove skin from fish, or rewrap your meat, fish, and poultry purchases in the portion sizes that you need most.

Tip: While you're chatting with the butcher, ask for suggestions on quick, tasty ways to prepare your purchases. The store staff often knows quick prep methods and is happy to share.

- Chicken breasts
- Deli meats
- Ground meat (beef, pork, or turkey, bulk or patties)
- Hot dogs
- Meat cut for stir-fries
- Pork chops
- Salmon
- Shrimp (cooked and peeled)
- Tenderloins (beef or pork)
- Tuna steaks

Dairy

- Butter and/or margarine
- Cheeses (chunk, sliced, or grated)
- Eggs
- Half-and-half
- Milk
- Sour cream and yogurt

Bread, Baked Goods

- Bagels
- Bread
- English muffins
- Tortillas (corn or flour, plain or flavored)

Refrigerator & Freezer Case

- Frozen fruit (berries, peaches, or rhubarb)
- Pasta
- Piecrust (ready to bake)
- Pizza shells (prebaked)
- Vegetables

Shelf & Canned Goods

- Beans (dried or canned)
- Biscuit mixes
- Bouillon cubes and/or base (beef or chicken)
- Bread crumbs
- Broth (chicken, beef, or vegetable)
- Brownie or cake mixes
- Chiles
- Corn bread mix
- Couscous
- Flour
- Honey
- Mushrooms (canned or dried)
- Nuts (almonds, pecans, walnuts, peanuts, or other nuts)
- Pasta, dried (various shapes)
- Refried beans
- Rice (white, brown, or wild)
- Roasted red peppers
- Soups
- Sugar (granulated, brown)
- Tomatoes (whole, diced, or stewed)
- Tomato paste
- Tomato sauce
- Tuna (canned or pouches, plain or seasoned)
- Vegetables (various kinds)
- Water chestnuts

Oils, Condiments, & Seasonings

- Barbecue sauce
- Herbs and spices
- Horseradish
- Hot sauce
- Ketchup
- Mustard (yellow, brown, Dijon-style, or specialty)
- Oil (vegetable, olive, sesame, or specialty)
- Olives
- Pickles
- Salad dressings, bottled
- Salsa
- Seasoning blends (Italian, taco, Cajun, lemon-pepper, or specialty)
- Soy sauce

- Vinegar (cider, white, wine, rice, or specialty)
- Worcestershire sauce

SIMPLE ACCOMPANIMENTS ARE SMART, QUICK

You'll eat better meals when you comple-ment your quick entrées with straight-forward accompaniments. Choose them to complement the flavor of your main dish. Think texture too. For appeal, foods should vary in shape and form.

Balance opposites:
- Hot—Cool (temperature and seasoning)
- Crunchy—Soft
- Salty—Sweet
- Complex—Mellow

Go-with ideas:
- Apples or pears
- Beans
- Cheese and crackers
- Chewy bread (sourdough, whole wheat, or specialty)

- Corn bread
- Cottage cheese topped with fresh sliced strawberries, raspberries, or blueberries
- Couscous
- Hard-cooked egg slices
- Heat-and-eat side dishes from a supermarket deli counter
- Melon wedges
- Olives
- Orange or grapefruit sections
- Pasta
- Peaches, plums, or nectarines
- Pineapple slices
- Potatoes (whole or half, they're a quick bake in the microwave)
- Rice
- Salads from a supermarket deli counter or salad bar
- Steamed or grilled vegetables
- Torn mixed greens tossed with bottled salad dressing
- Vegetable dippers with purchased dip
- Yogurt

IN THE KITCHEN

Your Supplies

A well-stocked kitchen serves any cook well. Take inventory of your supplies and shop sales at local discount and department stores, or online.

- Aluminum foil (standard and heavy duty)—line pans with foil to speed cleanup
- Bowls (multisize sets)
- Brown lunch bags for ripening pears and stone fruits
- Colander
- Cutting boards (polyethylene or wood—for safety sake, reserve one exclusively for use with raw meat or poultry)
- Grater/shredder
- Food thermometer
- Hot pads/trivets—flexible silicone va-rieties double as hot pads and nonskid trivets
- Kitchen shears
- Knives (chef, paring, and serrated)
- Liquid measuring cups (large and small sizes)
- Measuring cups set
- Measuring spoons set
- Mixing spoons
- Nonstick cooking spray
- Plastic wrap
- Refrigerator and freezer containers (various sizes)
- Spatulas
- Tape and markers for labeling leftovers
- Vegetable peeler
- Vegetable steamer—keep it in a saucepan on the stovetop ready to go
- Waxed paper
- Wooden spoons
- Zester for cutting citrus peels

embrace convenience

Who's not short on time? Convenience foods once had a reputation for being inferior, but grocers and food marketers eager to keep customers happy are responding with an increasing number of high-quality convenience products. Pricing is good too, especially when you consider the alternatives—dining out, food that has gone bad, and nutritious food groups missed altogether. Listed below are a number of timesaving food options; more appear every day. Invest a few minutes roaming the grocery store to find timesavers that you can use.

Chopped fresh fruits
Chopped fresh veggies
Deli-prepared potatoes, macaroni and cheese, and side-salads
Frozen meals including ethnic and vegetarian options
Frozen meal kits ready for the slow cooker
Frozen meal starters for a quick stir-fry
Frozen prepared desserts—remove a few portions to thaw during dinner
Marinated meat and poultry
Torn salad greens

CLEAR THE CLUTTER, DOUBLE UP

Don't waste any more time rummaging through the utensil drawer looking for tongs or wrestling a pan from the tangles of a lower cupboard. Get a few transparent tubs in small, medium, and large sizes and go through your cupboards and drawers. Remove everything that you don't use often. Be ruthless. Now, send those tubs to the basement or attic—get rid of the stuff if you want to or store it for later. The point is to get it out of your way.

Now that you can see the stuff you use, decide if you need more of what you have. No kidding. Having doubles or more of your most frequently used tools—cutting boards, liquid measures, and favorite-size saucepans—will speed your way through meal prep and cleanup.

IF YOU CAN, BUY A GOOD SINK & FAUCET

Meal prep and cleanup are a breeze when you're in sync with your sink—you probably won't even notice how well it serves you. But if you've ever been drenched trying to wash a big pot in a too-small sink, you understand. Low-profile faucets can make sink work awkward too. So when it's time to replace a sink or faucet—or if you're buying a new home—opt for a sink style with a small prep sink (fitted with a garbage disposal) on one side and an oversize deep bowl on the other. Also, choose a tall gooseneck-style faucet that won't get in your way as you wash large items or lift them from the sink.

APPLIANCE AND EQUIPMENT POINTERS

- Follow the will-it-make-a-difference rule: Are you thinking that buying washed and cut fresh vegetables is an indulgence? It's not, if having to wash and cut them yourself means that you'll skip them all together. Do you need a food processor? Not if the cleanup keeps you from using it, and you're buying prepped veggies anyway. And is that countertop grill an indulgence? If it's saving you from purchasing pricey, less healthful meals out, it's a bargain! Remember, Grandma might have loved to use these options had she the choice.

- Follow the golden dishwasher/sink rule: If you're buying a new piece of kitchen equipment, make sure that it's dishwasher safe and will fit in your machine. Similarly, if the item won't fit in your sink, skip it. You'll keep cleanup a cinch with this guideline.

- An increasing number of countertop appliances and tools are being produced with parts that are dishwasher-safe. Slow cookers, electric skillets, and grilling machines are among them. These can be great timesavers.

- Beware of oversize baking sheets and platters. Though they often hold a few more cookies or steaks, they often don't fit easily in the dishwasher or sink.

plug in!

While some electric countertop appliances are used a few times and then resigned to clutter the cupboard, others are reached for time and again, earning their keep while speeding and simplifying meal prep. The trick lies in knowing your personal preferences. Also, within each appliance type you'll find models that are compact, easy to slip in the dishwasher, and store—and others that don't have any of those qualities. Choose wisely. These appliances rate consideration but you be the final judge of whether each one will work for you:

- **Slow cookers** do meal prep while you're away. They also can stand unattended on buffet tables for parties.
- **Grilling machines** let you prepare meat, poultry, and seafood quickly and simply.
- **Electric skillets** add stovetop capacity and make fast work of whipping up a meal for the gang.
- **Food chopper/processors** shred cheese and chop veggies quickly.
- **Hand blenders** are favored by many for pureeing soups, mashing potatoes, and preparing beverages.

company-style steaks

Don't wait for company to try this recipe! These tender steaks with mushroom-wine sauce are incredibly quick to make and are great for everyday eating or special occasions.

START TO FINISH: 25 minutes **MAKES:** 4 servings

4	beef tenderloin steaks (about 1 pound total) or 1 pound beef top sirloin, cut ¾ inch thick
1	tablespoon Dijon-style mustard or coarse-grain brown mustard
2	tablespoons olive oil
3	cups sliced fresh mushrooms
⅓	cup dry red wine, sherry, or beef or chicken broth
1	tablespoon Worcestershire sauce for chicken
2	teaspoons snipped fresh thyme
½	cup beef broth
1	teaspoon cornstarch

one If using top sirloin, cut meat into 4 pieces. Spread mustard evenly over steaks. In a large skillet heat 1 tablespoon of the oil over medium heat. Add steaks; cook until desired doneness, turning once. (Allow 7 to 9 minutes for medium-rare [145°F] to medium doneness [160°F].) Transfer steaks to a serving platter. Keep warm.

two Add remaining 1 tablespoon oil to skillet drippings. Add mushrooms; cook and stir for 4 minutes. Stir in wine, Worcestershire sauce, and thyme. Simmer, uncovered, for 3 minutes. Combine the ½ cup broth and cornstarch. Stir into mushroom mixture. Cook and stir until thickened and bubbly. Cook and stir for 2 minutes more. Spoon over steaks.

NUTRITION FACTS PER SERVING: 263 cal., 14 g total fat (4 g sat. fat), 64 mg chol., 176 mg sodium, 5 g carbo., 1 g fiber, 23 g pro.

menu idea:

Spinach, Red Onion & Cherry Tomato Salad (see p. 245)

Vanilla ice cream topped with crushed purchased shortbread cookies and toasted chopped pecans

pasta with beef & asparagus

Fast enough for a weekday meal and fancy enough for casual company on weekends, this combination is sensational. Tarragon adds a touch of class but the bowtie pasta keeps it fun. If asparagus isn't available use broccoli florets or baby bok choy.

START TO FINISH: 30 minutes **MAKES:** 4 servings

1	pound fresh asparagus
8	ounces dried bowtie pasta
1	8-ounce carton dairy sour cream
2	tablespoons all-purpose flour
⅔	cup water
1	tablespoon honey
½	teaspoon salt
¼	teaspoon black pepper
1	teaspoon cooking oil
8	ounces beef top sirloin steak, trimmed and cut into thin bite-size strips
2	tablespoons finely chopped shallot
2	teaspoons snipped fresh tarragon

one Cut off and discard woody bases from asparagus. If desired, scrape off scales. Bias-slice asparagus into 1-inch pieces; set aside. Cook pasta according to package directions, adding asparagus for the last 3 minutes of cooking; drain well. Return pasta mixture to pan; cover and keep warm.

two In a medium bowl stir together sour cream and flour. Stir in the water, honey, salt, and pepper. Set aside.

three In a large nonstick skillet heat oil over medium-high heat. Add meat and shallot; cook and stir about 5 minutes or until meat is brown. Drain off fat.

four Stir sour cream mixture into meat mixture in skillet. Cook and stir until thickened and bubbly. Cook and stir for 1 minute more. Stir in drained pasta, asparagus, and tarragon. Heat through.

NUTRITION FACTS PER SERVING: 462 cal., 17 g total fat (9 g sat. fat), 113 mg chol., 358 mg sodium, 53 g carbo., 3 g fiber, 24 g pro.

test kitchen tip: For a lower-fat pasta, substitute light dairy sour cream for the regular sour cream.

NUTRITION FACTS PER SERVING: 421 cal., 11 g total fat (4 g sat. fat), 107 mg chol., 373 mg sodium, 54 g carbo., 3 g fiber, 26 g pro.

menu idea:

Purchased soft breadsticks served with butter and grated Parmesan cheese

Gooey Brownie Cups (see p. 262)

easy shepherd's pie

If you like, try this recipe with ground turkey or chicken for a great-tasting twist on an old favorite.

START TO FINISH: 30 minutes **MAKES:** 6 servings

1	pound lean ground beef or uncooked ground turkey or chicken
1	medium onion, chopped
1	10-ounce package frozen mixed vegetables, thawed
¼	cup water
1	10¾-ounce can condensed tomato soup
1	teaspoon Worcestershire sauce
¼	teaspoon dried thyme, crushed
1	20-ounce package refrigerated mashed potatoes or 3 cups leftover mashed potatoes
½	cup shredded cheddar cheese (2 ounces)

one In a large skillet cook ground meat and onion until meat is brown and onion is tender. Drain off fat. Stir mixed vegetables and the water into meat mixture in skillet. Bring to boiling; reduce heat. Cover and simmer about 5 minutes or until vegetables are tender.

two Stir in tomato soup, Worcestershire sauce, and thyme. Return to boiling; reduce heat. Drop mashed potatoes in 6 mounds on top of hot mixture. Sprinkle potatoes with cheese. Cover and simmer for 10 to 15 minutes or until potatoes are heated through.

NUTRITION FACTS PER SERVING: 301 cal., 12 g total fat (5 g sat. fat), 58 mg chol., 570 mg sodium, 27 g carbo., 3 g fiber, 20 g pro.

---

menu idea:

Torn fresh spinach tossed with crisp-cooked bacon, croutons, and purchased balsamic vinaigrette salad dressing

Apricot-Peach Cobbler (see p. 256)

white & green chili

Chili gets a fresh update with a dab of tangy sour cream and a sprinkle of refreshing cilantro.

PREP: 15 minutes **COOK:** 15 minutes **MAKES:** 4 servings

1	pound unseasoned meat loaf mix (⅓ pound each ground beef, pork, and veal), lean ground beef, or ground pork
1	small onion, chopped
2	15-ounce cans Great Northern beans or white beans, rinsed and drained
1	16-ounce jar green salsa
1	14-ounce can chicken broth
1½	teaspoons ground cumin
2	tablespoons snipped fresh cilantro
¼	cup dairy sour cream (optional)

one In a 4-quart Dutch oven combine meat loaf mix or ground meat and onion. Cook over medium heat about 5 minutes or until meat is brown and onion is tender, breaking up pieces of meat with a spoon. Drain off fat. Stir beans, salsa, chicken broth, and cumin into meat mixture in Dutch oven. Bring to boiling; reduce heat. Cover and simmer for 15 minutes.

two To serve, stir in 1 tablespoon of the cilantro. Divide among 4 serving bowls. Sprinkle with remaining 1 tablespoon cilantro. If desired, top individual servings with sour cream.

NUTRITION FACTS PER SERVING: 400 cal., 11 g total fat (4 g sat. fat), 73 mg chol., 1,404 mg sodium, 41 g carbo., 13 g fiber, 31 g pro.

menu idea:

Crackers and/or bagel chips served with assorted cheeses

Fruit-Filled Waffle Bowls (see p. 274)

quick skillet lasagna

Talk about quick! By using bottled pasta sauce and just one skillet, this typically labor-intensive family favorite is streamlined enough that you can make and enjoy it at a moment's notice.

START TO FINISH: 30 minutes **MAKES:** 6 servings

3	cups (6 ounces) dried mafalda (mini lasagna) noodles
12	ounces lean ground beef or bulk pork sausage
1	26- to 28-ounce jar red pasta sauce
1½	cups shredded mozzarella cheese (6 ounces)
¼	cup grated Parmesan cheese (1 ounce)

one Cook pasta according to package directions; drain well.

two Meanwhile, in a 10-inch nonstick skillet cook meat until brown. Drain off fat. Set meat aside. Wipe the skillet with the paper towels.

three Spread about half of the cooked pasta in the skillet. Cover with about half of the pasta sauce. Spoon cooked meat over sauce. Sprinkle with 1 cup of the mozzarella cheese. Top with remaining pasta and remaining sauce. Sprinkle remaining ½ cup mozzarella cheese and the Parmesan cheese on top.

four Cover and cook over medium heat for 5 to 7 minutes or until heated through and cheese melts. Remove skillet from heat. Let stand, covered, for 1 minute.

NUTRITION FACTS PER SERVING: 375 cal., 17 g total fat (6 g sat. fat), 50 mg chol., 1,046 mg sodium, 30 g carbo., 2 g fiber, 25 g pro.

menu idea:

Mixed greens tossed with sliced red and/or green sweet peppers and bottled creamy Italian salad dressing

Mocha Mousse Cups (see p. 279)

beef & black bean wraps

Hearty and satisfying, these wraps are not only delicious but go together in just 25 minutes. You can't go wrong serving this quick-to-fix meal.

START TO FINISH: 25 minutes **MAKES:** 6 servings

8	ounces lean ground beef
1	large onion, chopped
1	teaspoon bottled minced garlic (2 cloves)
1½	teaspoons ground cumin
1	teaspoon chili powder
½	teaspoon ground coriander
1	15-ounce can black beans, rinsed and drained
1	large tomato, chopped
¼	teaspoon salt
¼	teaspoon black pepper
6	8-inch whole wheat flour tortillas
1½	cups shredded lettuce
1	to 1½ cups shredded cheddar or Monterey Jack cheese (4 to 6 ounces)
	Bottled salsa (optional)

one In a large skillet cook ground beef, onion, and garlic about 5 minutes or until meat is brown and onion is tender. Drain off fat. Stir cumin, chili powder, and coriander into meat mixture in skillet. Cook and stir for 1 minute. Stir in black beans, tomato, salt, and pepper. Cover and cook for 5 minutes more, stirring occasionally.

two To serve, spoon some of the beef mixture down the center of each tortilla. Sprinkle with lettuce and cheese. Roll up. If desired, serve with salsa.

NUTRITION FACTS PER SERVING: 267 cal., 10 g total fat (5 g sat. fat), 44 mg chol., 593 mg sodium, 27 g carbo., 14 g fiber, 19 g pro.

menu idea:

Speedy Southwestern-Style Tomato Soup *(see p. 239)* served with corn tortilla chips

Lemon and/or lime sherbet

french onion & beef soup

Teaming a canned soup with additional ingredients is a quick way to boost flavor. Enhanced with golden onions, tender morsels of browned beef, and bubbling Gruyère cheese, this soup is so delicious no one will mind that it isn't homemade!

START TO FINISH: 25 minutes **MAKES:** 4 servings

3	tablespoons butter or margarine
1	medium onion, thinly sliced and separated into rings
2	10½-ounce cans condensed French onion soup
2½	cups water
8	ounces cooked roast beef, cubed
4	1-inch slices French bread
½	cup shredded Gruyère or Swiss cheese (2 ounces)

one In a large skillet melt butter over medium heat. Add onion; cook about 5 minutes or until very tender. Stir in French onion soup, the water, and cooked beef. Bring to boiling, stirring soup occasionally.

two Meanwhile, place the bread slices on a baking sheet. Broil 4 inches from the heat about 1 minute or until toasted on one side. Top the toasted sides of bread slices with shredded cheese; broil about 1 minute more or until cheese is melted.

three To serve, ladle soup into soup bowls. Top with bread slices, cheese sides up.

NUTRITION FACTS PER SERVING: 465 cal., 21 g total fat (10 g sat. fat), 82 mg chol., 1,701 mg sodium, 40 g carbo., 3 g fiber, 28 g pro.

menu idea:

Citrus Salad with Glazed Pecans *(see p. 247)*

Purchased oatmeal raisin cookies, spread with canned vanilla frosting and sprinkled with ground cinnamon

roast beef sandwiches
with horseradish slaw

Horseradish and beef, common sandwich partners, pair up once again. Here the horseradish seasons crunchy broccoli slaw.

START TO FINISH: 15 minutes **MAKES:** 4 servings

⅓   cup dairy sour cream

2   tablespoons snipped fresh chives

2   tablespoons spicy brown mustard

1   teaspoon prepared horseradish

½   teaspoon sugar

¼   teaspoon salt

1   cup packaged shredded broccoli (broccoli slaw mix)

8   ounces thinly sliced cooked roast beef

8   ½-inch slices sourdough bread, toasted

one In a medium bowl combine sour cream, chives, brown mustard, horseradish, sugar, and salt. Add shredded broccoli; toss to coat.

two To assemble, divide roast beef among 4 of the bread slices. Top with broccoli mixture and remaining bread slices.

NUTRITION FACTS PER SERVING: 312 cal., 12 g total fat (5 g sat. fat), 52 mg chol., 612 mg sodium, 29 g carbo., 2 g fiber, 21 g pro.

---

menu idea:

Orange Dream Fruit Salad *(see p. 249)*

Neapolitan ice cream served with purchased chocolate-filled sugar wafer cookies

pork chops with peppers & onions

Tempt your family with the mouthwatering aroma of pork chops and vibrantly colored sweet peppers sizzling in a pan.

START TO FINISH: 25 minutes **MAKES:** 4 servings

4	pork loin or rib chops, cut ½ to ¾ inch thick (about 1¼ pounds total)
1	tablespoon olive oil
1	medium red sweet pepper, cut into strips
1	medium green sweet pepper, cut into strips
1	medium yellow sweet pepper, cut into strips
1	large sweet onion, thinly sliced
¼	cup water
¼	cup dry white wine or chicken broth
1	teaspoon snipped fresh rosemary or ½ teaspoon dried rosemary, crushed
¼	teaspoon salt

one Trim fat from chops. In a large skillet heat oil over medium-high heat. Add chops; cook for 4 to 5 minutes or until brown, turning once. Add sweet peppers and onion to skillet. Add the water, wine, rosemary, and salt. Bring to boiling; reduce heat. Cover and simmer for 4 to 7 minutes or until pork is done (160°F) and juices run clear.

two Transfer chops to serving plates. Use a slotted spoon to remove pepper mixture from skillet; spoon over chops. If desired, drizzle with some of the skillet juices.

NUTRITION FACTS PER SERVING: 209 cal., 8 g total fat (2 g sat. fat), 58 mg chol., 205 mg sodium, 10 g carbo., 2 g fiber, 22 g pro.

menu idea:

Purchased refrigerated biscuits, baked and served with butter and maple syrup

Amaretto Peaches with Vanilla Yogurt *(see p. 285)*

gala pork chops

Keep a variety of nuts on hand for adding crunch, taste, and extra nutrients to everyday meals. Nuts can be stored in an airtight container in the refrigerator for up to 4 months or in the freezer up to 6 months.

PREP: 10 minutes **GRILL:** 12 minutes **MAKES:** 4 servings

4	boneless pork loin chops, cut ¾ inch thick (about 1 pound total)
1	teaspoon olive oil
½	teaspoon dried rosemary, crushed
½	teaspoon salt
¼	to ½ teaspoon black pepper
1½	cups sliced, peeled cooking apples
⅓	cup apple juice or apple cider
1	tablespoon lemon juice
1	tablespoon cold water
1½	teaspoons cornstarch
¼	cup crumbled feta cheese (1 ounce)
¼	cup chopped pecans, toasted

one Trim fat from chops. Rub both sides of each chop lightly with the oil. Sprinkle both sides of each chop with rosemary, salt, and pepper.

two Place chops on the rack of an uncovered grill directly over medium heat. Grill for 12 to 15 minutes or until tender (160° F) and juices run clear, turning once.

three Meanwhile, in a medium saucepan stir together apples, apple juice, and lemon juice. Bring to boiling; reduce heat. Cover and simmer for 3 minutes. In a small bowl stir together the cold water and cornstarch. Add to apple mixture. Cook and stir until thickened and bubbly. Cook and stir for 2 minutes more. Serve apple mixture over chops; top with feta and pecans.

NUTRITION FACTS PER SERVING: 278 cal., 14 g total fat (4 g sat. fat), 68 mg chol., 421 mg sodium, 11 g carbo., 2 g fiber, 27 g pro.

Broiler method: Place chops on unheated rack of a broiler pan. Broil 3 to 4 inches from heat for 9 to 11 minutes or until tender (160°F) and juices run clear.

menu idea:

Summer Spaghetti *(see p. 231)*

Pirouette cookies served with coffee ice cream

oven-fried pork chops

Coating the chops with the corn bread stuffing mix gives them a delightful crispy crust, keeping them juicy and moist inside.

PREP: 10 minutes **BAKE:** 20 minutes **MAKES:** 4 servings

3	tablespoons butter or margarine
1	egg
2	tablespoons milk
1	cup packaged corn bread stuffing mix
4	pork loin chops, cut ½ inch thick (about 1½ pounds total)
	Applesauce (optional)

one Place butter in a 13×9×2-inch baking pan; heat in a 425°F oven about 3 minutes or until butter melts.

two Meanwhile, in a shallow dish beat egg with a fork; stir in milk. Place dry stuffing mix in another shallow dish. Trim fat from chops. Dip pork chops into egg mixture. Coat both sides with stuffing mix. Place chops in the baking pan with the butter.

three Bake for 20 to 25 minutes or until tender (160°F) and juices run clear, turning once. If desired, serve with applesauce.

NUTRITION FACTS PER SERVING: 326 cal., 16 g total fat (8 g sat. fat), 131 mg chol., 392 mg sodium, 17 g carbo., 0 g fiber, 26 g pro.

menu idea:

Purchased chunky applesauce sprinkled with cinnamon-sugar

Raspberry & Chocolate Tulips (see p. 271)

soft shell pork tacos

These tacos get their pizzazz from chipotle chili powder. If you can't find it at your supermarket, crush a dried chipotle chile pepper. In a real pinch, regular chili powder will do.

START TO FINISH: 25 minutes **MAKES:** 4 servings

- 2 teaspoons cooking oil
- 8 ounces boneless pork loin, trimmed and cut into thin bite-size strips
- ¼ cup dairy sour cream
- ¼ teaspoon chipotle chili powder, crushed dried chipotle chile pepper, or chili powder
- 4 6-inch flour tortillas, warmed*
- ½ cup shredded lettuce
- ½ cup diced tomato
- ½ cup shredded cheddar cheese (2 ounces)
  Bottled salsa

one In a large skillet heat oil over medium-high heat. Add pork; cook until done. Set aside.

two In a small bowl combine sour cream and chipotle chili powder; set aside.

three Spoon one-fourth of the pork onto each tortilla just below the center. Top pork with lettuce, tomato, and cheese. Fold top half of each tortilla over filling. Serve with sour cream mixture and salsa.

NUTRITION FACTS PER SERVING: 255 cal., 14 g total fat (6 g sat. fat), 51 mg chol., 243 mg sodium, 13 g carbo., 1 g fiber, 18 g pro.

*NOTE: To warm tortillas, wrap them in white microwave-safe paper towels; microwave on 100% power (high) for 15 to 30 seconds or until tortillas are softened. (Or wrap tortillas in foil. Heat in a 350°F oven for 10 to 15 minutes or until warmed.)

test kitchen tip: For lower-fat tacos, substitute light dairy sour cream and reduced-fat cheddar cheese for the regular sour cream and cheddar cheese.

NUTRITION FACTS PER SERVING: 240 cal., 11 g total fat (4 g sat. fat), 48 mg chol., 263 mg sodium, 14 g carbo., 1 g fiber, 19 g pro.

menu idea:

Fried rice mix, prepared according to package directions and sprinkled with shredded cheese

Bananas Suzette over Pound Cake (see p. 263)

jamaican pork stir-fry

Make your meal lively by adding some Caribbean heat from Jerk seasoning. It's a heady and fragrant combination of chiles, garlic, onion, and other seasonings, such as thyme, cinnamon, ginger, allspice, and cloves.

START TO FINISH: 20 minutes **MAKES:** 4 servings

2	tablespoons cooking oil
1	16-ounce package loose-pack frozen peas, whole baby carrots, snow peas, and baby corn
12	ounces lean boneless pork, trimmed and cut into thin bite-size strips
2	to 3 teaspoons Jamaican jerk seasoning
¾	cup bottled plum sauce
	Hot cooked rice or pasta
	Crushed corn chips or chopped peanuts

one In a wok or large skillet heat oil over medium-high heat. Add frozen vegetables; cook and stir for 5 to 7 minutes or until vegetables are crisp-tender. Remove vegetables from wok.

two Toss pork strips with Jamaican jerk seasoning; add pork strips to wok. (Add more cooking oil if necessary.) Cook and stir for 2 to 3 minutes or until pork is tender and juices run clear.

three Add plum sauce to wok. Return vegetables to wok. Stir together to coat all ingredients with sauce. Heat through. Serve over hot cooked rice or pasta. Sprinkle with corn chips or peanuts.

NUTRITION FACTS PER SERVING: 419 cal., 11 g total fat (2 g sat. fat), 46 mg chol., 269 mg sodium, 51 g carbo., 3 g fiber, 24 g pro.

menu idea:

Fresh pineapple wedges served with purchased fruit dip

No-Drip Chocolate Dip (see p. 281)

pasta with ham-mushroom sauce

This creamy, satisfying dish resembles a vegetable-studded fettuccine Alfredo. Instead of the usual heavy cream, this rich-tasting sauce is made with evaporated milk. You save on calories and don't have to give up taste.

START TO FINISH: 30 minutes **MAKES:** 4 servings

2	cups sliced fresh shiitake or button mushrooms
1	small red or green sweet pepper, cut into thin strips
1	medium onion, chopped
½	teaspoon bottled minced garlic (1 clove)
1	tablespoon butter or margarine
1	12-ounce can (1½ cups) evaporated milk
2	tablespoons snipped fresh basil or ½ teaspoon dried basil, crushed
4	teaspoons cornstarch
¼	teaspoon black pepper
4	ounces cooked ham, cut into thin bite-size strips
1	9-ounce package refrigerated fettuccine
	Finely shredded Parmesan cheese (optional)

one For sauce, in a large skillet cook mushrooms, sweet pepper, onion, and garlic in hot butter until tender. In a medium bowl combine evaporated milk, basil, cornstarch, and black pepper. Stir into vegetable mixture in skillet. Cook and stir over medium heat until bubbly. Cook and stir for 2 minutes more. Stir in ham. Remove from heat.

two Meanwhile, cook pasta according to package directions. Drain. Serve sauce over pasta. If desired, sprinkle with Parmesan cheese.

NUTRITION FACTS PER SERVING: 432 cal., 14 g total fat (7 g sat. fat), 116 mg chol., 501 mg sodium, 60 g carbo., 4 g fiber, 20 g pro.

test kitchen tip: For a lower-fat sauce, substitute fat-free evaporated milk for the regular evaporated milk.

NUTRITION FACTS PER SERVING: 385 cal., 10 g total fat (4 g sat. fat), 96 mg chol., 600 mg sodium, 52 g carbo., 3 g fiber, 22 g pro.

menu idea:

Baguette-style French bread served with olive oil and cracked black pepper

Coffee & Almond Parfaits (see p. 264)

tex-mex skillet

Chorizo sausage, made with garlic, chili powder, and other spices, is the star here surrounded by the vibrant colors of tomatoes, green chile peppers, corn, and cheddar cheese.

START TO FINISH: 30 minutes **MAKES:** 4 servings

8	ounces ground pork
4	ounces uncooked chorizo sausage
1	10-ounce can diced tomatoes and green chile peppers, undrained
1	cup loose-pack frozen whole kernel corn
¾	cup water
1	small red sweet pepper, chopped
1	cup instant rice
½	cup shredded cheddar cheese or Monterey Jack cheese (2 ounces)
	Flour tortillas, warmed* (optional)
	Dairy sour cream (optional)

one In a large skillet cook pork and sausage until brown. Drain off fat. Stir undrained tomatoes, corn, the water, and sweet pepper into pork mixture in skillet. Bring to boiling.

two Stir uncooked rice into meat mixture in skillet. Remove from heat. Top with cheese. Cover and let stand about 5 minutes or until rice is tender. If desired, serve in flour tortillas and top with sour cream.

NUTRITION FACTS PER SERVING: 395 cal., 20 g total fat (9 g sat. fat), 66 mg chol., 748 mg sodium, 33 g carbo., 1 g fiber, 21 g pro.

***NOTE:** To warm tortillas, wrap them in white microwave-safe paper towels; microwave on 100% power (high) for 15 to 30 seconds or until tortillas are softened. (Or wrap tortillas in foil. Heat in a 350°F oven for 10 to 15 minutes or until warmed.)

menu idea:

Nacho Corn Soup (see p. 237)

Mixed fresh berries

beer, cheese & bacon soup

While the soup simmers, pop some popcorn to garnish the soup.

START TO FINISH: 15 minutes **MAKES:** 8 servings

1	medium onion, finely chopped
½	cup butter or margarine
⅔	cup all-purpose flour
1	teaspoon dry mustard
1	teaspoon paprika
⅛	teaspoon cayenne pepper
4	cups milk
1	12-ounce can beer
1	10½-ounce can condensed chicken broth
3	cups shredded sharp cheddar cheese (12 ounces)
10	slices bacon, crisp-cooked, drained, and crumbled
	Popcorn (optional)

one In a large saucepan cook onion in hot butter until tender. Stir in flour, dry mustard, paprika, and cayenne pepper. Gradually stir in milk, beer, and broth. Cook, stirring constantly, over medium heat until mixture comes to a boil. Cook and stir for 1 minute more. Reduce heat. Add cheese, stirring until smooth. Stir in bacon. If desired, top servings with popcorn.

NUTRITION FACTS PER SERVING: 463 cal., 34 g total fat (18 g sat. fat), 95 mg chol., 811 mg sodium, 16 g carbo., 1 g fiber, 20 g pro.

menu idea:

Purchased refrigerated or frozen biscuits, baked and served with a mixture of softened butter, black pepper, and snipped fresh chives

A Billow of Berries 'n' Brownies (see p. 261)

veal marsala

Though veal is the traditional meat of choice here, chicken makes an inexpensive substitute.

START TO FINISH: 30 minutes **MAKES:** 4 servings

4	teaspoons olive oil or cooking oil
3	cups sliced fresh mushrooms
4	veal cutlets (1 pound total)
¼	teaspoon salt
¼	teaspoon black pepper
¾	cup dry Marsala
4	green onions, sliced
1	tablespoon snipped fresh sage or ½ teaspoon dried sage, crushed
1	tablespoon cold water
1	teaspoon cornstarch
⅛	teaspoon salt

one In a 12-inch skillet heat 2 teaspoons of the oil over medium heat. Add mushrooms; cook and stir for 4 to 5 minutes or until tender. Remove from skillet. Set aside.

two Sprinkle meat with the ¼ teaspoon salt and the pepper. In the same skillet heat the remaining 2 teaspoons oil over medium-high heat. Add veal, half at a time; cook for 2 to 3 minutes or until done, turning once. Transfer to dinner plates. Keep warm.

three Add Marsala to drippings in skillet. Bring to boiling. Boil mixture gently for 1 minute, scraping up any browned bits. Return mushrooms to skillet; add green onions and sage. In a small bowl stir together the cold water, cornstarch, and the ⅛ teaspoon salt; add to skillet. Cook and stir until slightly thickened and bubbly; cook and stir for 1 minute more. To serve, spoon the mushroom mixture over meat. Serve immediately.

NUTRITION FACTS PER SERVING: 219 cal., 8 g total fat (1 g sat. fat), 88 mg chol., 288 mg sodium, 4 g carbo., 1 g fiber, 27 g pro.

menu idea:

Glazed Parsnips & Apples *(see p. 228)*

Purchased individual shortcakes topped with sliced bananas, strawberries, and vanilla ice cream, and drizzled with hot fudge sauce

tuscan lamb chop skillet

Americans always have had a love affair with Italian cooking. The fresh-and-simple appeal of Tuscan cooking and its quick yet stylish dishes, such as this one, fit right into today's fast-paced lifestyles.

START TO FINISH: 20 minutes **MAKES:** 4 servings

8	lamb rib chops, cut 1 inch thick (about 1½ pounds total)
2	teaspoons olive oil
1½	teaspoons bottled minced garlic (3 cloves)
1	19-ounce can cannellini (white kidney) beans, rinsed and drained
1	8-ounce can Italian-style stewed tomatoes, undrained
1	tablespoon balsamic vinegar
2	teaspoons snipped fresh rosemary

one Trim fat from chops. In a large skillet heat oil over medium heat. Add chops; cook for 9 to 11 minutes or until medium doneness (160°F), turning once. Transfer chops to a plate; keep warm.

two Stir garlic into drippings in skillet. Cook and stir for 1 minute. Stir in beans, undrained tomatoes, vinegar, and rosemary. Bring to boiling; reduce heat. Simmer, uncovered, for 3 minutes.

three Divide bean mixture among 4 dinner plates; arrange 2 chops on top of beans on each plate.

NUTRITION FACTS PER SERVING: 272 cal., 9 g total fat (3 g sat. fat), 67 mg chol., 466 mg sodium, 24 g carbo., 6 g fiber, 30 g pro.

menu idea:

Mushroom & Herb Rice *(see p. 236)*

Purchased baked mini phyllo tarts filled with canned fruit pie filling and topped with whipped cream

spicy chicken breasts with fruit

With its mild flavor, chicken is one of the most versatile meats available. There are so many delicious things you can do with it—pairing it with fruit, for example. This recipe brings together hot, sweet, spicy, and salty ingredients to create a dish that tastes as good as it looks.

START TO FINISH: 30 minutes **MAKES:** 4 servings

- 2 teaspoons Jamaican jerk seasoning
- 2 fresh serrano chile peppers,* seeded and finely chopped
- 4 skinless, boneless chicken breast halves (about 1¼ pounds total)

  Nonstick cooking spray
- ½ cup peach nectar
- 3 green onions, cut into 1-inch pieces
- 2 cups sliced, peeled peaches
- 1 cup sliced, pitted plums
- 1 tablespoon packed brown sugar
- ⅛ teaspoon salt
- ½ cup pitted dark sweet cherries

  Hot cooked rice (optional)

one For rub, in a small bowl combine Jamaican jerk seasoning and half of the serrano peppers. Sprinkle mixture evenly over all sides of chicken breasts; rub in with your fingers. Lightly coat an unheated large skillet with cooking spray. Preheat skillet over medium heat. Add chicken; cook for 8 to 10 minutes or until chicken is tender and no longer pink (170°F), turning once. Transfer to a serving platter; keep warm.

two Add 2 tablespoons of the peach nectar and the green onions to skillet. Cook and stir over medium heat for 4 to 5 minutes or just until green onions are tender.

three In a medium bowl combine remaining peach nectar, remaining chile pepper, half of the peaches, half of the plums, the brown sugar, and salt. Add to skillet. Cook and stir over medium heat about 2 minutes or until slightly thickened and bubbly. Remove from heat. Stir in cherries and remaining peaches and plums. Spoon over chicken. If desired, serve with hot cooked rice.

NUTRITION FACTS PER SERVING: 264 cal., 2 g total fat (1 g sat. fat), 82 mg chol., 304 mg sodium, 26 g carbo., 3 g fiber, 34 g pro.

*NOTE: Because chile peppers contain volatile oils that can burn your skin and eyes, avoid direct contact with them as much as possible. When working with chile peppers, wear plastic or rubber gloves. If your bare hands do touch the peppers, wash your hands and nails well with soap and warm water.

menu idea:

Sliced carrots, cooked and tossed with brown sugar and butter

Chocolate ice cream with Chocolate-Hazelnut Ice Cream Sauce *(see p. 284)*

chicken with buttermilk gravy

Don't let the name fool you. Buttermilk is actually quite low in fat and has a subtle tang and creamy texture. It gives body and richness to sauces and gravies without adding extra fat and calories.

PREP: 15 minutes **BROIL:** 12 minutes **MAKES:** 6 servings

⅓ cup fine dry seasoned bread crumbs

2 tablespoons grated Parmesan cheese

½ teaspoon paprika

6 skinless, boneless chicken breast halves (about 2 pounds total)

3 tablespoons butter or margarine, melted
   Salt (optional)
   Black pepper (optional)

1 1-ounce envelope chicken gravy mix

1 cup buttermilk

¼ teaspoon dried sage, crushed

one In a shallow dish combine bread crumbs, Parmesan cheese, and paprika; set aside. Brush chicken with some of the melted butter. If desired, sprinkle with salt and pepper. Dip chicken into crumb mixture, turning to coat evenly.

two Arrange chicken on the unheated rack of a broiler pan. Drizzle with any remaining melted butter. Broil 4 to 5 inches from the heat for 12 to 15 minutes or until chicken is tender and no longer pink (170°F), turning once.

three Meanwhile, for gravy, in a small saucepan prepare chicken gravy mix according to package directions, except use the 1 cup buttermilk in place of the water called for in the package directions. Stir sage into gravy. Serve with chicken.

NUTRITION FACTS PER SERVING: 288 cal., 9 g total fat (5 g sat. fat), 107 mg chol., 644 mg sodium, 10 g carbo., 0 g fiber, 38 g pro.

menu idea:

Purchased refrigerated large or Southern-style biscuits, baked

Strawberry Shortbread Sandwiches (see p. 269)

cucumber-yogurt chicken

Spice up chicken with cayenne pepper, then cool it down with a refreshing yogurt-cucumber sauce. If you're afraid the chicken is too zippy for your palate, start out with half of the cayenne pepper.

START TO FINISH: 25 minutes **MAKES:** 4 servings

1	8-ounce carton plain low-fat yogurt
1	cup chopped, peeled seedless cucumber
½	cup finely chopped radishes
2	tablespoons mayonnaise or salad dressing
¼	teaspoon finely shredded lemon peel
1	tablespoon lemon juice
½	teaspoon bottled minced garlic (1 clove)
¼	teaspoon bottled hot pepper sauce
4	skinless, boneless chicken breast halves (about 1¼ pounds total)
¼	teaspoon salt
¼	teaspoon cayenne pepper
2	teaspoons cooking oil

one For sauce, in a small bowl combine yogurt, cucumber, radishes, mayonnaise, lemon peel, lemon juice, garlic, and hot pepper sauce. Cover and chill until ready to serve.

two Sprinkle chicken with salt and cayenne pepper. In a large nonstick skillet heat oil over medium-high heat. Add chicken; cook for 8 to 10 minutes or until chicken is tender and no longer pink (170°F), turning once. Serve the chicken with the yogurt sauce.

NUTRITION FACTS PER SERVING: 276 cal., 11 g total fat (2 g sat. fat), 91 mg chol., 313 mg sodium, 6 g carbo., 0 g fiber, 36 g pro.

menu idea:

Curried Cherry Pilaf (see p. 234)

Purchased loaf pound cake iced with canned lemon frosting and garnished with lemon and/or orange wedges

pulled chicken-peanut salad

A mixture of orange-tangerine juice concentrate and sesame oil infuses the tender chicken breasts with citrus flavor as they steam.

START TO FINISH: 25 minutes **MAKES:** 4 servings

2	tablespoons frozen orange-tangerine or orange juice concentrate
1	tablespoon water
2	teaspoons toasted sesame oil
¼	teaspoon salt
⅛	teaspoon coarsely ground black pepper
12	ounces skinless, boneless chicken breasts
3	cups watercress sprigs or torn fresh spinach
¼	cup cocktail peanuts

one In a small bowl combine juice concentrate, the water, sesame oil, salt, and pepper. Reserve 1 tablespoon of the juice concentrate mixture. Cover remaining mixture; set aside.

two In a large skillet bring ½ inch water to boiling. (Water should come just below the bottom of a steamer basket.) Reduce heat to simmer. Arrange chicken in a single layer in steamer basket. Place basket in skillet. Brush chicken with the reserved 1 tablespoon juice concentrate mixture. Cover. Steam chicken for 10 to 12 minutes or until tender and no longer pink (170°F).

three Transfer chicken to cutting board. Cool slightly (about 5 minutes). Using a pair of forks, pull chicken into bite-size pieces about 1½ inches long.

four In a large salad bowl combine chicken, watercress, and peanuts. Stir remaining juice concentrate mixture. Pour over salad and toss to coat.

NUTRITION FACTS PER SERVING: 186 cal., 8 g total fat (1 g sat. fat), 49 mg chol., 241 mg sodium, 5 g carbo., 1 g fiber, 23 g pro.

---

menu idea:

Sticky Lemon Pinwheels (see p. 255)

Chocolate frozen yogurt topped with chocolate sprinkles and served with chocolate cream-filled wafer cookies

chicken with dried fruit & honey

A splash of color from the dried fruit and a dash of sweetness from the honey and pumpkin pie spice make this recipe a wonderful choice for a fall supper.

START TO FINISH: 25 minutes **MAKES:** 4 servings

8	skinless, boneless chicken thighs (about 1½ pounds total)
½	teaspoon pumpkin pie spice or ¼ teaspoon ground ginger
1	tablespoon butter or margarine
1	cup mixed dried fruit bits
⅓	cup water
¼	cup honey

one Sprinkle 1 side of each thigh with pumpkin pie spice. In a 12-inch skillet cook the thighs in hot butter about 4 minutes or until browned, turning once. Stir in dried fruit bits, the water, and honey. Bring to boiling; reduce heat. Cover and simmer for 10 to 15 minutes or until chicken is tender and no longer pink (180°F).

NUTRITION FACTS PER SERVING: 381 cal., 9 g total fat (4 g sat. fat), 149 mg chol., 171 mg sodium, 41 g carbo., 0 g fiber, 35 g pro.

menu idea:

Steamed broccoli topped with shredded American or cheddar cheese

Double Dippin' Fruit (see p. 280)

chicken fajitas

Cream of chicken soup adds a saucy consistency to this family-friendly dish.

START TO FINISH: 25 minutes **MAKES:** 4 servings

- 2 tablespoons cooking oil
- 1 medium onion, cut into thin wedges
- 1 teaspoon bottled minced garlic (2 cloves)
- 2 medium red and/or green sweet peppers, cut into thin bite-size strips
- 12 ounces skinless, boneless chicken breasts, cut into bite-size strips
- 1 10¾-ounce can condensed cream of chicken soup
- ⅓ cup bottled salsa
- 8 7- to 8-inch flour tortillas, warmed*
- 2 cups shredded lettuce

  Dairy sour cream, shredded cheddar cheese, and/or thinly sliced green onion (optional)

one In a large skillet heat 1 tablespoon of the oil over medium-high heat. Add onion and garlic; cook and stir for 2 minutes. Add sweet peppers; cook and stir for 1 to 2 minutes more or until vegetables are crisp-tender. Remove from skillet.

two Add remaining 1 tablespoon oil to skillet. Add chicken; cook and stir for 3 to 4 minutes or until chicken is no longer pink. Return vegetables to skillet. Add cream of chicken soup and salsa; cook and stir until heated through.

three To serve, divide chicken mixture evenly among warmed tortillas. Top with lettuce. If desired, top with sour cream, cheese, and/or green onion. Roll up tortillas.

NUTRITION FACTS PER SERVING: 491 cal., 13 g total fat (3 g sat. fat), 56 mg chol., 1,342 mg sodium, 62 g carbo., 5 g fiber, 27 g pro.

*NOTE: To warm tortillas, wrap them in white microwave-safe paper towels; microwave on 100% power (high) for 15 to 30 seconds or until tortillas are softened. (Or wrap tortillas in foil. Heat in a 350°F oven for 10 to 15 minutes or until warmed.)

menu idea:

Rice pilaf mix, prepared according to package directions

Tropical Fruit Cups (double the recipe) (see p. 278)

chili-flavored chicken soup

Bring out the flavor of the traditional chili seasonings in this hearty soup by serving it with vibrant Tex-Mex toppers, such as coarsely crushed tortilla chips, chopped avocado, diced tomato, shredded Monterey Jack cheese, and snipped fresh cilantro.

PREP: 10 minutes **COOK:** 10 minutes **MAKES:** 6 servings

1	15-ounce can whole kernel corn, drained
1	14-ounce can beef broth
1	14-ounce can chicken broth
1	14½-ounce can diced tomatoes, undrained
1	medium onion, chopped
¼	cup chopped green sweet pepper
1	teaspoon chili powder
½	teaspoon ground cumin
¼	teaspoon black pepper
1	pound skinless, boneless chicken breasts, cut into bite-size pieces

one In a Dutch oven combine corn, beef broth, chicken broth, undrained tomatoes, onion, sweet pepper, chili powder, cumin, and black pepper. Bring to boiling. Stir in chicken pieces. Return to boiling; reduce heat. Cover and simmer for 10 to 12 minutes or until chicken is no longer pink, stirring once or twice.

NUTRITION FACTS PER SERVING: 173 cal., 2 g total fat (1 g sat. fat), 44 mg chol., 762 mg sodium, 17 g carbo., 2 g fiber, 21 g pro.

menu idea:

Honey-Nut Corn Muffins (see p. 253)

Sliced watermelon and/or cantaloupe

chicken salad with strawberries

Chicken breast strips double-dipped in a lemon-and-herb flour, then flash-fried in a skillet have all the crunch of traditional fried chicken. This salad is especially delicious in the summer when strawberries are at their sweet and juicy peak.

START TO FINISH: 30 minutes **MAKES:** 6 servings

- ¾ cup all-purpose flour
- 4 tablespoons snipped fresh purple or green basil
- 1 tablespoon finely shredded lemon peel
- 2 eggs, beaten
- 1 pound skinless, boneless chicken breasts, cut into thin bite-size strips
- 2 tablespoons cooking oil
- 4 cups torn mixed spring salad greens
- 1 head radicchio, torn into bite-size pieces
- 2 cups sliced fresh strawberries
- ½ cup bottled balsamic vinaigrette salad dressing
- 6 butterhead (Bibb or Boston) lettuce leaves

one In a shallow dish combine flour, 2 tablespoons of the basil, and the lemon peel. Place eggs in another shallow dish. Dip chicken into flour mixture, then into eggs, and then again into flour mixture to coat.

two In a heavy 12-inch skillet heat cooking oil over medium-high heat. Add chicken; cook and stir for 6 to 8 minutes or until chicken is no longer pink. (If necessary, reduce heat to medium to prevent overbrowning and add more oil as needed during cooking.) Cool slightly.

three Meanwhile, in a large bowl toss together greens, radicchio, strawberries, and remaining 2 tablespoons basil. Drizzle vinaigrette over greens mixture; toss gently to coat. To serve, line salad bowls with lettuce leaves. Add greens mixture. Top with chicken.

NUTRITION FACTS PER SERVING: 261 cal., 13 g total fat (2 g sat. fat), 79 mg chol., 295 mg sodium, 16 g carbo., 2 g fiber, 21 g pro.

menu idea:

Sourdough rolls served with flavored cream cheese

Cookies & Cream *(see p. 270)*

asian chicken sandwich

Daikon is a large Asian radish with a pleasant, sweet, and zesty flavor and a mild bite. It is available year-round in many supermarkets and in Asian specialty stores.

START TO FINISH: 30 minutes **MAKES:** 8 servings

1	2- to 2¼-pound deli-roasted chicken
8	8- to 10-inch flour tortillas
½	cup bottled hoisin sauce
¼	cup finely chopped peanuts
¼	cup finely chopped green onions
½	cup shredded daikon, well drained
3	tablespoons soy sauce
3	tablespoons Chinese black vinegar or rice vinegar
1	tablespoon water
1	teaspoon chili oil or toasted sesame oil

one Remove skin from chicken and discard. Remove chicken from bones and shred chicken (you should have about 4 cups); set aside.

two Spread one side of each tortilla with some of the hoisin sauce; sprinkle with peanuts and green onions. Top with shredded chicken and shredded daikon. Roll up; halve crosswise.

three In a small bowl combine soy sauce, vinegar, the water, and chili oil or sesame oil. Serve as a dipping sauce with chicken roll-ups.

NUTRITION FACTS PER SERVING: 283 cal., 9 g total fat (2 g sat. fat), 50 mg chol., 869 mg sodium, 26 g carbo., 1 g fiber, 20 g pro.

menu idea:

Asian Pea Pod Salad (double the recipe) *(see p. 242)*

Vanilla ice cream, sliced strawberries, and a dash of cinnamon placed in a blender container and blended until nearly smooth

dried tomato & basil chicken wraps

Make dinner fun with different colored tortillas. The kids will love filling up their red, green, or white shells with the tomatoes, chicken, cheese, nuts, and basil leaves.

START TO FINISH: 20 minutes **MAKES:** 6 servings

- ½ of a 3-ounce package (about ¾ cup) dried tomatoes (not oil-packed)
- 3 cups shredded roasted or grilled chicken (about 1 pound)
- 1 cup shredded mozzarella or Monterey Jack cheese (4 ounces)
- ½ cup chopped pecans, toasted
- ⅓ cup bottled creamy Italian or ranch salad dressing
- 6 10-inch dried tomato, spinach, and/or plain flour tortillas, warmed*
- 1 cup large fresh basil leaves

one Soak dried tomatoes in enough hot water to cover for 10 minutes. Drain and chop tomatoes.

two In a large bowl combine chopped dried tomatoes, chicken, cheese, pecans, and salad dressing.

three Line each tortilla with some of the basil leaves. Divide chicken mixture among the tortillas. Fold in sides and roll up; cut each diagonally in half to serve.

NUTRITION FACTS PER SERVING: 449 cal., 24 g total fat (6 g sat. fat), 73 mg chol., 701 mg sodium, 29 g carbo., 3 g fiber, 30 g pro.

*NOTE: To warm tortillas, wrap them in white microwave-safe paper towels; microwave on 100% power (high) for 15 to 30 seconds or until tortillas are softened. (Or wrap tortillas in foil. Heat in a 350°F oven for 10 to 15 minutes or until warmed.)

menu idea:

Salt-and-vinegar potato chips or kettle-cooked potato chips

Fast & Fruity Banana Split Tarts *(see p. 273)*

prize winning sunday salad

This scrumptious fruit-and-chicken salad makes a guaranteed-to-be-gone addition to any buffet table.

START TO FINISH: 20 minutes **MAKES:** 6 to 8 servings

1	20-ounce can pineapple chunks, drained
2	cups cubed cooked chicken breast (about 10 ounces)
2	cups cubed cooked ham (about 10 ounces)
4	stalks celery, diced
1	medium green sweet pepper, chopped
¾	cup slivered almonds
½	cup mayonnaise or salad dressing
2	to 3 tablespoons lemon juice
½	teaspoon ground ginger
½	teaspoon ground nutmeg
	Dash salt
	Lettuce leaves

one In a large bowl combine pineapple chunks, chicken, ham, celery, sweet pepper, and almonds.

two For dressing, in a small bowl combine mayonnaise, lemon juice, ginger, nutmeg, and salt. Pour dressing over salad; toss lightly to coat. Serve on lettuce-lined plates.

NUTRITION FACTS PER SERVING: 461 cal., 29 g total fat (5 g sat. fat), 78 mg chol., 901 mg sodium, 22 g carbo., 4 g fiber, 30 g pro.

menu idea:

Sliced fresh watermelon and honeydew melon

Ultimate Chocolate Sundaes (see p. 286)

italian turkey sandwiches

An aromatic basil-flavored spread takes these sandwiches out of an ordinary realm and puts them into an extraordinary one. Fresh basil is the key here; dried simply doesn't work.

START TO FINISH: 20 minutes **MAKES:** 4 sandwiches

- ⅓ cup fine dry bread crumbs
- 2 teaspoons dried Italian seasoning, crushed
- 2 turkey breast tenderloins, halved horizontally (about 1 pound total)
- 2 teaspoons olive oil
- 2 tablespoons snipped fresh basil
- ¼ cup mayonnaise or salad dressing
- 8 ½-inch slices Italian bread, toasted
- 1 cup bottled roasted red and/or yellow sweet peppers, cut into thin strips

one In a large resealable plastic bag combine bread crumbs and Italian seasoning. Place a turkey tenderloin piece in the bag; seal and shake to coat. Repeat with remaining turkey tenderloin pieces.

two In a 12-inch nonstick skillet heat oil over medium heat. Add turkey; cook about 10 minutes or until tender and no longer pink (170°F), turning once.

three In a small bowl stir 1 tablespoon of the basil into mayonnaise. Spread mayonnaise mixture on one side of each of 4 of the bread slices; top with turkey pieces, sweet pepper strips, and the remaining 1 tablespoon basil. Top with remaining bread slices.

NUTRITION FACTS PER SANDWICH: 457 cal., 18 g total fat (3 g sat. fat), 78 mg chol., 728 mg sodium, 39 g carbo., 3 g fiber, 33 g pro.

test kitchen tip: For a lower-fat sandwich, substitute light mayonnaise dressing for the mayonnaise.

NUTRITION FACTS PER SANDWICH: 399 cal., 11 g total fat (2 g sat. fat), 73 mg chol., 671 mg sodium, 40 g carbo., 3 g fiber, 33 g pro.

menu idea:

Purchased frozen seasoned potato wedges, cooked according to package directions and served with warm spaghetti or pizza sauce

Mocha Cookies (see p. 267)

five-spice turkey stir-fry

Five-spice powder lends a wonderfully exotic and aromatic element to this stir-fry. Used extensively in Chinese cooking, the powder is a pungent mixture of five ground spices—cinnamon, cloves, fennel seeds, star anise, and Szechwan peppercorns. You can find it in Asian markets and most supermarkets.

START TO FINISH: 25 minutes **MAKES:** 4 servings

1	4.4-ounce package beef lo-mein noodle mix
12	ounces turkey breast tenderloin, cut into thin bite-size strips
¼	teaspoon five-spice powder
¼	teaspoon salt
¼	teaspoon black pepper
2	tablespoons cooking oil
½	of a 16-ounce package frozen pepper stir-fry vegetables (yellow, green, and red peppers and onion)
2	tablespoons chopped honey-roasted peanuts or plain peanuts

one Prepare noodle mix according to package directions. Set aside. In a small bowl toss together turkey strips, five-spice powder, salt, and pepper; set aside.

two Pour 1 tablespoon of the oil into a wok or large skillet. Heat over medium-high heat. Carefully add frozen vegetables to wok; cook and stir for 3 minutes. Remove vegetables from wok. Add remaining 1 tablespoon oil to hot wok. Add turkey mixture to wok or skillet; cook and stir for 2 to 3 minutes or until turkey is done. Return cooked vegetables to wok. Cook and stir about 1 minute more or until heated through.

three To serve, divide noodle mixture among 4 dinner plates. Top with turkey mixture; sprinkle with peanuts.

NUTRITION FACTS PER SERVING: 314 cal., 11 g total fat (2 g sat. fat), 76 mg chol., 670 mg sodium, 26 g carbo., 3 g fiber, 27 g pro.

menu idea:

Mixed Greens Salad with Ginger Vinaigrette
(see p. 244)

Strawberry frozen yogurt topped with sliced strawberries

turkey & spinach salad

How do you turn baby spinach into a meal? Add cubed turkey, grapefruit and orange sections, and sliced almonds. Toss them all together with a homemade poppy seed dressing and enjoy.

START TO FINISH: 25 minutes **MAKES:** 4 servings

8	cups fresh baby spinach or torn fresh spinach
8	ounces cooked turkey, cubed
2	grapefruits, peeled and sectioned
2	oranges, peeled and sectioned
¼	cup orange juice
2	tablespoons olive oil
1	teaspoon honey
½	teaspoon poppy seeds
¼	teaspoon salt
¼	teaspoon dry mustard
2	tablespoons sliced almonds, toasted (optional)

one Place spinach in a large bowl. Add turkey, grapefruit sections, and orange sections.

two For dressing, in a screw-top jar combine orange juice, oil, honey, poppy seeds, salt, and dry mustard. Cover and shake well. Pour the dressing over salad; toss gently. If desired, sprinkle with almonds.

NUTRITION FACTS PER SERVING: 228 cal., 10 g total fat (2 g sat. fat), 43 mg chol., 261 mg sodium, 16 g carbo., 8 g fiber, 20 g pro.

menu idea:

Blueberry Gems *(see p. 252)*

Purchased apple crisp served with caramel ice cream

smoked turkey & blue cheese pasta salad

Sharp blue cheese and sweet mandarin orange sections give this pasta salad some punch.

START TO FINISH: 25 minutes **MAKES:** 4 servings

- 1   cup medium dried bow ties or medium shell macaroni (about 2½ ounces)
- ½   cup crumbled blue cheese (2 ounces)
- ⅓   cup bottled balsamic vinaigrette or oil and vinegar salad dressing
- 6   ounces smoked turkey, cut into bite-size pieces
- 3   cups torn mixed salad greens
- ¼   cup walnut or pecan pieces
- 1   11-ounce can mandarin orange sections, drained

one Cook pasta in lightly salted water according to package directions. Drain in colander. Rinse with cold water; drain again.

two Meanwhile, in a large bowl combine blue cheese and vinaigrette. Add smoked turkey, salad greens, and nuts. Add pasta; toss gently to coat. Top individual servings with mandarin orange sections.

NUTRITION FACTS PER SERVING: 284 cal., 16 g total fat (4 g sat. fat), 29 mg chol., 887 mg sodium, 25 g carbo., 2 g fiber, 14 g pro.

menu idea:

Purchased refrigerated soft breadsticks, baked

Purchased pound cake with Apricot-Orange Sauce
(see p. 283)

beer-chili bean soup

Looking for something to serve after the game or for Sunday football in front of the television? This turkey chili soup will have your sports fans coming back for seconds.

START TO FINISH: 20 minutes **MAKES:** 4 servings

1	15-ounce can hot-style chili beans with chili gravy
1	12-ounce can (1½ cups) beer
1	11¼-ounce can condensed chili beef soup
1½	cups chopped cooked turkey (about 8 ounces)
1	cup hot water
1	teaspoon dried minced onion
1	teaspoon Worcestershire sauce
½	teaspoon garlic powder
	Shredded cheddar cheese
	Dairy sour cream (optional)

one In a large saucepan combine undrained chili beans, beer, chili beef soup, turkey, the hot water, dried minced onion, Worcestershire sauce, and garlic powder.

two Bring to boiling; reduce heat. Simmer, uncovered, for 5 minutes. Serve with cheese and, if desired, sour cream.

NUTRITION FACTS PER SERVING: 353 cal., 10 g total fat (5 g sat. fat), 57 mg chol., 1,154 mg sodium, 35 g carbo., 12 g fiber, 27 g pro.

---

menu idea:

Packaged corn muffin mix, baked and served with honey

Cherry Trifles (see p. 265)

mock monte cristo sandwiches

There is nothing like the savory flavors of turkey, ham, Swiss cheese, and sweet-tangy honey mustard nestled between French toast slices.

PREP: 10 minutes **BAKE:** 15 minutes **MAKES:** 6 half sandwiches

6   slices frozen French toast

2   tablespoons honey mustard

3   ounces sliced cooked turkey breast

3   ounces sliced cooked ham

3   ounces thinly sliced Swiss cheese

one Lightly grease a baking sheet; set aside. To assemble sandwiches, spread 1 side of each of the frozen French toast slices with honey mustard. Layer 3 of the toast slices, mustard sides up, with the turkey, ham, and cheese. Cover with remaining toast slices, mustard sides down.

two Place sandwiches on prepared baking sheet. Bake in a 400°F oven for 15 to 20 minutes or until sandwiches are heated through, turning sandwiches once. Cut each sandwich in half diagonally.

NUTRITION FACTS PER HALF SANDWICH: 221 cal., 9 g total fat (4 g sat. fat), 75 mg chol., 704 mg sodium, 21 g carbo., 1 g fiber, 14 g pro.

menu idea:

Mashed Potato Soup (double the recipe) *(see p. 241)*

Purchased angel food cake served with assorted mixed berries

california club sandwich

Take advantage of the latest convenience products to cut the prep time for this colorful and flavor-packed sandwich. Buy presliced mushrooms, prewashed spinach leaves, and precooked bacon, if they are available.

START TO FINISH: 25 minutes **MAKES:** 4 servings

- 1 8-ounce tub cream cheese
- 2 tablespoons honey mustard
- 1 6½-ounce jar marinated artichoke hearts, drained and chopped
- ¼ cup chopped pitted ripe olives, pitted green olives, or Greek black olives
- 1 16-ounce loaf crusty French bread
- 2 cups loosely packed fresh spinach leaves, stems removed
- 2 cups sliced fresh mushrooms
- 1 small red onion, thinly sliced
- 8 ounces thinly sliced cooked turkey breast
- 4 slices bacon, crisp-cooked, drained, and crumbled
- ¼ cup roasted and salted sunflower seeds

one In a small bowl stir together cream cheese and honey mustard. Gently stir in artichokes and olives; set aside.

two Cut bread loaf in half lengthwise. Hollow out bottom half of bread loaf, leaving a ½-inch-thick shell (reserve bread crumbs for another use). Spread bread shell with ⅔ cup of the cream cheese mixture. Layer spinach leaves, sliced mushrooms, red onion, and turkey into bottom half of loaf. Sprinkle with bacon and sunflower seeds.

three Spread another ⅔ cup cream cheese mixture onto cut side of top half of bread loaf. Reserve any remaining cream cheese mixture for another use. Place top half of bread, cream cheese mixture side down, on top of sandwich. Cut into 4 serving-portions.

NUTRITION FACTS PER SERVING: 665 cal., 34 g total fat (16 g sat. fat), 85 mg chol., 1,941 mg sodium, 62 g carbo., 5 g fiber, 31 g pro.

menu idea:

Purchased pasta salad

Citrus Freeze (see p. 287)

broiled halibut with dijon cream

Mild tasting with a firm texture, halibut is an excellent choice for the zesty mustard sauce.

PREP: 10 minutes **BROIL:** 8 minutes **MAKES:** 4 servings

4	fresh or frozen halibut steaks, cut 1 inch thick (1 to 1½ pounds)
1	teaspoon Greek-style or Mediterranean seasoning blend
¼	teaspoon coarsely ground black pepper
¼	cup dairy sour cream
¼	cup creamy Dijon-style mustard blend
1	tablespoon milk
½	teaspoon dried oregano, crushed

one Thaw fish, if frozen. Rinse fish; pat dry with paper towels. Grease the rack of an unheated broiler pan; place fish on rack. Sprinkle fish with Greek-style seasoning blend and pepper.

two Broil 4 inches from the heat for 8 to 12 minutes or until fish flakes easily when tested with a fork, turning once. Invert fish onto serving platter.

three Meanwhile, for sauce, in a small bowl stir together sour cream, mustard blend, milk, and oregano. Serve sauce over fish.

NUTRITION FACTS PER SERVING: 168 cal., 5 g total fat (2 g sat. fat), 42 mg chol., 300 mg sodium, 4 g carbo., 0 g fiber, 24 g pro.

---

menu idea:

Mushroom & Herb Rice *(see p. 236)*

Vanilla ice cream drizzled with pourable cherry all-fruit topping and sprinkled with dried cherries or cranberries

lime-poached mahi mahi

Simply prepared with fruity olive oil and tangy margarita mix concentrate, this dish can be on the table in 20 minutes.

START TO FINISH: 20 minutes **MAKES:** 4 servings

- 4 6-ounce fresh or frozen mahi mahi or catfish fillets, ½ to ¾ inch thick
- 2 teaspoons seasoned pepper
- 1 tablespoon olive oil
- ⅓ cup frozen margarita mix concentrate, thawed
   Hot cooked rice

one Thaw fish, if frozen. Skin fish, if necessary. Rinse fish; pat dry with paper towels.

two Rub both sides of each fish fillet with seasoned pepper. In a large nonstick skillet heat oil over medium-high heat. Add fish; cook for 2 to 4 minutes or until lightly browned on both sides, turning once. Reduce heat to medium-low. Carefully add margarita mix concentrate to skillet.

three Cover and cook for 6 to 8 minutes or until fish flakes easily when tested with a fork. Serve with rice.

NUTRITION FACTS PER SERVING: 336 cal., 5 g total fat (1 g sat. fat), 124 mg chol., 150 mg sodium, 41 g carbo., 0 g fiber, 34 g pro.

menu idea:

Steamed sugar snap peas tossed with butter and shredded orange peel

Tropical Fruit Shortcakes (see p. 260)

fish with black bean sauce

Bottled teriyaki and hoisin sauces give this
Asian-inspired dish outstanding flavor.

START TO FINISH: 30 minutes **MAKES:** 6 servings

1½	pounds fresh or frozen skinless sea bass or orange roughy fillets
1	15-ounce can black beans, rinsed and drained
3	tablespoons bottled teriyaki sauce
2	tablespoons bottled hoisin sauce
	Nonstick cooking spray
	Hot cooked rice

one Thaw fish, if frozen. Rinse fish; pat dry with paper towels. Cut into 6 serving-size pieces; set aside. In a food processor/blender combine drained beans, teriyaki sauce, and hoisin sauce. Cover and blend until nearly smooth.

two Lightly coat an unheated 12-inch skillet with cooking spray. Preheat skillet over medium-high heat. Carefully place fish portions in skillet and cook about 4 minutes or until browned on both sides, turning once. Add bean mixture to fish. Bring to boiling; reduce heat to medium. Cover and simmer about 8 minutes or until fish flakes easily when tested with a fork. Serve with rice.

NUTRITION FACTS PER SERVING: 276 cal., 3 g total fat (1 g sat. fat), 46 mg chol., 617 mg sodium, 35 g carbo., 4 g fiber, 28 g pro.

menu idea:

Cooked sliced carrots tossed with snipped fresh chives

Purchased pound cake with Golden Citrus Sauce
(see p. 282)

tilapia with chili cream sauce

Originally from the waters surrounding Africa, tilapia is raised commercially everywhere from North America to Asia. In this recipe, the sweet, mild fish—sometimes called Hawaiian sun fish—fries up crisp and tender, and soaks up all the glorious flavor of the sassy sauce.

START TO FINISH: 25 minutes **MAKES:** 4 servings

1	pound fresh or frozen tilapia or other firm-flesh fish fillets, ½ to 1 inch thick
2	tablespoons cornmeal
2	tablespoons all-purpose flour
	Nonstick cooking spray
1	teaspoon cooking oil
2	teaspoons butter or margarine
2	teaspoons all-purpose flour
1	teaspoon chili powder
¼	teaspoon salt
¼	teaspoon ground cumin
¾	cup half-and-half or light cream
2	tablespoons snipped fresh parsley or cilantro (optional)

one Thaw fish, if frozen. Rinse fish; pat dry with paper towels. Cut into 4 serving-size pieces. In a small bowl stir together cornmeal and the 2 tablespoons flour. Sprinkle over both sides of each fish piece. Lightly coat an unheated 12-inch nonstick skillet with cooking spray. Add the oil to skillet. Preheat over medium-high heat. Add fish pieces. Cook over medium to medium-high heat for 4 to 6 minutes or until fish flakes easily when tested with a fork, turning once. Remove fish from skillet. Cover and keep warm.

two For sauce, melt butter in the same skillet. Stir in the 2 teaspoons flour, the chili powder, salt, and cumin. Stir in half-and-half. Cook and stir until thickened and bubbly. Cook and stir for 1 minute more. To serve, spoon sauce over fish. If desired, sprinkle with parsley.

NUTRITION FACTS PER SERVING: 229 cal., 11 g total fat (4 g sat. fat), 22 mg chol., 240 mg sodium, 11 g carbo., 1 g fiber, 21 g pro.

test kitchen tip: For a lower-fat dish, substitute fat-free half-and-half for the regular half-and-half.

NUTRITION FACTS PER SERVING: 187 cal., 4 g total fat (2 g sat. fat), 60 mg chol., 258 mg sodium, 12 g carbo., 1 g fiber, 23 g pro.

menu idea:

Frozen or canned Spanish-style rice, prepared according to package or can directions

Tropical Fruit Cups (double the recipe) *(see p. 278)*

browned butter salmon

Browning the butter lends a subtle nutty flavor that complements the maple syrup and orange peel, giving the salmon a sweet richness.

PREP: 20 minutes **BROIL:** 5 minutes + 3 minutes **MAKES:** 4 servings

- 4 fresh or frozen salmon or halibut steaks, cut 1 inch thick (about 1½ pounds total)
  Salt
  Black pepper
- 2 tablespoons butter or margarine
- 2 tablespoons pure maple syrup
- 1 teaspoon finely shredded orange peel

one Thaw fish, if frozen. Rinse fish and pat dry with paper towels. Sprinkle both sides of each fish steak with salt and pepper; set aside. In a small saucepan cook the butter over medium heat about 3 minutes or until golden brown, stirring occasionally. Remove from heat. Cool for 10 minutes. Stir in maple syrup and orange peel (mixture may thicken).

two Meanwhile, line unheated broiler pan with foil; grease rack. Place fish on prepared rack of broiler pan. Spread both sides of each fish steak with the browned butter mixture. Broil 4 inches from the heat for 5 minutes. Using a wide spatula, carefully turn fish over. Broil for 3 to 7 minutes more or until fish flakes easily when tested with a fork.

NUTRITION FACTS PER SERVING: 277 cal., 12 g total fat (5 g sat. fat), 105 mg chol., 322 mg sodium, 7 g carbo., 0 g fiber, 34 g pro.

---

menu idea:

Glazed Parsnips & Apples (see p. 228)

New York-style cheesecake served with mixed fresh berries

salmon-broccoli chowder

Salmon and broccoli make a great pair because they taste wonderful together and are chockful of nutrients.

START TO FINISH: 20 minutes **MAKES:** 4 servings

2½	cups milk
1	10¾-ounce can condensed broccoli-cheese soup or cream of chicken soup
¾	cup shredded sharp cheddar cheese or process American cheese (3 ounces)
1	cup loose-pack frozen cut broccoli
½	cup loose-pack frozen whole kernel corn
1	15-ounce can salmon, drained, flaked, and skin and bones removed

one In a medium saucepan stir together milk and broccoli-cheese soup. Stir in cheese. Stir in broccoli and corn. Cook and stir just until mixture boils. Stir in salmon. Heat through.

NUTRITION FACTS PER SERVING: 401 cal., 22 g total fat (10 g sat. fat), 65 mg chol., 1,257 mg sodium, 19 g carbo., 2 g fiber, 31 g pro.

menu idea:

Citrus Salad with Glazed Pecans *(see p. 247)*

Purchased shortbread or butter cookies

tuna & pasta alfredo

This easy tuna recipe gives you maximum flavor with minimum cleanup.

START TO FINISH: 25 minutes **MAKES:** 6 servings

3	cups dried mini lasagna, broken mafalda, or medium noodles
1	tablespoon butter or margarine
2	cups chopped broccoli rabe or broccoli
1	medium red sweet pepper, chopped
1	10-ounce container refrigerated Alfredo pasta sauce
2	teaspoons snipped fresh dillweed
1	to 2 tablespoons milk (optional)
1	9½-ounce can tuna (water-pack), drained and broken into chunks
½	cup sliced almonds, toasted (optional)

one Cook pasta according to package directions; drain well. Return pasta to hot pan. Cover and keep warm.

two Meanwhile, in a large saucepan melt butter over medium heat. Add broccoli rabe or broccoli and sweet pepper; cook until tender. Stir in Alfredo sauce and dillweed. If necessary, stir in enough of the milk to make sauce of desired consistency. Gently stir cooked pasta and tuna into broccoli rabe mixture. Heat through.

three To serve, if desired, sprinkle with almonds.

NUTRITION FACTS PER SERVING: 387 cal., 12 g total fat (5 g sat. fat), 63 mg chol., 568 mg sodium, 48 g carbo., 3 g fiber, 20 g pro.

menu idea:

Frozen or refrigerated large biscuits, prepared according to package directions and sprinkled with shredded Asiago or Parmesan cheese

Lemon Meringue Cookie Tarts *(see p. 272)*

creamy tuna mac

Everyone loves a good mac and cheese! In this version canned tuna is added to a quick mac and cheese dinner mix. It's so easy to prepare and so satisfying.

START TO FINISH: 25 minutes **MAKES:** 4 to 6 servings

- 1 7¼-ounce package macaroni and cheese dinner mix
- 1 cup loose-pack frozen peas
- ½ cup ranch-, onion-, or chive-flavor sour cream dip
- 1 6-ounce can solid white tuna, drained and broken into chunks

   Crushed potato chips (optional)

one Cook macaroni from dinner mix according to package directions, except add peas for the last 2 minutes of cooking. Drain. Continue according to dinner mix package directions.

two Stir dip into macaroni mixture; stir tuna into mixture. Heat through. If desired, sprinkle with crushed potato chips.

NUTRITION FACTS PER SERVING: 368 cal., 9 g total fat (4 g sat. fat), 47 mg chol., 888 mg sodium, 50 g carbo., 2 g fiber, 23 g pro.

menu idea:

Curried Carrots *(see p. 226)*

Ice cream served in sugar ice cream cones and sprinkled with chopped nuts, miniature chocolate pieces, or colored sprinkles

tuna tortellini soup

Refrigerated or frozen tortellini ranks with canned soup as a great convenience product.

START TO FINISH: 20 minutes **MAKES:** 6 servings

3	cups milk
2	10¾-ounce cans condensed cream of potato soup
1	cup loose-pack frozen peas
1	teaspoon dried basil, crushed
1	9-ounce package refrigerated cheese tortellini
1	12-ounce can tuna (water pack), drained and flaked
⅓	cup dry white wine

one In a large saucepan combine milk, cream of potato soup, peas, and basil; bring just to boiling. Add tortellini. Simmer, uncovered, for 6 to 8 minutes or until tortellini is tender, stirring frequently to prevent sticking. Stir in tuna and wine; heat through.

NUTRITION FACTS PER SERVING: 351 cal., 9 g total fat (4 g sat. fat), 59 mg chol., 1,267 mg sodium, 38 g carbo., 2 g fiber, 27 g pro.

menu idea:

BLT Salad *(see p. 243)*

Purchased individual graham cracker tart crusts filled with canned lemon pie filling and topped with vanilla yogurt or whipped cream

spicy jalapeño-shrimp pasta

Fresh jalapeño peppers spice up this dish that pairs plump, juicy shrimp, garlic, and tomatoes, all tossed with perfectly cooked linguine. Tailor the amount of jalapeño to suit your family's taste.

START TO FINISH: 30 minutes **MAKES:** 4 servings

12	ounces fresh or frozen large shrimp in shells
8	ounces dried linguine
2	tablespoons olive oil
1	or 2 fresh jalapeño chile peppers, finely chopped*
1	teaspoon bottled minced garlic (2 cloves)
½	teaspoon salt
⅛	teaspoon black pepper
2	cups chopped tomatoes and/or cherry tomatoes, halved or quartered
	Finely shredded Parmesan cheese (optional)

one Thaw shrimp, if frozen. Peel and devein shrimp. Rinse shrimp; pat dry with paper towels. Cook linguine according to package directions; drain well. Return to pan. Cover and keep warm.

two In a large skillet heat oil over medium-high heat. Add chile peppers, garlic, salt, and black pepper; cook and stir for 1 minute. Add shrimp; cook about 3 minutes more or until shrimp are opaque. Stir in tomatoes; heat through.

three Toss cooked linguine with shrimp mixture. If desired, sprinkle with Parmesan cheese.

NUTRITION FACTS PER SERVING: 363 cal., 9 g total fat (1 g sat. fat), 97 mg chol., 396 mg sodium, 48 g carbo., 3 g fiber, 21 g pro.

*NOTE: Because chile peppers contain volatile oils that can burn your skin and eyes, avoid direct contact with them as much as possible. When working with chile peppers, wear plastic or rubber gloves. If your bare hands do touch the peppers, wash your hands and nails well with soap and warm water.

menu idea:

Broiled Summer Squash & Onions *(see p. 229)*

Canned apple pie filling, warmed, sprinkled with granola, and topped with butter pecan ice cream

chipotle-topped crab cakes

The distinctive smoky flavor of the chipotle chile pepper gives the sauce for these subtly seasoned crab cakes zing. If you haven't used chipotle peppers in adobo sauce before, start with half of a pepper, taste, and then add the other half if you wish.

START TO FINISH: 30 minutes **MAKES:** 4 servings

1	egg, slightly beaten
¾	cup soft bread crumbs (1 slice)
1	green onion, sliced
2	tablespoons mayonnaise or salad dressing
1	tablespoon milk
½	teaspoon lemon-pepper seasoning
2	6- to 7-ounce cans crabmeat, drained, flaked, and cartilage removed
	Nonstick cooking spray
4	cups torn mixed salad greens
1	recipe Chipotle Sauce
	Lime wedges

one In a large bowl stir together egg, bread crumbs, green onion, mayonnaise, milk, and lemon-pepper seasoning. Add crabmeat; mix well. Shape into 8 patties.

two Lightly coat an unheated large nonstick skillet with cooking spray. Preheat over medium heat. Add patties. Cook for 6 to 8 minutes or until browned on both sides, turning once. Serve over greens with Chipotle Sauce. Pass lime wedges.

NUTRITION FACTS PER SERVING: 348 cal., 25 g total fat (5 g sat. fat), 153 mg chol., 719 mg sodium, 7 g carbo., 1 g fiber, 21 g pro.

*NOTE: Because chile peppers contain volatile oils that can burn your skin and eyes, avoid direct contact with them as much as possible. When working with chile peppers, wear plastic or rubber gloves. If your bare hands do touch the peppers, wash your hands and nails well with soap and warm water.

chipotle sauce: In a small bowl stir together ⅓ cup mayonnaise or salad dressing; ¼ cup dairy sour cream; 2 tablespoons milk; 2 teaspoons snipped fresh cilantro; 1 canned chipotle chile pepper in adobo sauce, drained and finely chopped;* and dash salt.

test kitchen tip: For lower-fat crab cakes and sauce, substitute light mayonnaise dressing for the mayonnaise or salad dressing and light dairy sour cream for the regular sour cream.

NUTRITION FACTS PER SERVING: 255 cal., 13 g total fat (3 g sat. fat), 144 mg chol., 739 mg sodium, 12 g carbo., 1 g fiber, 22 g pro.

menu idea:

Skewered bite-size pieces of fresh fruit, such as pineapple, grapes, strawberries, banana, melon, and/or kiwifruit

Triple Dipster Strawberries *(see p. 277)*

crab bisque

Canned soups make this crab bisque extra fast and easy, but just as rich as made-from-scratch versions.

START TO FINISH: 20 minutes **MAKES:** 6 servings

1	10¾-ounce can condensed cream of asparagus soup
1	10¾-ounce can condensed cream of mushroom soup
2¾	cups milk
1	cup half-and-half or light cream
1	6- to 7-ounce can crabmeat, drained, flaked, and cartilage removed
3	tablespoons dry sherry or milk

one In a large saucepan combine cream of asparagus soup, cream of mushroom soup, milk, and half-and-half. Cook over medium heat just until boiling, stirring frequently. Stir in crabmeat and dry sherry; heat through.

NUTRITION FACTS PER SERVING: 227 cal., 12 g total fat (6 g sat. fat), 63 mg chol., 921 mg sodium, 16 g carbo., 1 g fiber, 12 g pro.

menu idea:

Purchased sourdough rolls

A Billow of Berries 'n' Brownies *(see p. 261)*

seared scallops with tropical salsa

The sweetness of the papaya complements the delicate flavor of the scallops, and the freshly made salsa makes them extra colorful.

START TO FINISH: 25 minutes **MAKES:** 4 servings

12	ounces fresh or frozen scallops
1	cup finely chopped strawberry papaya or papaya
½	cup seeded and finely chopped cucumber
1	small tomato, seeded and chopped
2	tablespoons snipped fresh cilantro
1	fresh jalapeño chile pepper, seeded and finely chopped*
4	teaspoons lime juice
1	teaspoon olive oil
	Salt
	Black pepper
1	teaspoon butter or margarine
½	teaspoon bottled minced garlic (1 clove)

one Thaw scallops, if frozen. Rinse scallops; pat dry with paper towels. Set aside. For salsa, in a small bowl stir together papaya, cucumber, tomato, cilantro, chile pepper, lime juice, and oil. Let stand at room temperature for at least 15 minutes to allow flavors to blend.

two Meanwhile, halve any large scallops. Lightly sprinkle with salt and black pepper.

three In a large nonstick skillet melt butter over medium heat. Add garlic; cook for 30 seconds. Add scallops. Cook and stir for 2 to 3 minutes or until scallops are opaque. Use a slotted spoon to remove scallops; drain on paper towels. Serve scallops with the salsa.

NUTRITION FACTS PER SERVING: 116 cal., 3 g total fat (0 g sat. fat), 31 mg chol., 151 mg sodium, 8 g carbo., 1 g fiber, 15 g pro.

*NOTE: Because chile peppers contain volatile oils that can burn your skin and eyes, avoid direct contact with them as much as possible. When working with chile peppers, wear plastic or rubber gloves. If your bare hands do touch the peppers, wash your hands and nails well with soap and warm water.

menu idea:

Cooked linguine or fettuccine tossed with olive oil, lime juice, and minced garlic

Fast & Fruity Banana Split Tarts *(see p. 273)*

peachy lobster pasta salad

Herbs, especially the basil, dillweed, and thyme trio, make this salad a standout. Feel free to try your favorites. Serve the salad with garlic bread or crusty sourdough rolls and glasses of iced tea.

START TO FINISH: 30 minutes **MAKES:** 4 to 6 servings

6	ounces dried medium shell macaroni
½	cup snipped mixed fresh herbs (such as basil, dillweed, and thyme)
¼	cup olive oil
1	teaspoon finely shredded lime peel
3	tablespoons lime juice
3	tablespoons orange juice
1	tablespoon honey
1	teaspoon bottled minced garlic (2 cloves)
¼	teaspoon salt
¼	teaspoon black pepper
3	medium peaches, peeled and sliced
2	cups cut-up, cooked lobster or crabmeat (cartilage removed) or flake-style imitation lobster (about 12 ounces)
1	cup watercress
	Salt
	Black pepper

one Cook pasta according to package directions; drain well. Rinse with cold water; drain again.

two Meanwhile, in a large salad bowl combine herbs, oil, lime peel, lime juice, orange juice, honey, garlic, the ¼ teaspoon salt, and the ¼ teaspoon pepper. Add peach slices. Toss gently to combine. Add cooked pasta, lobster, and watercress. Toss gently to combine. Season with additional salt and pepper.

NUTRITION FACTS PER SERVING: 422 cal., 15 g total fat (2 g sat. fat), 61 mg chol., 509 mg sodium, 49 g carbo., 3 g fiber, 24 g pro.

menu idea:

Garlic bread loaf, toasted
Cannoli (see p. 276)

clam chowder

Canned clams are something every busy cook should keep in the pantry—especially if your family loves good chowder, like this one.

PREP: 15 minutes **COOK:** 15 minutes **MAKES:** 4 to 6 servings

2   10¾-ounce cans condensed cream of celery soup

2   cups loose-pack frozen diced hash brown potatoes with onion and peppers

1   8-ounce bottle clam juice

1   6½-ounce can minced or chopped clams, undrained

2   teaspoons Worcestershire sauce

1   teaspoon dried thyme, crushed

1   cup half-and-half or light cream

3   slices packaged ready-to-serve cooked bacon, chopped

Black pepper (optional)

one In a large saucepan combine cream of celery soup, hash browns, clam juice, undrained clams, Worcestershire sauce, and thyme. Bring to boiling; reduce heat. Cover and simmer about 15 minutes or until potatoes are tender, stirring frequently.

two Stir in half-and-half; heat through. Sprinkle individual servings with bacon. If desired, season to taste with pepper.

NUTRITION FACTS PER SERVING: 383 cal., 20 g total fat (9 g sat. fat), 62 mg chol., 1,410 mg sodium, 29 g carbo., 3 g fiber, 19 g pro.

menu idea:

Rye or pumpernickel bread, spread with herb butter and toasted

Caramel Apple Pastry (see p. 257)

tomato-brown rice frittata

Mustard greens, tomato, and fontina cheese make this simple omelet a masterpiece. Remember it when you have leftover brown rice.

START TO FINISH: 30 minutes **MAKES:** 4 servings

6	egg whites
3	eggs
¼	teaspoon salt
⅛	teaspoon black pepper
½	cup cooked brown rice
¼	cup chopped onion
½	teaspoon bottled minced garlic (1 clove)
1	tablespoon olive oil
2	cups packed fresh mustard greens, stems trimmed and torn into 1-inch pieces
1	medium tomato, seeded and chopped
⅓	cup shredded fontina, provolone, or Gruyère cheese

one In a medium bowl beat together egg whites, eggs, salt, and pepper. Stir in brown rice; set aside. In a large broilerproof skillet cook onion and garlic in oil until tender. Stir in mustard greens; cook and stir about 2 minutes or until wilted. Stir in tomato; cook for 1 minute more.

two Pour egg mixture into skillet over vegetables. Cook over medium-low heat. As mixture sets, run a spatula around edge of skillet, lifting egg mixture so uncooked portion flows underneath. Continue cooking and lifting edge until egg mixture is almost set (surface will be moist). Sprinkle with cheese. Place the skillet under broiler 4 to 5 inches from heat. Broil for 1 to 2 minutes or just until top is set and cheese is melted.

NUTRITION FACTS PER SERVING: 197 cal., 11 g total fat (4 g sat. fat), 172 mg chol., 370 mg sodium, 11 g carbo., 2 g fiber, 14 g pro.

menu idea:

Purchased muffins served with maple butter or jam

Baked Fruit Ambrosia *(see p. 258)*

egg salad sandwiches

If you think one egg salad sandwich is like another, you'll be surprised and delighted when you taste this one. It is dressed up with Colby Jack cheese and sweet red pepper.

START TO FINISH: 20 minutes **MAKES:** 5 sandwiches

4	hard-cooked eggs, chopped
¼	cup shredded Colby Jack cheese (1 ounce)
2	tablespoons sweet or dill pickle relish
2	tablespoons finely chopped red sweet pepper
¼	cup mayonnaise or salad dressing
1	tablespoon prepared mustard
10	slices whole wheat and/or white bread
5	small romaine leaves
	Halved cherry tomatoes and/or thin bite-size carrot strips
	(optional)

one In a medium bowl stir together eggs, cheese, relish, and sweet pepper. Stir in mayonnaise and mustard.

two If desired, use large cookie cutters to cut bread slices into shapes. Top 5 slices of the bread with lettuce leaves. Spread on egg mixture. Top with remaining bread slices. If desired, garnish sandwiches with cherry tomatoes and/or carrots, using wooden toothpicks to secure.

NUTRITION FACTS PER SANDWICH: 431 cal., 20 g total fat (4 g sat. fat), 183 mg chol., 551 mg sodium, 50 g carbo., 6 g fiber, 14 g pro.

test kitchen tip: For a lower-fat sandwich, substitute reduced-fat Colby Jack cheese for the Colby Jack cheese and light mayonnaise dressing or salad dressing for the mayonnaise or salad dressing.

NUTRITION FACTS PER SANDWICH: 365 cal., 11 g total fat (3 g sat. fat), 176 mg chol., 599 mg sodium, 54 g carbo., 6 g fiber, 15 g pro.

menu idea:

Tortilla or corn chips

Chewy Granola Bars (see p. 268)

alfredo & sweet pepper pizza

Creamy garlicky Alfredo sauce instead of pizza sauce is a great change of pace for pizza. Buy two or three Italian bread shells and freeze them for quick-to-fix, satisfying pizzas.

PREP: 15 minutes **BAKE:** 10 minutes **MAKES:** 4 servings

1   16-ounce Italian bread shell (Boboli)

½   of a 10-ounce container (about ⅔ cup) refrigerated Alfredo pasta sauce

½   teaspoon dried Italian seasoning, crushed

1   8-ounce package shredded 4-cheese pizza cheese (2 cups)

1   16-ounce package frozen pepper stir-fry vegetables (yellow, green, and red peppers and onion), thawed and well drained

one Place bread shell on an ungreased baking sheet. In a small bowl stir together Alfredo sauce and Italian seasoning. Spread Alfredo sauce mixture over bread shell.

two Sprinkle bread shell with 1 cup of the cheese. Top with stir-fry vegetables. Sprinkle with remaining 1 cup cheese. Bake in a 425°F oven about 10 minutes or until heated through.

NUTRITION FACTS PER SERVING: 626 cal., 30 g total fat (8 g sat. fat), 63 mg chol., 1,136 mg sodium, 60 g carbo., 3 g fiber, 30 g pro.

menu idea:

Mixed greens tossed with seasoned croutons, tomato wedges, and bottled Italian salad dressing

Quick Strawberry Shortcakes (see p. 259)

grilled cheese with caramelized onions

This comfort food classic is made even better with the addition of mushrooms and caramelized onions. Sourdough bread complements the bold flavors of the berry-balsamic vinegar and the golden brown onions.

START TO FINISH: 30 minutes **MAKES:** 4 sandwiches

- 6   tablespoons butter or margarine, softened
- 1   large onion, sliced
- 1   cup sliced fresh mushrooms
- 1   teaspoon berry-balsamic vinegar
- ⅛   teaspoon salt
- 8   slices sourdough bread
- 8   slices cheddar cheese, Swiss cheese, Monterey Jack cheese, and/or other desired cheese

one In a large skillet melt 2 tablespoons of the butter over medium heat. Add onion slices; cook about 10 minutes or until onion is soft and golden brown, stirring occasionally. Stir in mushrooms. Cook and stir for 2 minutes more. Remove from heat. Sprinkle onions and mushrooms with balsamic vinegar and salt.

two Butter 1 side of each slice of the bread with 1 tablespoon of the remaining butter. Place 2 slices of the desired cheese on the unbuttered side of each of 4 slices of the sourdough bread. Top each with some of the onion-mushroom mixture and another slice of sourdough bread, buttered side up. In a large skillet cook sandwiches over medium heat for 4 to 6 minutes or until cheese is melted, turning once.

NUTRITION FACTS PER SANDWICH: 552 cal., 39 g total fat (22 g sat. fat), 108 mg chol., 861 mg sodium, 32 g carbo., 2 g fiber, 20 g pro.

---

menu idea:

Fruited Wild Rice & Spinach Salad (see p. 251)

Chocolate fudge ice cream sprinkled with toasted sliced almonds

potato-cauliflower chowder

Topping bowls of this chowder with cheesy slices of toasted rye bread is a simple way to add eye appeal that invites hungry eaters to dig in.

START TO FINISH: 30 minutes **MAKES:** 6 servings

1	large onion, chopped
2	tablespoons butter or margarine
4	cups chicken or vegetable broth
2	cups diced, peeled Yukon gold or white potatoes
2½	cups cauliflower florets
1	cup half-and-half, light cream, or milk
2	tablespoons all-purpose flour
2½	cups shredded Jarlsberg cheese or Swiss cheese (10 ounces)
	Salt
	Black pepper
3	slices dark rye or pumpernickel bread, halved crosswise (optional)
½	cup shredded Jarlsberg cheese or Swiss cheese (2 ounces) (optional)
2	tablespoons snipped fresh flat-leaf parsley (optional)

one In a large saucepan or Dutch oven cook onion in hot butter until tender. Carefully add broth and potatoes. Bring to boiling; reduce heat. Cover and simmer for 6 minutes. Add cauliflower. Return to boiling; reduce heat. Cover and simmer for 4 to 6 minutes or until vegetables are tender.

two In a small bowl whisk half-and-half into flour until smooth; add to soup mixture. Cook and stir until mixture is thickened and bubbly. Reduce heat to low. Add the 2½ cups cheese, stirring until melted. Do not allow mixture to boil. Season to taste with salt and pepper.

three Meanwhile, if using bread, if desired, trim crusts from bread. Place the halved bread slices on a baking sheet. Bake in a 350°F oven about 3 minutes or until crisp on top. Turn slices over. If desired, sprinkle with the ½ cup cheese and the parsley. Bake about 5 minutes more or until cheese melts.

four Float cheese-topped bread slices on individual servings.

NUTRITION FACTS PER SERVING: 267 cal., 17 g total fat (12 g sat. fat), 58 mg chol., 533 mg sodium, 14 g carbo., 2 g fiber, 15 g pro.

menu idea:

Peanut Butter Fruit Salad *(see p. 248)*

Purchased unfrosted brownies spread with canned chocolate frosting and sprinkled with mini marshmallows and chopped nuts

bean & cheese quesadillas

These packed-full-of-veggies quesadillas are quick, colorful, and irresistible. The diced peaches add a hint of sweetness.

PREP: 15 minutes **BAKE:** 12 minutes **MAKES:** 4 servings

½ of a 16-ounce can refried beans (¾ cup)

1 8-ounce can whole kernel corn, drained

¼ cup bottled salsa

1 canned chipotle chile pepper in adobo sauce, drained and chopped* (optional)

8 8-inch flour tortillas

2 tablespoons cooking oil

1 cup packaged shredded broccoli (broccoli slaw mix)

1 4- to 4¼-ounce can or container diced peaches, drained

1 cup finely shredded Mexican cheese blend (4 ounces)

Purchased guacamole dip, dairy sour cream, and/or bottled salsa

one In a small bowl combine refried beans, corn, the ¼ cup salsa, and, if desired, chipotle chile pepper. Brush 1 side of each tortilla with some of the oil. Spread bean mixture over the unoiled side of 4 of the tortillas; set aside.

two In another bowl combine broccoli slaw and peaches. Top bean mixture on tortillas with broccoli mixture. Top with cheese. Top with remaining tortillas, oiled sides up; press down lightly. Place on a large baking sheet.

three Bake in a 400°F oven for 12 to 15 minutes or until golden brown and cheese is melted. Cut into quarters to serve. Serve with guacamole dip, sour cream, and/or additional salsa.

NUTRITION FACTS PER SERVING: 444 cal., 21 g total fat (7 g sat. fat), 25 mg chol., 825 mg sodium, 50 g carbo., 5 g fiber, 14 g pro.

*****NOTE:** Because chile peppers contain volatile oils that can burn your skin and eyes, avoid direct contact with them as much as possible. When working with chile peppers, wear plastic or rubber gloves. If your bare hands do touch the peppers, wash your hands and nails well with soap and warm water.

menu idea:

Tomato-Barley Soup with Garden Vegetables
(see p. 240)

Vanilla frozen yogurt served with sliced fresh mango

easy cheesy macaroni

The name says it all—this Alfredo-sauced macaroni laced with toasted nuts is easy and cheesy!

START TO FINISH: 20 minutes **MAKES:** 4 servings

8	ounces dried penne, rotini, or gemelli pasta
2	cups loose-pack frozen cauliflower, broccoli, and carrots
1	10-ounce container refrigerated light Alfredo pasta sauce
¼	cup milk
1	cup shredded cheddar cheese (4 ounces)
½	cup finely shredded Parmesan cheese (2 ounces)
¼	cup chopped walnuts, toasted

one In a 4-quart Dutch oven cook pasta according to package directions, adding frozen vegetables for the last 4 minutes of cooking; drain well. Return to the Dutch oven; cover and keep warm.

two Meanwhile, in a medium saucepan combine Alfredo sauce and milk; heat and stir just until bubbly. Gradually add cheddar and Parmesan cheeses, stirring until melted. Add cheese mixture to pasta mixture in Dutch oven; stir to coat. Heat through. Top with toasted walnuts.

NUTRITION FACTS PER SERVING: 586 cal., 28 g total fat (15 g sat. fat), 70 mg chol., 1,054 mg sodium, 57 g carbo., 3 g fiber, 26 g pro.

menu idea:

Rosy Tangerine-Scented Cabbage *(see p. 225)*

Sliced green and/or red apples served with caramel dip and sprinkled with granola

cheese & vegetable-filled focaccia

Brimming with zesty pickled vegetables and herbed cheese, this stuffed focaccia makes an instant meal. Save time by buying prewashed spinach from the produce department and getting the cheese at the deli counter so you can have it very thinly sliced or shaved.

START TO FINISH: 20 minutes **MAKES:** 4 servings

⅓	cup mayonnaise or salad dressing
2	tablespoons honey mustard
1	8- to 10-inch tomato or onion focaccia bread, halved horizontally
1	cup lightly packed fresh spinach leaves
6	ounces dilled Havarti cheese, very thinly sliced
1	16-ounce jar pickled mixed vegetables, drained and chopped

one In a small bowl stir together mayonnaise and honey mustard. Spread mayonnaise mixture over bottom half of focaccia. Top with spinach leaves and half of the cheese. Spoon vegetables over; top with remaining cheese. Replace bread top. Cut into quarters.

NUTRITION FACTS PER SERVING: 364 cal., 32 g total fat (2 g sat. fat), 67 mg chol., 1,251 mg sodium, 10 g carbo., 0 g fiber, 10 g pro.

menu idea:

Creamy Carrot Soup *(see p. 238)*

Fresh strawberries topped with vanilla or strawberry frozen yogurt and served with purchased sugar cookies

creamy penne & mushrooms

Turn the heat to low or take the skillet off of the burner before adding the sour cream to the sauce. The sour cream will curdle if it gets too hot.

START TO FINISH: 25 minutes **MAKES:** 4 servings

8	ounces dried penne pasta
3	cups sliced fresh button mushrooms (8 ounces)
1½	cups sliced fresh shiitake mushrooms (4 ounces)
2	teaspoons bottled minced garlic (4 cloves)
1	tablespoon butter or margarine
½	cup dry white wine
1	teaspoon instant chicken bouillon granules
¼	teaspoon coarsely ground black pepper
½	cup light dairy sour cream
¼	cup finely shredded Parmesan cheese (1 ounce)

one Cook pasta according to package directions; drain. Return to hot pan; cover and keep warm.

two In a large skillet cook and stir mushrooms and garlic in hot butter for 3 minutes. Stir in white wine, bouillon granules, and pepper. Bring to boiling; reduce heat. Simmer, uncovered, for 5 minutes. Reduce heat to low. Stir in sour cream; add hot cooked pasta. Cook and stir until heated through (do not boil).

three To serve, transfer pasta to shallow pasta bowls or dinner plates. Sprinkle servings with Parmesan cheese.

NUTRITION FACTS PER SERVING: 360 cal., 9 g total fat (5 g sat. fat), 24 mg chol., 408 mg sodium, 51 g carbo., 2 g fiber, 14 g pro.

menu idea:

Lemon-Almond Broccoli *(see p. 224)*

Purchased individual shortcakes topped with canned apple pie filling and drizzled with purchased warm caramel sauce

soft shell pork tacos
Recipe on page 160

veal marsala
Recipe on page 165

tilapia with chili cream sauce
Recipe on page 188

italian turkey sandwiches
Recipe on page 178

peanut butter fruit salad
Recipe on page 248

roasted asparagus parmesan
Recipe on page 223

fruit-filled waffle bowls
Recipe on page 274

spicy chicken breasts with fruit
Recipe on page 167

vegetable fried rice

With this no-hassle recipe, you can enjoy a Chinese classic at home in just minutes.

START TO FINISH: 20 minutes **MAKES:** 4 servings

1	teaspoon toasted sesame oil or cooking oil
2	eggs, slightly beaten
1/3	cup rice vinegar
1/4	cup soy sauce
1/8	teaspoon ground ginger
1/8	teaspoon crushed red pepper
1	tablespoon cooking oil
1	cup sliced fresh mushrooms
1	teaspoon bottled minced garlic (2 cloves)
2	8.8-ounce pouches cooked long grain rice
1/2	cup loose-pack frozen peas
1	2-ounce jar diced pimientos, drained
1/4	cup chopped peanuts (optional)

one In a large skillet heat sesame oil over medium heat. Add half of the egg, lifting and tilting the skillet to form a thin layer (egg may not completely cover the bottom of the skillet). Cook about 1 minute or until set. Invert skillet over a baking sheet to remove cooked egg; cut into strips and set aside. Repeat with remaining egg. In a small bowl stir together vinegar, soy sauce, ginger, and crushed red pepper; set aside.

two In the same skillet heat cooking oil over medium-high heat. Add mushrooms and garlic; cook about 3 minutes or until mushrooms are tender. Stir in vinegar mixture. Stir in rice, frozen peas, and pimientos. Cook and stir about 2 minutes or until heated through and liquid is nearly evaporated. Stir in egg strips. If desired, sprinkle servings with chopped peanuts.

NUTRITION FACTS PER SERVING: 314 cal., 10 g total fat (1 g sat. fat), 106 mg chol., 999 mg sodium, 45 g carbo., 3 g fiber, 10 g pro.

menu idea:

Asian Pea Pod Salad (see p. 242)

Instant pistachio pudding mix, prepared according to package directions and topped with flaked coconut

white beans
with tomato, basil & parmesan

A fresh combination of Great Northern beans, sweet juicy red tomatoes, and fragrant basil makes a quick-and-easy meatless main dish. The bow tie pasta adds an element of fun.

START TO FINISH: 30 minutes **MAKES:** 4 servings

8	ounces dried bow tie pasta
1	tablespoon olive oil
1½	teaspoons bottled minced garlic (3 cloves)
2	15-ounce cans Great Northern or white kidney (cannellini) beans, rinsed and drained
2	large tomatoes, chopped (about 3 cups)
¼	cup snipped fresh basil or 2 teaspoons dried basil, crushed
1	tablespoon lemon juice
¼	teaspoon salt (optional)
½	cup grated Parmesan cheese (2 ounces)
	Freshly ground black pepper

one Cook pasta according to package directions; drain well. Return to hot pan; cover and keep warm.

two Meanwhile, in a large nonstick skillet heat oil over medium-low heat. Add garlic; cook, stirring occasionally, for 1 to 2 minutes or until golden brown. Stir in beans, tomatoes, and basil. Cook, uncovered, for 5 minutes. Stir in lemon juice and, if desired, salt.

three Serve bean mixture over hot cooked pasta. Sprinkle servings with Parmesan cheese and freshly ground pepper.

NUTRITION FACTS PER SERVING: 480 cal., 9 g total fat (3 g sat. fat), 10 mg chol., 247 mg sodium, 77 g carbo., 12 g fiber, 25 g pro.

menu idea:

Honey & Poppy Seed Biscuits *(see p. 254)*

Coffee or mocha ice cream served with purchased fudge stick cookies

minestrone

There is nothing more energizing than a hot steaming bowl of hearty soup on a cold day.

START TO FINISH: 25 minutes **MAKES:** 8 servings

3	14-ounce cans chicken broth or vegetable broth
2	14½-ounce cans stewed tomatoes, undrained
1	15-ounce can white kidney (cannellini) beans, rinsed and drained
1	15-ounce can garbanzo beans (chickpeas), rinsed and drained
1	6-ounce can tomato paste
2	teaspoons dried Italian seasoning, crushed
2	cups loose-pack frozen mixed vegetables (such as Italian blend)
2	cups fresh spinach leaves, cut into strips
2	cups cooked medium pasta (such as medium shell macaroni or mostaccioli)
	Finely shredded Parmesan cheese (optional)

one In a 4-quart Dutch oven combine broth, undrained tomatoes, white kidney beans, garbanzo beans, tomato paste, and Italian seasoning. Bring to boiling; add mixed vegetables. Reduce heat. Cover and simmer about 10 minutes or until vegetables are tender.

two Stir in spinach and cooked pasta; heat through. If desired, sprinkle with Parmesan cheese.

NUTRITION FACTS PER SERVING: 219 cal., 2 g total fat (0 g sat. fat), 2 mg chol., 1,081 mg sodium, 41 g carbo., 8 g fiber, 12 g pro.

make-ahead directions: Prepare Minestrone as directed through step one. Cover and chill for up to 24 hours. To serve, reheat soup over medium heat. Stir in spinach and cooked pasta; heat through.

menu idea:

Sourdough rolls

A Billow of Berries 'n' Brownies (see p. 261)

skillet eggplant parmigiana

This range-top version of Parmigiana satisfies diners as much as the classic long-baking casserole. A bonus topping of heady basil and crunchy walnuts gives the dish extra appeal.

START TO FINISH: 30 minutes **MAKES:** 4 servings

1	medium eggplant (1 pound)
¼	cup seasoned fine dry bread crumbs
½	cup grated Parmesan cheese (2 ounces)
1	egg
1	tablespoon water
2	tablespoons olive oil or cooking oil
1¼	cups bottled meatless spaghetti sauce
1	cup shredded mozzarella cheese (4 ounces)
¼	cup snipped fresh basil
2	tablespoons finely chopped walnuts

one If desired, peel eggplant. Cut eggplant into ¾-inch slices. In a shallow dish combine bread crumbs and ¼ cup of the Parmesan cheese. In another shallow dish whisk together egg and the water. Dip eggplant slices into the egg mixture and then into the crumb mixture to coat.

two In a 12-inch skillet heat oil over medium heat. Add eggplant slices; cook for 6 to 8 minutes or until golden brown, turning once. Add spaghetti sauce; sprinkle with mozzarella cheese and remaining ¼ cup Parmesan cheese. Reduce heat to medium-low. Cover and cook for 5 minutes.

three Sprinkle the basil and walnuts over eggplant just before serving.

NUTRITION FACTS PER SERVING: 295 cal., 20 g total fat (7 g sat. fat), 48 mg chol., 850 mg sodium, 18 g carbo., 5 g fiber, 15 g pro.

menu idea:

Spinach, Red Onion & Cherry Tomato Salad *(see p. 245)*

Purchased carrot cake

french bread egg breakfast

This meatless version of eggs Benedict features French bread instead of the traditional English muffin. A no-cook mustard and sour cream sauce is a quick alternative to Hollandaise.

START TO FINISH: 20 minutes **MAKES:** 4 servings

- ¼ cup dairy sour cream or crème fraîche
- 1 teaspoon lemon juice
- ¾ to 1 teaspoon dry mustard
- 3 to 4 teaspoons milk
- 4 eggs
- 4 ½-inch slices artisanal French bread, lightly toasted
- 4 ounces thinly sliced smoked salmon (optional)
- Salt
- Black pepper

one In a small bowl combine sour cream, lemon juice, and dry mustard. Add enough milk to make desired consistency. Set aside.

two Lightly grease 4 cups of an egg poaching pan. Place poacher cups over the pan of boiling water (water should not touch bottoms of cups); reduce heat to simmering. Break an egg into a measuring cup. Carefully slide egg into a poacher cup. Repeat with remaining eggs. Cover and cook for 6 to 8 minutes or until the whites are completely set and yolks begin to thicken but are not hard. Run a knife around edges to loosen eggs. Invert poacher cups to remove eggs.

three If desired, top each bread slice with smoked salmon. Top with poached egg. Top with sour cream mixture. Season with salt and pepper.

NUTRITION FACTS PER SERVING: 172 cal., 8 g total fat (3 g sat. fat), 217 mg chol., 303 mg sodium, 14 g carbo., 1 g fiber, 9 g pro.

saucepan method: Lightly grease a 2-quart saucepan with cooking oil or shortening. Half fill the pan with water. Bring the water to boiling; reduce heat to simmering (bubbles should begin to break surface). Break an egg into a measuring cup. Carefully slide egg into simmering water, holding the lip of the cup as close to the water as possible. Repeat with remaining eggs, allowing each egg an equal amount of space. Simmer eggs, uncovered, for 3 to 5 minutes or until whites are completely set and yolks begin to thicken but are not hard. Remove eggs with a slotted spoon.

menu idea:

Baked Fruit Ambrosia *(see p. 258)*

Espresso or flavored coffee

pumpkin pancakes with orange syrup

Canned pumpkin is the magic ingredient that makes these pancakes moist and hard to resist.

START TO FINISH: 30 minutes **MAKES:** 8 pancakes

2	cups all-purpose flour
2	tablespoons packed brown sugar
1	tablespoon baking powder
½	teaspoon salt
½	teaspoon pumpkin pie spice
1½	cups milk
1	cup canned pumpkin
2	eggs, beaten
2	tablespoons cooking oil
	Nonstick cooking spray
1	recipe Orange Syrup
1	orange, peeled and sectioned (optional)

one In a medium bowl stir together flour, brown sugar, baking powder, salt, and pumpkin pie spice. Make a well in the center of flour mixture.

two In another medium bowl combine milk, pumpkin, eggs, and oil. Add the milk mixture all at once to flour mixture. Stir just until moistened (batter should be lumpy).

three Lightly coat an unheated nonstick griddle or heavy skillet with cooking spray. Preheat over medium heat. For each pancake, pour about ¼ cup of the batter onto the hot griddle or skillet. Cook over medium heat about 4 minutes or until pancakes are golden brown, turning to second sides when pancakes have bubbly surfaces and edges are slightly dry. Serve warm with Orange Syrup and, if desired, orange sections.

NUTRITION FACTS PER PANCAKE: 233 cal., 6 g total fat (1 g sat. fat), 57 mg chol., 278 mg sodium, 38 g carbo., 2 g fiber, 7 g pro.

orange syrup: In a small saucepan stir together 1 cup orange juice, 2 tablespoons honey, 2½ teaspoons cornstarch, and ¼ teaspoon ground cinnamon. Cook and stir until thickened and bubbly. Cook and stir for 2 minutes more. Serve warm.

menu idea:

Refrigerated or frozen diced potatoes with onions and peppers, prepared according to package directions

Hot Gingered Cider *(see p. 288)*

roasted asparagus parmesan

Parmesan cheese is something a busy cook should not be without. Nicely pungent and salty, it adds a quick flavor boost to crisp-tender asparagus.

PREP: 10 minutes **BAKE:** 15 minutes **MAKES:** 6 servings

- 2 pounds fresh asparagus
- 2 tablespoons olive oil
  Salt
  Black pepper
- ½ cup finely grated Parmesan cheese (2 ounces)

one Snap off and discard woody bases from asparagus spears. If desired, scrape off scales. Place asparagus in a 15×10×1-inch baking pan. Drizzle with oil, tossing gently to coat. Spread out into a single layer. Sprinkle with salt and pepper.

two Bake in a 400°F oven about 15 minutes or until asparagus is crisp-tender. Transfer to a serving platter; sprinkle with Parmesan cheese.

NUTRITION FACTS PER SERVING: 95 cal., 7 g total fat (2 g sat. fat), 8 mg chol., 102 mg sodium, 4 g carbo., 2 g fiber, 5 g pro.

lemon-almond broccoli

Toasted nuts and broccoli are an appealing combination that is quick and easy to put together. Here a dash of lemon peel makes the broccoli even better while the nuts add some satisfying crunch.

START TO FINISH: 20 minutes **MAKES:** 4 servings

8	ounces broccoli, cut into ¾-inch pieces, or 2 cups loose-pack frozen cut broccoli
1	tablespoon butter or margarine
¾	cup sliced fresh mushrooms
1	green onion, thinly sliced
2	tablespoons slivered almonds or chopped pecans, toasted
½	teaspoon finely shredded lemon peel

one If using fresh broccoli, in a covered medium saucepan cook broccoli in a small amount of boiling lightly salted water about 8 minutes or until crisp-tender. If using frozen broccoli, cook according to package directions. Drain. Meanwhile, for sauce, in a small saucepan melt butter over medium heat. Add mushrooms and green onion; cook until tender, stirring occasionally. Remove from heat. Stir in nuts and lemon peel. Toss with broccoli.

NUTRITION FACTS PER SERVING: 69 cal., 6 g total fat (2 g sat. fat), 8 mg chol., 34 mg sodium, 4 g carbo., 2 g fiber, 3 g pro.

rosy tangerine-scented cabbage

Red cabbage adds the wonderful deep pinky-purple color that makes this dish appealing!

START TO FINISH: 20 minutes **MAKES:** 4 servings

2	tangerines
1	tablespoon lemon juice
1	teaspoon olive oil
4	cups shredded red cabbage
1	large red onion, cut into thin slivers
1	tablespoon sugar
¼	teaspoon coarsely ground peppercorn blend
1	tablespoon finely snipped fresh cilantro

one Finely shred ½ teaspoon peel from one of the tangerines; set peel aside. Peel, seed, and section tangerines over a bowl to catch the juice.

two In a large nonstick skillet combine 1 tablespoon of the tangerine juice, the lemon juice, and oil. Bring to boiling. Add red cabbage and onion. Reduce heat to medium. Cover and cook for 3 to 5 minutes or until cabbage is slightly wilted but still crisp, stirring occasionally. Remove from heat. Stir in sugar, coarsely ground peppercorn blend, and ½ teaspoon salt. Gently stir in tangerine peel and sections and the cilantro.

NUTRITION FACTS PER SERVING: 72 cal., 1 g total fat (0 g sat. fat), 0 mg chol., 300 mg sodium, 15 g carbo., 3 g fiber, 2 g pro.

curried carrots

Keep a supply of frozen vegetables on hand for days when you need speedy side dishes such as these can't miss carrots.

START TO FINISH: 15 minutes **MAKES:** 6 servings

1	16-ounce package frozen crinkle-cut carrots
¼	cup chopped onion
2	tablespoons butter or margarine
1	teaspoon sugar
1	teaspoon curry powder
½	teaspoon salt
⅛	teaspoon cayenne pepper
	Dash ground allspice or nutmeg

one In a covered medium saucepan cook carrots and onion in a small amount of boiling salted water for 5 to 7 minutes or until crisp-tender. Drain; set aside.

two In the same saucepan melt butter over medium heat. Stir in sugar, curry powder, salt, cayenne pepper, and allspice. Stir in carrot mixture; heat through.

NUTRITION FACTS PER SERVING: 73 cal., 4 g total fat (2 g sat. fat), 11 mg chol., 275 mg sodium, 9 g carbo., 2 g fiber, 1 g pro.

skillet scalloped corn

If you think preparing scalloped corn takes too much time for weeknight dinners, try this skillet version. Thick and cheesy, it's ready to serve in just 10 minutes.

START TO FINISH: 10 minutes **MAKES:** 3 servings

2	teaspoons butter or margarine
⅓	cup crushed wheat or rye crackers
1	11-ounce can whole kernel corn with sweet peppers, drained
2	1-ounce slices process Swiss cheese, torn
¼	cup milk
⅛	teaspoon onion powder
	Dash black pepper

one For crumb topping, in a large skillet melt butter over medium heat. Add 1 tablespoon of the crushed crackers to the skillet. Cook and stir until lightly browned; remove and set aside.

two In the same skillet combine remaining crushed crackers, corn, cheese, milk, onion powder, and pepper. Cook, stirring frequently, until cheese melts. Transfer to a serving dish; sprinkle with crumb topping.

NUTRITION FACTS PER SERVING: 199 cal., 9 g total fat (5 g sat. fat), 25 mg chol., 697 mg sodium, 24 g carbo., 3 g fiber, 8 g pro.

glazed parsnips & apples

Parsnips are a versatile root vegetable that can be prepared by almost any cooking method, including baking, boiling, frying, and steaming. Pairing them with apples and brown sugar is a winning combination guaranteed to have you enjoying them more often.

START TO FINISH: 20 minutes **MAKES:** 4 or 5 servings

- ¾ cup apple cider or apple juice
- 1 pound small parsnips, peeled and cut into ¼-inch slices
- 2 tablespoons butter or margarine
- 2 tablespoons packed brown sugar
- 2 medium cooking apples, cored and thinly sliced

one In a large skillet bring apple cider just to boiling. Add parsnips; reduce heat. Cover and simmer for 7 to 8 minutes or until crisp-tender. Remove parsnips and any liquid from skillet.

two In the same skillet combine butter and brown sugar. Cook, uncovered, over medium-high heat about 1 minute or until mixture begins to thicken. Add apples and undrained parsnips; cook, uncovered, about 2 minutes or until glazed, stirring frequently.

NUTRITION FACTS PER SERVING: 206 cal., 7 g total fat (4 g sat. fat), 16 mg chol., 74 mg sodium, 38 g carbo., 7 g fiber, 1 g pro.

broiled summer squash & onions

Bottled vinaigrettes and other salad dressings are really convenient as fast and flavorful marinades for vegetables. You get great taste without having to fuss over the food.

PREP: 10 minutes **BROIL:** 8 minutes **MAKES:** 4 servings

- ¼ cup bottled olive oil vinaigrette or balsamic vinaigrette salad dressing
- ½ teaspoon dried basil or oregano, crushed
- ⅛ teaspoon black pepper
- 2 medium yellow summer squash or zucchini, quartered lengthwise
- 1 small onion, cut into thin wedges

one In a small bowl whisk together salad dressing, basil, and pepper. Brush summer squash and onion with some of the salad dressing mixture.

two Place summer squash and onion on unheated rack of a broiler pan. Broil about 4 inches from the heat for 8 to 10 minutes or until crisp-tender, turning and brushing occasionally with salad dressing mixture.

three Cut broiled vegetables into bite-size pieces; transfer to a serving bowl. Toss with any remaining salad dressing mixture.

NUTRITION FACTS PER SERVING: 91 cal., 8 g total fat (1 g sat. fat), 0 mg chol., 77 mg sodium, 4 g carbo., 1 g fiber, 1 g pro.

baked pineapple casserole

This easy fruit-and-cheese side dish brings out the best in pork, poultry, or fish.

PREP: 10 minutes **BAKE:** 20 minutes **MAKES:** 4 to 6 servings

- 1   15¼-ounce can pineapple chunks (juice pack)
- ½   cup sugar
- 3   tablespoons all-purpose flour
- 1   cup shredded cheddar cheese (4 ounces)
- ½   cup crushed rich round crackers (about 12 crackers)
- 3   tablespoons butter or margarine, melted

one Grease 1-quart au gratin dish or casserole; set aside. Drain pineapple, reserving juice (you should have about ⅔ cup juice). In a medium bowl stir together sugar and flour. Stir in reserved juice until smooth. Stir in pineapple and cheese. Pour into prepared dish.

two In a small bowl stir together crackers and melted butter; sprinkle over pineapple mixture. Bake in a 325°F oven for 20 to 25 minutes or until top is golden brown.

NUTRITION FACTS PER SERVING: 426 cal., 21 g total fat (10 g sat. fat), 45 mg chol., 375 mg sodium, 53 g carbo., 1 g fiber, 9 g pro.

summer spaghetti

Even though it has a pared-down ingredient list and a speedy preparation time, this recipe rewards you with magnificent flavors. Serve it with roasted meats or fish.

START TO FINISH: 20 minutes **MAKES:** 4 servings

- 8 ounces dried spaghetti
- 2 cups cut-up fresh vegetables (such as sliced yellow summer squash, halved baby sunburst squash, chopped carrots, and sliced green onions)
- 2 tablespoons butter, melted, or olive oil
- ¼ cup finely shredded Asiago or Parmesan cheese (1 ounce)
- ⅛ teaspoon freshly ground black pepper

one Cook pasta according to package directions. Meanwhile, place the vegetables in a colander. Pour pasta mixture over vegetables in colander; drain.

two Transfer pasta and vegetable mixture to a serving bowl. Drizzle with butter or olive oil; toss to coat. Sprinkle with cheese and pepper.

NUTRITION FACTS PER SERVING: 320 cal., 10 g total fat (6 g sat. fat), 24 mg chol., 152 mg sodium, 48 g carbo., 3 g fiber, 10 g pro.

broken pasta with italian parsley

Simple pasta dishes, such as this one tossed with tiny super-sweet tomatoes, are popular in Italy. If small tomatoes aren't available, use fresh ripe plum or Roma tomatoes, cut into wedges.

START TO FINISH: 20 minutes **MAKES:** 4 servings

6	ounces dried lasagna noodles (about 7 noodles)
2	tablespoons olive oil*
½	teaspoon snipped fresh rosemary*
⅔	cup red and/or gold grape tomatoes, teardrop tomatoes, or cherry tomatoes, halved lengthwise
¼	cup snipped fresh flat-leaf parsley
	Salt
	Coarsely ground black pepper
	Parmesan or other hard cheese, crumbled

one Break lasagna noodles into irregular pieces (2 to 3 inches long). In a Dutch oven or large saucepan bring 3 quarts (12 cups) salted water to boiling. Add broken lasagna noodles. Cook, uncovered, for 8 to 10 minutes or until tender but still firm (al dente). Drain and rinse pasta.

two Meanwhile, in a small bowl stir together oil and snipped rosemary.

three Toss the cooked pasta with oil-rosemary mixture, tomatoes, and parsley. Season to taste with salt and pepper. Top with crumbled cheese.

NUTRITION FACTS PER SERVING: 251 cal., 10 g total fat (2 g sat. fat), 6 mg chol., 77 mg sodium, 33 g carbo., 1 g fiber, 7 g pro.

*NOTE: If desired, substitute 2 tablespoons purchased rosemary-flavor oil for the oil and rosemary mixture.

spicy peanut noodles

What could be more fun than curly ramen noodles teamed with bright vegetables and crunchy peanuts? Ready in just 15 minutes, this recipe has it all.

START TO FINISH: 15 minutes **MAKES:** 4 servings

1	9-ounce package frozen cut green beans
2	3-ounce packages Oriental-flavor ramen noodles
1	medium red or yellow sweet pepper, cut into bite-size strips
½	cup bottled peanut sauce or stir-fry sauce
¼	cup chopped peanuts

one In a large saucepan bring 5 cups water to boiling. Add green beans; cook, uncovered, for 3 minutes. Add ramen noodles with seasoning from packets and sweet pepper strips. Cook, uncovered, about 3 minutes more or until noodles and vegetables are tender. Drain. Return noodle mixture to saucepan. Stir in peanut sauce. Heat through. Sprinkle with peanuts.

NUTRITION FACTS PER SERVING: 372 cal., 19 g total fat (2 g sat. fat), 0 mg chol., 1,269 mg sodium, 40 g carbo., 3 g fiber, 11 g pro.

curried cherry pilaf

Fennel with its fresh and delicate hint of licorice becomes even sweeter when cooked with curry powder and tart red cherries in this festive dish.

START TO FINISH: 30 minutes **MAKES:** 6 to 8 servings

1	8-ounce fennel bulb with top leaves
1	medium onion, chopped
1	tablespoon butter or margarine
1	14-ounce can chicken broth
1	cup long grain rice
½	cup water
½	teaspoon curry powder
½	cup dried tart red cherries, halved

one Cut off upper stalks of fennel, reserving the top feathery leaves. Remove wilted outer layer of stalks; cut off a thin layer from base. Wash fennel bulb and chop (you should have about 1 cup).

two In a medium saucepan cook chopped fennel and onion in hot butter about 3 minutes or until crisp-tender. Carefully stir in broth, uncooked rice, the water, and curry powder. Bring to boiling; reduce heat. Cover and simmer about 15 minutes or until rice is tender.

three Snip 1 tablespoon of the reserved fennel leaves. Stir dried cherries and snipped fennel leaves into rice mixture. Remove from heat. Cover and let stand for 5 minutes.

NUTRITION FACTS PER SERVING: 179 cal., 2 g total fat (1 g sat. fat), 6 mg chol., 294 mg sodium, 35 g carbo., 2 g fiber, 3 g pro.

lemon pesto rice with sugar snap peas

Rice has never had it so good—or so tasty! Fragrant garlicky pesto, fresh lemon, and sweet, crisp, plump sugar snap peas give rice the ultimate spring treatment.

START TO FINISH: 25 minutes **MAKES:** 8 servings

¼	cup dry sherry
3	tablespoons purchased basil pesto
1	teaspoon finely shredded lemon peel
1	tablespoon lemon juice
1	tablespoon olive oil
2	stalks celery, sliced
¾	cup coarsely chopped walnuts
1½	teaspoons bottled minced garlic (3 cloves)
½	teaspoon salt
8	ounces fresh sugar snap peas, halved crosswise if desired
3	cups hot cooked rice
	Freshly ground black pepper
	Finely shredded Parmesan cheese

one In a small bowl stir together sherry, basil pesto, lemon peel, and lemon juice; set aside.

two In a large skillet heat oil over medium-high heat. Add celery; cook and stir for 3 to 4 minutes or until tender. Stir in walnuts, garlic, and salt; cook and stir for 30 seconds. Add sugar snap peas; cook and stir about 2 minutes more or until peas are crisp-tender.

three Stir cooked rice into vegetable mixture. Add pesto mixture. Stir to coat well. Heat through. Sprinkle with pepper and Parmesan cheese.

NUTRITION FACTS PER SERVING: 234 cal., 13 g total fat (3 g sat. fat), 4 mg chol., 242 mg sodium, 23 g carbo., 2 g fiber, 6 g pro.

mushroom & herb rice

The pairing of mushrooms with rice and Italian seasoning makes a savory side dish that takes almost no time at all to go from skillet to plate.

START TO FINISH: 20 minutes **MAKES:** 4 servings

1	tablespoon olive oil or butter
8	ounces fresh mushrooms, sliced
1	8.8-ounce pouch cooked whole grain brown rice or long grain rice
⅓	cup shredded carrot
2	green onions, chopped
2	tablespoons water
1	teaspoon dried Italian seasoning or thyme, crushed
¼	teaspoon salt
¼	cup finely shredded Parmesan cheese (1 ounce)

one In a large skillet heat oil over medium heat. Add mushrooms; cook until almost tender. Add rice, carrot, green onions, the water, Italian seasoning, and salt. Cook until heated through and vegetables are tender, stirring occasionally. Top servings with Parmesan cheese.

NUTRITION FACTS PER SERVING: 299 cal., 8 g total fat (3 g sat. fat), 4 mg chol., 241 mg sodium, 50 g carbo., 3 g fiber, 11 g pro.

nacho corn soup

If your kids love nachos, they will adore this quick-to-fix and spicy soup.

START TO FINISH: 15 minutes **MAKES:** 4 servings

- 2 cups milk
- 1 11-ounce can whole kernel corn with sweet peppers, drained
- 1 11-ounce can condensed nacho cheese soup
- ½ of a 4-ounce can (2 tablespoons) diced green chile peppers, undrained
- 1 tablespoon dried minced onion
- ¼ teaspoon ground cumin
- ¼ teaspoon dried oregano, crushed

  Tortilla chips, broken (optional)

one In a large saucepan stir together milk, corn, nacho cheese soup, chile peppers, dried minced onion, cumin, and oregano. Cook over medium heat until heated through, stirring frequently.

two If desired, top servings with tortilla chips.

NUTRITION FACTS PER SERVING: 219 cal., 8 g total fat (4 g sat. fat), 20 mg chol., 898 mg sodium, 29 g carbo., 4 g fiber, 10 g pro.

creamy carrot soup

For a touch of elegance, swirl sour cream or yogurt onto this rich, delicate-flavored soup. Put the sour cream or yogurt into a plastic squeeze bottle to make the swirling easy.

START TO FINISH: 15 minutes **MAKES:** 4 servings

2	cups half-and-half, light cream, or milk
4	teaspoons all-purpose flour
2	6-ounce jars junior carrot baby food
1½	teaspoons instant chicken bouillon granules
½	teaspoon curry powder or ¼ teaspoon dried dillweed
⅛	teaspoon onion salt
⅛	teaspoon black pepper

one In a medium saucepan stir together half-and-half and flour. Stir in carrot baby food, chicken bouillon granules, curry powder or dillweed, onion salt, and pepper. Cook and stir over medium-high heat until thickened and bubbly. Cook and stir for 1 minute more.

NUTRITION FACTS PER SERVING: 195 cal., 14 g total fat (9 g sat. fat), 44 mg chol., 471 mg sodium, 14 g carbo., 2 g fiber, 5 g pro.

speedy southwestern-style tomato soup

Purchased tomato soup will never be the same! Southwestern-style seasonings give it extra character and punch. For even more flavor, pass additional snipped cilantro to sprinkle on top.

START TO FINISH: 10 minutes **MAKES:** 5 or 6 servings

1	32-ounce jar ready-to-serve tomato soup
1	14½-ounce can Mexican-style stewed tomatoes, undrained
⅛	teaspoon ground cumin
	Dash cayenne pepper or several dashes bottled hot pepper sauce
2	tablespoons snipped fresh cilantro
¼	cup dairy sour cream

one In a large saucepan combine tomato soup, undrained tomatoes, cumin, and cayenne pepper or hot pepper sauce. Cover and cook over medium heat until heated through, stirring occasionally. Stir in cilantro. Top servings with sour cream.

NUTRITION FACTS PER SERVING: 125 cal., 2 g total fat (1 g sat. fat), 7 mg chol., 788 mg sodium, 23 g carbo., 2 g fiber, 3 g pro.

tomato-barley soup
with garden vegetables

Start with a can of soup; add zucchini, carrot, and green beans for freshness and color and barley for extra flavor. Serve the combo with crusty rolls and a cheese-and-meat tray, and Sunday night's supper is on the table!

START TO FINISH: 30 minutes **MAKES:** 4 servings

2   14-ounce cans vegetable broth

¾   cup quick-cooking barley

¾   cup thinly sliced carrot

1   teaspoon dried thyme, crushed

⅛   teaspoon black pepper

1   19-ounce can ready-to-serve tomato basil soup

2   cups coarsely chopped zucchini and/or yellow summer squash

1   cup loose-pack frozen cut green beans

one In a large saucepan combine broth, barley, carrot, thyme, and pepper. Bring to boiling; reduce heat. Cover and simmer for 10 minutes.

two Stir in tomato basil soup, zucchini, and green beans. Return to boiling; reduce heat. Cover and simmer for 8 to 10 minutes more or until vegetables and barley are tender.

NUTRITION FACTS PER SERVING: 197 cal., 3 g total fat (0 g sat. fat), 0 mg chol., 1,265 mg sodium, 40 g carbo., 6 g fiber, 7 g pro.

mashed potato soup

Thick, creamy, and topped with a dollop of
sour cream, this creative soup is like having
a well-dressed mashed potato in a bowl!

START TO FINISH: 15 minutes **MAKES:** 3 servings

1 20-ounce package refrigerated mashed potatoes

1 14-ounce can chicken broth

2 green onions, sliced

2 ounces Swiss, cheddar, or smoked Gouda cheese,
shredded (½ cup)

Dairy sour cream (optional)

one In a medium saucepan combine mashed potatoes,
broth, and green onions. Cook over medium-high heat just
until mixture reaches boiling, whisking to make nearly smooth.
Add cheese; whisk until cheese is melted. If desired, serve
with sour cream.

NUTRITION FACTS PER SERVING: 239 cal., 9 g total fat (4 g sat. fat),
17 mg chol., 917 mg sodium, 27 g carbo., 2 g fiber, 11 g pro.

asian pea pod salad

Fresh pea pods make this salad a real treat. Look for plump, crisp pods with a bright green color.

START TO FINISH: 20 minutes **MAKES:** 6 servings

- 6 cups torn romaine
- 2 cups fresh pea pods, trimmed and halved crosswise
- ⅓ cup bottled Italian salad dressing
- 1 tablespoon bottled hoisin sauce
- 1 tablespoon sesame seeds, toasted

one In a large salad bowl toss together romaine and pea pods. In a small bowl stir together salad dressing and hoisin sauce. Pour salad dressing mixture over romaine mixture; toss to coat. Sprinkle with sesame seeds.

NUTRITION FACTS PER SERVING: 98 cal., 7 g total fat (1 g sat. fat), 0 mg chol., 153 mg sodium, 6 g carbo., 2 g fiber, 2 g pro.

b.l.t. salad

If you think you'll miss the bread, top the salad with baked whole wheat croutons or serve with fresh crusty rolls.

START TO FINISH: 20 minutes **MAKES:** 8 servings

- 5 cups torn mixed salad greens or fresh spinach
- 2 cups grape or cherry tomatoes, halved
- 8 ounces bacon (about 10 slices), crisp-cooked, drained, and crumbled
- 2 hard-cooked eggs, peeled and chopped
- ⅓ cup bottled poppy seed salad dressing

one In a large bowl top greens with tomatoes, bacon, and chopped eggs. Drizzle with dressing. Toss well.

NUTRITION FACTS PER SERVING: 126 cal., 10 g total fat (3 g sat. fat), 62 mg chol., 231 mg sodium, 4 g carbo., 1 g fiber, 5 g pro.

mixed greens salad
with ginger vinaigrette

To make squash ribbons, draw a vegetable peeler down the length of the squash, cutting it into thin bands.

START TO FINISH: 20 minutes **MAKES:** 4 servings

¼	cup salad oil
¼	cup rice vinegar
2	teaspoons honey
1	teaspoon soy sauce
1	teaspoon grated fresh ginger
4	cups mixed baby salad greens
4	ounces fresh enoki mushrooms
1	small yellow summer squash or zucchini, cut into thin ribbons
1	small tomato, chopped

one For vinaigrette, in a screw-top jar combine oil, rice vinegar, honey, soy sauce, and ginger. Cover and shake well.

two On 4 salad plates, arrange greens, mushrooms, squash, and tomato. Drizzle with vinaigrette.

NUTRITION FACTS PER SERVING: 98 cal., 7 g total fat (1 g sat. fat), 0 mg chol., 51 mg sodium, 8 g carbo., 2 g fiber, 2 g pro.

make-ahead tip: Prepare vinaigrette up to 1 week ahead. Cover and store in the refrigerator. Shake well before using.

spinach, red onion & cherry tomato salad

Baby spinach dressed up with a fresh tarragon vinaigrette and a sprinkling of blue cheese is the perfect serve-along for chicken or pork.

START TO FINISH: 20 minutes **MAKES:** 4 servings

⅓	cup olive oil
3	tablespoons rice vinegar
2	tablespoons snipped fresh tarragon
1	tablespoon finely chopped shallot
¼	teaspoon salt
	Dash black pepper
8	cups fresh baby spinach
1	cup cherry tomatoes and/or yellow pear-shape cherry tomatoes, halved or quartered
¼	cup thinly sliced red onion
2	ounces blue cheese, crumbled

one For dressing, in a screw-top jar combine oil, rice vinegar, tarragon, shallot, salt, and pepper. Cover and shake well.

two Arrange the spinach and tomatoes on a platter. Top with red onion and blue cheese. Drizzle with dressing.

NUTRITION FACTS PER SERVING: 236 cal., 22 g total fat (5 g sat. fat), 13 mg chol., 449 mg sodium, 5 g carbo., 2 g fiber, 5 g pro.

cheesy apple coleslaw

This simple slaw, dressed up with apple and cheddar cheese, is scrumptious with roasted or grilled beef or pork. Refrigerate any leftovers in an airtight container and use within a day or so.

START TO FINISH: 30 minutes **MAKES:** 10 servings

4	cups finely shredded cabbage (12 ounces)
4	ounces cheddar cheese, cubed
2	medium carrots, shredded
1	large apple, cored and chopped
1	stalk celery, sliced
½	cup mayonnaise or salad dressing
1	tablespoon vinegar
1	teaspoon sugar
½	teaspoon salt
½	teaspoon black pepper

one In a large bowl combine cabbage, cheese, carrots, apple, and celery. In a small bowl combine mayonnaise, vinegar, sugar, salt, and pepper. Pour mayonnaise mixture over the cabbage mixture; toss to combine.

NUTRITION FACTS PER SERVING: 149 cal., 13 g total fat (4 g sat. fat), 18 mg chol., 265 mg sodium, 6 g carbo., 2 g fiber, 4 g pro.

make-ahead tip: Cover and chill salad for up to 4 hours. Stir before serving.

citrus salad with glazed pecans

Maple syrup works magic here. It brings out the sweetness of the pecans and oranges and is a marvelous complement to the tangy spinach and savory bacon.

START TO FINISH: 30 minutes **MAKES:** 4 servings

3	tablespoons red wine vinegar
3	tablespoons olive oil
2	tablespoons Dijon-style mustard
1	tablespoon pure maple syrup or maple-flavored syrup
⅓	cup coarsely chopped pecans
2	tablespoons pure maple syrup or maple-flavored syrup
2	slices bacon, cut up
½	of a medium red onion, cut into thin wedges
6	ounces fresh baby spinach, washed and stems removed
4	blood oranges or oranges, peeled, seeded, and thinly sliced

one In a screw-top jar combine red wine vinegar, oil, Dijon-style mustard, and the 1 tablespoon maple syrup. Cover and shake well. Set aside.

two In a medium skillet cook pecans in the 2 tablespoons maple syrup over medium heat for 3 to 4 minutes or until lightly toasted. Spread nuts on foil; cool. Break nuts into clusters.

three Meanwhile, in a small saucepan cook bacon and red onion wedges until bacon is crisp, stirring occasionally. Remove from heat.

four To serve, divide spinach and oranges among 4 salad plates. Top with bacon-onion mixture and pecans; drizzle with dressing.

NUTRITION FACTS PER SERVING: 254 cal., 19 g total fat (3 g sat. fat), 3 mg chol., 142 mg sodium, 20 g carbo., 6 g fiber, 14 g pro.

peanut butter fruit salad

This fruity and fun dish makes a great kid-friendly snack or side dish.

START TO FINISH: 15 minutes **MAKES:** 6 servings

- 1   8-ounce can pineapple tidbits (juice pack)
- 2   medium carrots, shredded
- 1   11-ounce can mandarin orange sections, drained
- ⅔   cup chopped apple
- ½   cup raisins and/or dried tart cherries
- ⅓   cup apple-cinnamon low-fat yogurt
- 2   tablespoons peanut butter
- 1   tablespoon shelled sunflower seeds

one Drain the pineapple tidbits, reserving 1 tablespoon of the juice; set juice aside. If desired, set aside some of the shredded carrots for garnish. In a medium bowl stir together pineapple tidbits, the remaining carrots, oranges, apple, and raisins and/or cherries.

two In a small bowl stir together yogurt, peanut butter, and reserved pineapple juice. Add to fruit mixture; stir to coat. Sprinkle with sunflower seeds and, if desired, reserved carrots.

NUTRITION FACTS PER SERVING: 152 cal., 4 g total fat (1 g sat. fat), 1 mg chol., 44 mg sodium, 29 g carbo., 3 g fiber, 3 g pro.

orange dream fruit salad

Combining orange yogurt with sweet mandarin orange sections and other fruits is a refreshing way to perk up a meal.

START TO FINISH: 15 minutes **MAKES:** 4 to 6 servings

1	cup chopped, peeled, seeded mango or papaya
1	11-ounce can mandarin orange sections, drained
1	cup seedless red and/or green grapes, halved
½	cup orange yogurt
¼	teaspoon poppy seeds

one In a medium bowl combine mango or papaya, mandarin oranges, and grapes. In a small bowl stir together yogurt and poppy seeds. Gently stir yogurt mixture into fruit mixture until combined.

NUTRITION FACTS PER SERVING: 136 cal., 1 g total fat (0 g sat. fat), 2 mg chol., 26 mg sodium, 32 g carbo., 2 g fiber, 2 g pro.

raspberry pecan salad

This inventive salad is perfect for summer when you can find fresh raspberries in the store or pluck them from your backyard raspberry patch. Buttery-rich toasted pecans deliver some crunch to complement the soft textures of the fruit and mixed greens.

START TO FINISH: 25 minutes **MAKES:** 8 servings

- ⅓ cup raspberry spreadable fruit
- ¼ cup raspberry vinegar
- ¼ cup salad oil
- 1 tablespoon honey
- 1 teaspoon poppy seeds
- 8 cups torn mixed salad greens
- 1 cup fresh raspberries
- 1 medium avocado, pitted, peeled, and sliced
- 1 cup sliced fresh mushrooms
- ½ cup pecans, toasted

one For dressing, in a blender combine spreadable fruit, raspberry vinegar, oil, honey, and poppy seeds. Cover and blend until combined. (Or in a medium bowl whisk together the ingredients.) Set aside.

two In a large salad bowl combine greens, raspberries, avocado, mushrooms, and pecans. Drizzle dressing over the salad. Toss to combine.

NUTRITION FACTS PER SERVING: 201 cal., 16 g total fat (2 g sat. fat), 0 mg chol., 10 mg sodium, 16 g carbo., 4 g fiber, 2 g pro.

fruited wild rice & spinach salad

The beguiling combination of fruit and wild rice will have you hooked with the first bite. Fresh blueberries make a lovely substitute if raspberries aren't available.

START TO FINISH: 30 minutes **MAKES:** 6 servings

6	cups torn fresh spinach
2	cups cooled, cooked wild rice
1	cup seedless green grapes, halved
¼	cup shelled sunflower seeds
¼	cup white balsamic vinegar or cider vinegar
¼	cup olive oil
1	tablespoon honey
2	teaspoons snipped fresh basil
	or ½ teaspoon dried basil, crushed
¼	teaspoon salt
¼	teaspoon freshly ground black pepper
1	cup fresh raspberries
2	oranges, peeled and sectioned

one In a large salad bowl combine spinach, wild rice, grapes, and sunflower seeds. For dressing, in a screw-top jar combine vinegar, oil, honey, basil, salt, and pepper. Cover and shake well. Pour over spinach mixture; toss to coat.

two Gently fold in raspberries and orange sections.

NUTRITION FACTS PER SERVING: 235 cal., 13 g total fat (2 g sat. fat), 0 mg chol., 139 mg sodium, 28 g carbo., 7 g fiber, 5 g pro.

blueberry gems

Plump and deliciously sweet blueberries make these orange-accented muffins scrumptious. Serve them plain or with a dab of honey. For a special treat, combine honey with some light cream cheese and spread the mixture on the muffin tops.

PREP: 10 minutes **BAKE:** 15 minutes **COOL:** 5 minutes **MAKES:** 36 muffins

	Nonstick cooking spray
1½	cups all-purpose flour
¼	cup sugar
1½	teaspoons baking powder
2	egg whites
⅔	cup orange juice
2	tablespoons cooking oil
1	teaspoon vanilla
1	cup fresh or frozen blueberries

one Lightly coat thirty-six 1¾-inch muffin cups with cooking spray. In a medium bowl stir together flour, sugar, baking powder, and ¼ teaspoon salt. Make a well in center of flour mixture; set aside. In bowl stir together egg whites, orange juice, oil, and vanilla. Add egg white mixture all at once to flour mixture; stir just until moistened. Fold in blueberries. Spoon into prepared muffin cups, filling each about **two-thirds** full.

two Bake in a 400°F oven for 15 to 18 minutes or until toothpick inserted into centers comes out clean. Cool in pans on wire racks for 5 minutes.

NUTRITION FACTS PER MUFFIN: 35 cal., 1 g total fat (0 g sat. fat), 0 mg chol., 36 mg sodium, 6 g carbo., 0 g fiber, 1 g pro.

honey-nut corn muffins

In only minutes you can transform plain corn muffins into a special treat that your family won't be able to resist. Chopped pecans add a rich nutty flavor while honey provides a touch of sweetness to complement the earthy cornmeal.

PREP: 10 minutes **BAKE:** 15 minutes **MAKES:** 6 to 8 muffins

1	8½-ounce package corn muffin mix
½	cup chopped pecans
2	tablespoons honey

one Grease six to eight 2½-inch muffin cups; set aside.

two Prepare corn muffin mix according to package directions, except stir in nuts and honey. Spoon batter into prepared muffin cups, filling each about three-fourths full.

three Bake in a 400°F oven about 15 minutes or until golden brown.

NUTRITION FACTS PER MUFFIN: 262 cal., 12 g total fat (1 g sat. fat), 36 mg chol., 298 mg sodium, 36 g carbo., 1 g fiber, 5 g pro.

honey & poppy seed biscuits

Cream-style cottage cheese, honey, and poppy seeds transform plain biscuits made from a mix into an irresistible treat.

PREP: 15 minutes **BAKE:** 10 minutes **MAKES:** 10 to 12 biscuits

½	cup cream-style cottage cheese
¼	cup milk
2	tablespoons honey
2¼	cups packaged biscuit mix
1	tablespoon poppy seeds

one In a food processor/ blender combine cottage cheese, milk, and honey. Cover and blend until nearly smooth.

two Prepare biscuit mix according to package directions for rolled biscuits, except substitute the pureed mixture and poppy seeds for the liquid called for on the package.

three Bake in a 450°F oven about 10 minutes or until bottoms are lightly browned.

NUTRITION FACTS PER BISCUIT: 148 cal., 5 g total fat (1 g sat. fat), 3 mg chol., 394 mg sodium, 21 g carbo., 1 g fiber, 4 g pro.

sticky lemon pinwheels

Creamy, luscious lemon curd is a wonderfully versatile ingredient to have on hand. It brings a touch of the sun to these pinwheels with its cheerful yellow color and its rich and tangy flavor. Serve these pinwheels at holiday breakfasts, special brunches, and summer tea parties!

PREP: 10 minutes **BAKE:** 15 minutes **MAKES:** 12 pinwheels

⅓ cup purchased lemon curd or orange curd

¼ cup sliced almonds, toasted

1 11-ounce package (12) refrigerated breadsticks

one Grease an 8x1½-inch round baking pan; set aside. In a small bowl stir together lemon curd and almonds. Spread mixture evenly into the bottom of the prepared baking pan.

two Separate, but do not uncoil, the breadsticks. Arrange coiled dough over the lemon mixture in the baking pan.

three Bake in a 375°F oven for 15 to 18 minutes or until golden brown. Immediately invert onto a platter. Spread any remaining lemon mixture in the pan over the pinwheels. Serve warm.

NUTRITION FACTS PER PINWHEEL: 118 cal., 4 g total fat (1 g sat. fat), 7 mg chol., 200 mg sodium, 19 g carbo., 2 g fiber, 3 g pro.

apricot-peach cobbler

Biscuit mix is the key to this sunny cobbler that is ready in only minutes. Chances are it will take less than that for your happy diners to eat it up!

PREP: 10 minutes **BAKE:** per package directions **MAKES:** 6 servings

- 1 15-ounce can unpeeled apricot halves in light syrup
- 1 7.75-ounce packet cinnamon swirl biscuit mix (Bisquick® complete)
- 1 21-ounce can peach pie filling
- 1 teaspoon vanilla

   Vanilla ice cream (optional)

one Drain apricot halves, reserving syrup. Prepare biscuit mix according to package directions, except use ½ cup of the reserved apricot syrup in place of the water called for on the package. Bake according to package directions.

two Meanwhile, in a medium saucepan combine pie filling, drained apricots, and any remaining apricot syrup. Heat through. Remove from heat; stir in vanilla. Spoon fruit mixture into bowls. Top with warm biscuits. If desired, serve with vanilla ice cream.

NUTRITION FACTS PER SERVING: 284 cal., 4 g total fat (0 g sat. fat), 0 mg chol., 346 mg sodium, 59 g carbo., 2 g fiber, 3 g pro.

caramel apple pastry

Refrigerated piecrust is a dessert lover's best friend. It's versatile, convenient, and best of all—it tastes wonderful, especially when paired with the sweet ingredients in this delectable recipe.

PREP: 15 minutes **BAKE:** 15 minutes **COOL:** 5 minutes **MAKES:** 6 servings

- ½ of a 15-ounce package (1 crust) rolled refrigerated unbaked piecrust
- 1 tablespoon butter
- 2 20-ounce cans sliced apples, well drained
- ½ cup packed brown sugar
- 1 tablespoon lemon juice
- 1 teaspoon apple pie spice or ground cinnamon
- 1 tablespoon purchased cinnamon-sugar*

  Cinnamon or vanilla ice cream (optional)

  Caramel ice cream topping (optional)

one Bring piecrust to room temperature in microwave oven according to package directions; set aside. In a large ovenproof skillet melt butter; stir in drained apple slices, brown sugar, lemon juice, and apple pie spice. Spread evenly in skillet. Cook over high heat until bubbly.

two Meanwhile, on a lightly floured surface, unroll piecrust. Sprinkle piecrust with cinnamon-sugar; rub into piecrust with your fingers. Carefully place the piecrust over bubbly apple mixture in skillet, cinnamon-sugar side up. Tuck in piecrust around edge of skillet using a spatula to press edge down slightly.

three Bake in a 450°F oven about 15 minutes or until piecrust is golden. Cool for 5 minutes. Carefully invert skillet onto a serving platter; remove skillet. Serve warm. If desired, serve with ice cream and caramel topping.

NUTRITION FACTS PER SERVING: 381 cal., 12 g total fat (5 g sat. fat), 12 mg chol., 159 mg sodium, 69 g carbo., 3 g fiber, 1 g pro.

*test kitchen tip: To make your own cinnamon-sugar, in a small bowl stir together 1 tablespoon granulated sugar and ¼ teaspoon ground cinnamon.

baked fruit ambrosia

Although it's an awesome dessert, this warm cinnamon-spiced fruit makes a delightful side dish for breakfast or brunch too.

PREP: 10 minutes **BAKE:** 15 minutes **MAKES:** 4 servings

2   medium oranges

1   8-ounce can pineapple tidbits (juice pack), drained

¼   teaspoon ground cinnamon

2   tablespoons shredded coconut

     Fresh raspberries (optional)

one Finely shred ½ teaspoon peel from one of the oranges; set peel aside. Peel and section oranges. Cut orange sections into bite-size pieces. Divide orange pieces and pineapple among four 6-ounce custard cups. Sprinkle with orange peel and cinnamon. Top with coconut.

two Bake in a 350°F oven about 15 minutes or until fruit is heated through and coconut is golden brown. If desired, garnish with fresh raspberries. Serve warm.

NUTRITION FACTS PER SERVING: 66 cal., 1 g total fat (1 g sat. fat), 0 mg chol., 12 mg sodium, 14 g carbo., 2 g fiber, 1 g pro.

quick strawberry shortcakes

When you're really in a hurry to savor these shortcakes, use purchased whipped cream that is available in a handy pressurized can.

PREP: 10 minutes **BAKE:** per package directions **MAKES:** 4 servings

- 4 frozen unbaked buttermilk biscuits
- ⅓ cup strawberry jelly
- 1 pint fresh strawberries, sliced
- ½ cup whipping cream
- ⅓ cup purchased lemon curd or strawberry curd

one Bake biscuits according to package directions. Cool. Meanwhile, in a small saucepan heat the strawberry jelly just until melted. Place berries in a bowl; add jelly. Toss until mixed. Set aside. In a chilled medium bowl beat whipping cream with chilled beaters of an electric mixer on medium speed just until soft peaks form (tips curl).

two Split biscuits horizontally. Spread bottoms with fruit curd; replace tops. Place biscuits on dessert plates. Spoon on berry mixture and whipped cream.

NUTRITION FACTS PER SERVING: 472 cal., 22 g total fat (10 g sat. fat), 61 mg chol., 619 mg sodium, 48 g carbo., 5 g fiber, 5 g pro.

tropical fruit shortcakes

Shortcake isn't just for the summer anymore. With this inspired and easy recipe, you can enjoy it whenever you wish.

PREP: 10 minutes **BAKE:** per package directions **MAKES:** 5 servings

1	10.2-ounce package (5) refrigerated large homestyle buttermilk biscuits
	Milk
1	to 2 teaspoons coarse sugar or granulated sugar
1	8-ounce container low-fat vanilla yogurt
¼	cup coconut
¼	of an 8-ounce container frozen whipped dessert topping, thawed
1½	cups sliced or chopped fresh fruit (such as kiwifruit, bananas, and/or refrigerated mango or papaya)

one Place biscuits on an ungreased baking sheet. Brush tops with milk; sprinkle with sugar. Bake according to package directions. Meanwhile, in a small bowl stir together yogurt and coconut. Fold in whipped dessert topping. Split warm biscuits. Divide fruit among biscuit bottoms; top with some of the yogurt mixture. Replace biscuit tops. Top with remaining yogurt mixture.

NUTRITION FACTS PER SERVING: 328 cal., 13 g total fat (6 g sat. fat), 2 mg chol., 689 mg sodium, 47 g carbo., 3 g fiber, 7 g pro.

a billow of berries 'n' brownies

A dazzling dessert doesn't get much easier—or
more delicious—than this.

START TO FINISH: 15 minutes **MAKES:** 12 servings

4 cups fresh red raspberries

4 to 5 tablespoons sugar

2 teaspoons finely shredded orange peel

2 cups whipping cream

¼ cup raspberry liqueur (Chambord) (optional)

4 3-inch squares purchased unfrosted brownies
(such as milk chocolate, blond, or marbled brownies),
cut into irregular chunks

one Set aside 8 to 10 of the raspberries. In a medium bowl
combine the remaining berries, the sugar, and orange peel.
Spoon berry mixture into a 1- to 1½-quart compote dish or
serving bowl.

two In a chilled bowl beat whipping cream and liqueur (if
using) with chilled beaters of an electric mixer on medium
speed until soft peaks form (tips curl). Spoon on top of
raspberry mixture. Top whipped cream with brownie
chunks and the reserved raspberries.

NUTRITION FACTS PER SERVING: 263 cal., 19 g total fat (10 g sat. fat),
69 mg chol., 63 mg sodium, 23 g carbo., 5 g fiber, 3 g pro.

gooey brownie cups

Toss together brownies, marshmallows, and peanut butter pieces for a to-die-for dessert.

PREP: 10 minutes **BAKE:** 7 minutes **MAKES:** 4 servings

- 4 purchased unfrosted chocolate brownies, cut into irregular-size chunks
- 1 cup tiny marshmallows
- ¼ cup peanut butter flavored pieces and/or milk chocolate pieces
- 2 tablespoons chopped cocktail peanuts
     Chocolate or vanilla ice cream
     Chocolate-flavored syrup

one In a large bowl toss together brownie chunks, marshmallows, peanut butter flavored pieces, and peanuts. Divide among 4 baking dishes.

two Bake in a 350°F oven for 7 to 8 minutes or until warm and marshmallows are golden brown. Serve with ice cream and drizzle with chocolate syrup.

NUTRITION FACTS PER SERVING: 581 cal., 28 g total fat (9 g sat. fat), 63 mg chol., 280 mg sodium, 78 g carbo., 3 g fiber, 9 g pro.

bananas suzette over pound cake

The "suzette" portion of this dessert refers to the classic combination of orange-butter sauce and orange liqueur. Here it gives bananas the royal treatment.

START TO FINISH: 15 minutes **MAKES:** 4 servings

- 2 tablespoons butter or margarine
- ½ of a 10¾-ounce package frozen pound cake, thawed and cut into 4 slices
- 2 medium ripe, yet firm, bananas
- 3 tablespoons sugar
- 2 tablespoons orange liqueur or orange juice
- 2 tablespoons orange juice
- ⅛ teaspoon ground nutmeg
- 1 cup vanilla ice cream

one In a medium skillet melt 1 tablespoon of the butter over medium heat. Add pound cake slices; cook for 1 to 2 minutes or until browned, turning once. Remove from skillet; set aside.

two Peel bananas; bias-slice each banana into 8 pieces. In the same skillet combine sugar, 2 tablespoons liqueur or orange juice, 2 tablespoons orange juice, and the remaining 1 tablespoon butter. Heat about 1 minute or until butter melts and sugar begins to dissolve. Add the bananas; heat for 2 to 4 minutes more or just until bananas are tender, stirring once. Stir in nutmeg.

three To serve, place a small scoop of vanilla ice cream on each pound cake slice. Spoon bananas and sauce over ice cream and pound cake slices.

NUTRITION FACTS PER SERVING: 394 cal., 18 g total fat (11 g sat. fat), 74 mg chol., 229 mg sodium, 53 g carbo., 2 g fiber, 4 g pro.

coffee & almond parfaits

If you don't have parfait glasses, use clear glass dessert bowls or short drinking glasses to achieve the lovely layered effect.

START TO FINISH: 30 minutes **MAKES:** 4 servings

½ of a 10¾-ounce package frozen pound cake, cut into ¾-inch cubes

2 8-ounce cartons vanilla low-fat yogurt

½ of an 8-ounce container frozen whipped dessert topping, thawed

2 tablespoons coffee liqueur or strong brewed coffee

4 amaretti cookies, coarsely crushed

one In a shallow baking pan arrange cake cubes in an even layer. Bake in a 350°F oven about 15 minutes or until golden brown, stirring twice. Cool. Meanwhile, in a medium bowl stir together yogurt and whipped topping.

two Layer ¼ cup of the cake cubes in each of four parfait glasses. Top with half of the yogurt mixture and remaining cake cubes. Stir liqueur or coffee into remaining yogurt mixture; spoon over cake cubes. Sprinkle with the coarsely crushed cookies. Serve immediately.

NUTRITION FACTS PER SERVING: 368 cal., 14 g total fat (10 g sat. fat), 47 mg chol., 212 mg sodium, 46 g carbo., 0 g fiber, 8 g pro.

cherry trifles

Although you can make them in a flash, these cherry trifles also are a great make-ahead choice for days when you know you'll be pressed for time during the dinner hour.

START TO FINISH: 10 minutes **MAKES:** 4 servings

1	8-ounce container plain low-fat yogurt
2	tablespoons cherry preserves
½	teaspoon vanilla
2	cups angel food cake cubes (about 4 ounces purchased cake)
1	15-ounce can pitted dark sweet cherries, drained
¼	cup purchased glazed walnuts, chopped

one In a small bowl stir together yogurt, cherry preserves, and vanilla; set aside.

two Divide half of the cake cubes among 4 parfait glasses or dessert dishes. Top cake cubes in parfait glasses or dessert dishes with half of the dark sweet cherries; spoon half of the yogurt mixture over cherries. Sprinkle with half of the nuts. Repeat layers.

NUTRITION FACTS PER SERVING: 280 cal., 7 g total fat (2 g sat. fat), 5 mg chol., 198 mg sodium, 51 g carbo., 2 g fiber, 7 g pro.

make-ahead tip: Cover and chill for up to 4 hours before serving.

piecrust cookies

These cookies are the ultimate in convenience and taste great too. Another time, try the cookies with ground cinnamon or chocolate sprinkles in place of the pumpkin pie spice.

PREP: 15 minutes **BAKE:** 8 minutes **MAKES:** about 25 cookies

- ½ of a 15-ounce package rolled refrigerated unbaked piecrust (1 crust)
- 1 tablespoon butter or margarine, melted
- 2 tablespoons packed brown sugar
- ½ to 1 teaspoon pumpkin pie spice or apple pie spice

one Unroll piecrust according to package directions using the microwave method. Place on a lightly floured surface. Brush piecrust with melted butter. Sprinkle with brown sugar and pumpkin pie spice. Use a pastry wheel or pizza cutter to cut dough into 1½- to 2-inch square cookies (some of the edges may be smaller). Place on an ungreased large cookie sheet, leaving a small space between cookies.

two Bake in a 400°F oven about 8 minutes or until golden brown. Serve warm or cooled.

NUTRITION FACTS PER COOKIE: 47 cal., 3 g total fat (1 g sat. fat), 3 mg chol., 35 mg sodium, 5 g carbo., 0 g fiber, 0 g pro.

mocha cookies

Refrigerated sugar cookie dough makes these chocolate morsels super easy. Put on a fresh pot of java while the cookies bake and you'll soon be ready for a relaxing afternoon coffee break.

PREP: 10 minutes **BAKE:** 10 minutes per batch **MAKES:** 20 cookies

- 3 tablespoons sugar
- 2 tablespoons unsweetened cocoa powder
- 1 tablespoon instant espresso coffee powder or 2 tablespoons instant coffee crystals, crushed
- 1 18-ounce package refrigerated portioned sugar cookie dough
- 2 tablespoons milk

one In a small bowl stir together sugar, cocoa powder, and espresso powder. Break cookie dough into portions. Roll each cookie dough portion in milk, then in the sugar mixture. Place cookie dough portions on an ungreased large cookie sheet.

two Bake in a 350°F oven for 10 to 12 minutes or until edges are set. Transfer to a wire rack; cool.

NUTRITION FACTS PER COOKIE: 123 cal., 5 g total fat (1 g sat. fat), 10 mg chol., 82 mg sodium, 18 g carbo., 1 g fiber, 1 g pro.

chewy granola bars

Pop these homemade snacks into lunch bags or knapsacks for lunchtime treats. Or leave some out on the kitchen counter alongside some fresh fruit for kids to enjoy as an afterschool pick-me-up.

PREP: 15 minutes **CHILL:** 5 minutes **MAKES:** 16 bars

  3   cups tiny marshmallows (½ of a 10-ounce bag)
  2   tablespoons butter or margarine
  2   cups granola with raisins
  ¾   cup crisp rice cereal
  ¼   cup sunflower nuts

one Line a 9×9×2-inch baking pan with foil. Butter foil; set aside. In a medium saucepan combine marshmallows and butter. Cook and stir over medium heat until marshmallows are melted. Stir in granola, rice cereal, and sunflower nuts. Press mixture into prepared pan.

two Cool in refrigerator about 5 minutes or until set. Lift by foil to remove from pan. Peel off foil and cut into bars.

NUTRITION FACTS PER BAR: 105 cal., 3 g total fat (1 g sat. fat), 4 mg chol., 75 mg sodium, 19 g carbo., 1 g fiber, 2 g pro.

strawberry shortbread sandwiches

A little cream cheese and some strawberry preserves turn ordinary shortbread cookies into a scrumptious treat. Serve the sandwiches with afternoon tea or with a glass of milk.

START TO FINISH: 15 minutes **MAKES:** 16 cookie sandwiches

2   ounces tub-style reduced-fat cream cheese
1   tablespoon strawberry preserves
    Red food coloring (optional)
32 plain and/or chocolate shortbread cookies

one In a small bowl stir together cream cheese and preserves. If desired, stir in a drop of red food coloring. Spread cheese mixture on flat sides of half of the cookies. Top with the remaining cookies, flat sides down.

NUTRITION FACTS PER COOKIE SANDWICH: 36 cal., 1 g total fat (1 g sat. fat), 2 mg chol., 38 mg sodium, 6 g carbo., 0 g fiber, 1 g pro.

cookies & cream

If oatmeal cookies are not available, use your favorite kind as long as they are soft enough to be cut with a fork.

START TO FINISH: 15 minutes **MAKES:** 6 to 8 servings

- ½ cup whipping cream
- 2 tablespoons honey
- ½ cup dairy sour cream
- 18 to 24 purchased large soft oatmeal cookies

  Honey

one In a small chilled bowl beat whipping cream and the 2 tablespoons honey with chilled beaters of an electric mixer on medium speed until soft peaks form (tips curl). Fold in sour cream.

two To serve, lay 1 oatmeal cookie on each of 6 to 8 dessert plates. Top each with a spoonful of the whipped cream mixture. Top each with another cookie and another spoon of whipped cream mixture. Top each stack with a third cookie and more whipped cream mixture. Drizzle with additional honey.

NUTRITION FACTS PER SERVING: 456 cal., 21 g total fat (10 g sat. fat), 43 mg chol., 310 mg sodium, 61 g carbo., 2 g fiber, 5 g pro.

make-ahead tip: Prepare whipped cream mixture; cover and chill for up to 1 hour before serving. Assemble individual desserts just before serving.

raspberry & chocolate tulips

Miniature phyllo dough shells are a real time saver for making desserts and appetizers. Here they're filled with raspberries, chocolate syrup, and whipped cream for elegant bite-size mini tarts.

START TO FINISH: 15 minutes **MAKES:** 15 tulips

½	cup frozen raspberries
2	tablespoons sugar
1	2.1-ounce package (15) miniature phyllo dough shells
4	teaspoons chocolate-flavored syrup
15	small squirts from a 7-ounce can pressurized whipped dessert topping
1½	tablespoons sliced almonds (optional)

one In a small saucepan combine raspberries and sugar. Cook over medium heat, stirring frequently, for 3 to 5 minutes or just until the sugar is melted and raspberries are completely thawed. Remove from heat; cool until slightly warm or room temperature.

two To serve, place the phyllo dough shells on a platter. Spoon about ½ teaspoon of the raspberry mixture into the bottom of each shell. Top with about ¼ teaspoon of the chocolate-flavored syrup and a squirt of whipped dessert topping. If desired, sprinkle with almonds. Serve immediately.

NUTRITION FACTS PER TULIP: 46 cal., 2 g total fat (0 g sat. fat), 0 mg chol., 11 mg sodium, 6 g carbo., 0 g fiber, 0 g pro.

lemon meringue cookie tarts

Refreshing lemon pudding is the easy base for these darling and delicious meringue tarts.

START TO FINISH: 20 minutes **MAKES:** 6 tarts

2   3½- to 4-ounce containers lemon pudding (prepared pudding cups), chilled

1   teaspoon finely shredded lemon peel (optional)

¼   of an 8-ounce container frozen whipped dessert topping, thawed

12   vanilla-flavored bite-size meringue cookies

6   3½-inch graham cracker tart shells (one 4-ounce package)

one Stir together chilled pudding and, if desired, lemon peel. Fold in whipped topping. Coarsely crush half of the cookies. Spoon half of the pudding mixture into tart shells; sprinkle with crushed cookies. Top with remaining pudding mixture and whole cookies.

NUTRITION FACTS PER TART: 221 cal., 9 g total fat (3 g sat. fat), 0 mg chol., 176 mg sodium, 33 g carbo., 1 g fiber, 2 g pro.

fast & fruity banana split tarts

Banana, strawberry, pineapple, and chocolate flavors meld to create a tantalizing filling for phyllo dough shells. They're perfect for a kid's birthday party or as a sweet ending to a summer meal.

START TO FINISH: 10 minutes **MAKES:** 15 tarts

1	8-ounce tub cream cheese with pineapple
¼	cup strawberry preserves
1	2.1-ounce package (15) miniature phyllo dough shells
1	banana, thinly sliced
⅓	cup chocolate ice cream topping

one For filling, in a small bowl combine cream cheese and preserves; beat with an electric mixer on medium speed until light and fluffy. Spoon filling into phyllo shells.

two To serve, divide banana slices among shells. Drizzle with ice cream topping. Serve immediately.

NUTRITION FACTS PER TART: 115 cal., 6 g total fat (3 g sat. fat), 13 mg chol., 63 mg sodium, 14 g carbo., 0 g fiber, 1 g pro.

make-ahead directions: Prepare and spoon filling into tarts as directed. Cover and refrigerate for up to 4 hours. Just before serving, add banana slices and drizzle with ice cream topping.

fruit-filled waffle bowls

These cones are a great way to get your kids to eat more fruit. Let them choose their favorite pudding flavor and their favorite fruits.

START TO FINISH: 15 minutes **MAKES:** 4 servings

1	4-serving-size package instant lemon or white chocolate pudding mix
1⅓	cups milk
1	cup fresh fruit (such as blueberries, sliced kiwi fruit, sliced strawberries, sliced bananas, or raspberries)
4	waffle ice cream bowls or large waffle ice cream cones
	Fresh mint leaves (optional)

one Prepare pudding according to package directions, except use the 1⅓ cups milk. Spoon fruit into waffle bowls or cones. Top with pudding. If desired, garnish with fresh mint. Serve immediately.

NUTRITION FACTS PER SERVING: 196 cal., 3 g total fat (1 g sat. fat), 6 mg chol., 399 mg sodium, 40 g carbo., 1 g fiber, 3 g pro.

banana tostadas

Tortillas—great with meat, chiles, and cheese—are just as nice piled on top of the crisp rounds. Think of these as quick-and-easy Mexican dessert pizzas!

START TO FINISH: 20 minutes **MAKES:** 4 servings

- 1 cup sliced strawberries
- ½ cup cubed honeydew melon or cantaloupe
- 2 kiwifruit, peeled and sliced
- 2 tablespoons snipped fresh mint
- 2 teaspoons honey
- 2 teaspoons lime juice
- 2 7- to 8-inch whole wheat flour tortillas
- 2 tablespoons tub-style cream cheese with strawberries
- 1 medium banana, sliced
- 2 tablespoons crushed graham crackers
  Ground cinnamon
  Honey (optional)
  Vanilla yogurt (optional)

one In a medium bowl combine strawberries, melon, and kiwifruit. Stir in mint, the 2 teaspoons honey, and the lime juice. Set aside.

two In a large skillet heat each of the tortillas over medium heat for 2 to 4 minutes or until browned and crisp, turning once. Cool.

three Spread each tortilla with 1 tablespoon of the cream cheese. Top each tortilla with half of the banana slices, half of the crushed graham crackers, and a dash cinnamon. Top with fruit mixture. If desired, drizzle with additional honey and/or yogurt. Cut into wedges to serve.

NUTRITION FACTS PER SERVING: 189 cal., 4 g total fat (2 g sat. fat), 8 mg chol., 235 mg sodium, 36 g carbo., 4 g fiber, 4 g pro.

cannoli

Rich ricotta cheese gives this traditional Italian pastry its distinctive and delicious flavor. Using purchased cannoli shells, you can easily make these treats for holiday buffets and dessert parties.

START TO FINISH: 15 minutes **MAKES:** 6 servings

¾	cup ricotta cheese
⅓	cup miniature semisweet chocolate pieces
3	tablespoons sugar
¾	teaspoon vanilla
¼	teaspoon ground cinnamon
¾	cup frozen whipped dessert topping, thawed
6	purchased cannoli shells

one In a small bowl combine ricotta, chocolate pieces, sugar, vanilla, and cinnamon. Fold in whipped topping. Spoon mixture into a heavy plastic bag.

two Snip off corner of bag; pipe filling into shells.

NUTRITION FACTS PER SERVING: 263 cal., 16 g total fat (6 g sat. fat), 16 mg chol., 36 mg sodium, 26 g carbo., 2 g fiber, 6 g pro.

triple dipster strawberries

Raw sugar is usually available in the baking products aisle of supermarkets. There are two popular types—Demerara and Turbinado. Either one will be delicious with the fresh strawberries.

START TO FINISH: 20 minutes **MAKES:** 4 servings

4	cups large strawberries with stems
1	8-ounce carton dairy sour cream
½	teaspoon ground cinnamon
½	cup coarsely chopped macadamia nuts, toasted
½	cup raw sugar or packed brown sugar
¼	cup chocolate-covered coffee beans, coarsely chopped

one Wash strawberries; drain well on paper towels. Place in a serving bowl.

two In a small bowl stir together sour cream and cinnamon. Place sour cream mixture, macadamia nuts, raw or brown sugar, and coffee beans in separate small serving dishes or bowls.

three To serve, dip strawberries first in sour cream mixture, then in macadamia nuts, sugar, and/or coffee beans, as desired.

NUTRITION FACTS PER SERVING: 415 cal., 27 g total fat (10 g sat. fat), 25 mg chol., 87 mg sodium, 45 g carbo., 5 g fiber, 4 g pro.

tropical fruit cups

Fresh mango and strawberries layered with yogurt and whipped dessert topping make terrific sundaes for youngsters and adults alike.

START TO FINISH: 10 minutes **MAKES:** 2 servings

1	8-ounce carton piña colada yogurt or other flavor low-fat yogurt
¼	teaspoon vanilla
¼	cup frozen whipped dessert topping, thawed
1	cup cubed mango or papaya
½	cup sliced fresh strawberries
1	tablespoon coconut, toasted

one In a small bowl stir together yogurt and vanilla. Fold in whipped topping.

two Divide the mango between 2 parfait glasses. Top each with one-fourth of the yogurt mixture. Top with strawberries and remaining yogurt mixture. Sprinkle with coconut. Serve immediately.

NUTRITION FACTS PER SERVING: 238 cal., 4 g total fat (4 g sat. fat), 5 mg chol., 79 mg sodium, 46 g carbo., 3 g fiber, 6 g pro.

mocha mousse cups

This simple yet sumptuous mousse will be an instant hit with the coffee lovers in your clan.

START TO FINISH: 15 minutes **MAKES:** 6 servings

2	teaspoons instant espresso powder or 1 tablespoon instant coffee crystals
1	tablespoon hot water
4	3½- to 4-ounce containers chocolate pudding (prepared pudding cups), chilled
½	of an 8-ounce container frozen whipped dessert topping, thawed
9	chocolate wafer cookies, coarsely crushed

one In a medium bowl stir espresso powder into hot water until dissolved. Stir in chilled pudding. Fold in whipped topping. Divide half of the pudding mixture among 6 dessert dishes. Sprinkle with half of the coarsely crushed cookies. Repeat layers.

NUTRITION FACTS PER SERVING: 187 cal., 7 g total fat (5 g sat. fat), 0 mg chol., 164 mg sodium, 27 g carbo., 0 g fiber, 2 g pro.

double dippin' fruit

Dip makes everything taste better to kids. Entice them to eat fresh fruit by letting them dip it twice—once in creamy caramel mixture and then in crunchy granola. They won't be able to resist!

START TO FINISH: 15 minutes **MAKES:** 6 servings

1	3½- to 4-ounce container vanilla pudding (prepared pudding cup)
3	tablespoons caramel ice cream topping
½	teaspoon vanilla
¼	of an 8-ounce container frozen whipped dessert topping, thawed
¾	cup granola
	Assorted fresh fruit (such as sliced apples, banana chunks, or strawberries)

one For caramel dip, in a medium bowl stir together pudding, caramel topping, and vanilla until smooth. Fold in whipped topping.

two To serve, spoon caramel dip into a serving bowl. Place granola in another serving bowl. Serve with fruit. Dip fruit into caramel dip, then into granola.

NUTRITION FACTS PER SERVING: 131 cal., 3 g total fat (2 g sat. fat), 0 mg chol., 82 mg sodium, 23 g carbo., 1 g fiber, 1 g pro.

no-drip chocolate dip

Take care to chop the chocolate into uniform pieces so it will melt evenly without burning. You won't want to waste a single drop of this sensational dip.

START TO FINISH: 15 minutes **MAKES:** 2 cups

8	ounces unsweetened chocolate, chopped
1	14-ounce can (1¼ cups) sweetened condensed milk
2	tablespoons light-colored corn syrup
½	cup milk
1	teaspoon vanilla
½	teaspoon ground cinnamon
	Milk
	Assorted cut-up fresh fruit (such as strawberries, pineapple cubes, banana slices, and/or kiwi fruit slices)

one In a heavy medium saucepan melt chocolate over low heat, stirring constantly. Stir in the sweetened condensed milk and corn syrup until combined. Gradually stir in the ½ cup milk until combined. Stir in vanilla and cinnamon. Stir in additional milk as necessary to make dipping consistency.

two Serve dip warm, using fruit as dippers.

NUTRITION FACTS PER 2 TABLESPOONS DIP: 166 cal., 10 g total fat (6 g sat. fat), 8 mg chol., 40 mg sodium, 20 g carbo., 2 g fiber, 4 g pro.

make-ahead directions: Prepare dip as directed; cool slightly. Cover and chill for up to 3 weeks. To reheat dip, transfer chocolate mixture to a medium saucepan. Cook and stir over low heat until smooth and heated through. (Or transfer to a microwave-safe dish. Microwave, uncovered, on 100% power [high] for 35 to 60 seconds or until smooth and heated through, stirring halfway through cooking.) Serve warm, stirring in additional milk as necessary to make dipping consistency.

golden citrus sauce

Be sure to include this heavenly dessert sauce in your recipe repertoire. Spooned warm over pound cake or angel food cake, it makes a sunny finish to any meal.

START TO FINISH: 15 minutes **MAKES:** about 1⅓ cups sauce

- ¾ cup orange marmalade
- ⅓ cup golden raisins
- 1 tablespoon water
- 1 4-ounce container mandarin orange sections, drained (about ⅓ cup)
- 1 tablespoon dry or cream sherry (optional)

  Pound cake or angel food cake

one In a small saucepan combine orange marmalade, golden raisins, and the water; heat and stir until marmalade is melted. Gently fold in orange sections and, if desired, sherry.

two Serve warm sauce over pound or angel food cake slices.

NUTRITION FACTS PER 2 TABLESPOONS SAUCE: 79 cal., 0 g total fat (0 g sat. fat), 0 mg chol., 15 mg sodium, 21 g carbo., 0 g fiber, 0 g pro.

apricot-orange sauce

In an instant this lively sauce turns ordinary desserts into something special.

START TO FINISH: 15 minutes **MAKES:** 2 cups sauce

1	21-ounce can apricot pie filling
1	cup mixed dried fruit bits
¾	cup orange juice
½	cup chopped pecans, toasted
1	tablespoon orange liqueur (optional)
	Pound cake or vanilla ice cream

one In a medium saucepan combine pie filling, fruit bits, and orange juice; cook and stir until warm. Stir in pecans and, if desired, liqueur.

two Serve warm sauce over pound cake or ice cream.

NUTRITION FACTS PER 2 TABLESPOONS SAUCE: 93 cal., 2 g total fat (0 g sat. fat), 0 mg chol., 8 mg sodium, 17 g carbo., 1 g fiber, 1 g pro.

chocolate-hazelnut ice cream sauce

Chocolate and hazelnut is a classic dessert flavor combination. One bite of this simple yet luscious sauce and you'll know why. With only 10 minutes of prep time, you'll be tempted to make it often.

START TO FINISH: 10 minutes **MAKES:** about ¾ cup sauce

- ½ cup chocolate-hazelnut spread
- ¼ cup half-and-half or light cream
- 1 teaspoon instant coffee crystals (optional)
- ¼ cup hazelnuts, toasted and coarsely chopped

  Vanilla, coffee-flavor, or other favorite ice cream

one In a small saucepan combine chocolate-hazelnut spread, half-and-half, and, if desired, coffee crystals. Heat over low heat until spread is melted, whisking to make smooth. Stir in nuts. Serve warm over ice cream.

NUTRITION FACTS PER 2 TABLESPOONS SAUCE: 155 cal., 11 g total fat (1 g sat. fat), 4 mg chol., 24 mg sodium, 14 g carbo., 1 g fiber, 2 g pro.

amaretto peaches with vanilla yogurt

In the summertime, this dessert is a perfect way to use an abundance of fresh peaches. In the winter, try it with frozen fruit.

PREP: 20 minutes **STAND:** 10 minutes **MAKES:** 4 servings

3   peaches, pitted, peeled, and sliced, or 2 cups frozen unsweetened peach slices, thawed and drained

1   tablespoon amaretto

2   teaspoons vanilla

2   8-ounce cartons plain low-fat yogurt

¼   cup sugar

⅓   cup coarsely chopped whole almonds, or slivered almonds, toasted

one In a medium bowl toss together peach slices, amaretto, and 1 teaspoon of the vanilla. Let stand for 10 minutes.

two Meanwhile, in another bowl stir together yogurt, sugar, and the remaining 1 teaspoon vanilla. Spoon about half of the yogurt mixture into 4 dessert dishes or stemmed glasses; top with the flavored peaches and the remaining yogurt. Spoon any remaining liquid from peaches over the tops. Sprinkle with almonds.

NUTRITION FACTS PER SERVING: 233 cal., 7 g total fat (2 g sat. fat), 7 mg chol., 80 mg sodium, 33 g carbo., 3 g fiber, 9 g pro.

ultimate chocolate sundaes

It's important that the water and chocolate are together from the very beginning of cooking, otherwise they won't blend properly when heated.

START TO FINISH: 30 minutes **MAKES:** 8 servings

8	ounces bittersweet chocolate, coarsely chopped
⅓	cup water
¼	cup sugar
¼	cup pear liqueur or pear nectar
4	small Forelle or Bosc pears (about 1 pound total)
3	tablespoons butter or margarine
2	tablespoons sugar
1	quart premium vanilla ice cream

one For chocolate sauce, in a small saucepan combine chocolate, the water, and the ¼ cup sugar. Cook over low heat until melted, stirring slowly and constantly. Stir in pear liqueur or nectar. Set aside to cool slightly.

two If desired, peel pears; cut into halves and remove cores.* If desired, leave stem on one portion. In a large skillet melt butter over medium heat. Add pear halves; cook about 12 minutes or until browned and tender, turning once. Add the 2 tablespoons sugar, stirring gently until sugar is dissolved and pears are glazed.

three To assemble, place scoops of ice cream in 8 dessert bowls. Spoon a pear half and some of the butter mixture around the ice cream in each bowl. Top with chocolate sauce.

NUTRITION FACTS PER SERVING: 466 cal., 27 g total fat (16 g sat. fat), 80 mg chol., 81 mg sodium, 56 g carbo., 5 g fiber, 5 g pro.

*NOTE: If pears are large, cut into sixths or eighths.

citrus freeze

Cool and thirst-quenching, this quick and simple slush is impossible to resist on hot summer days.

START TO FINISH: 10 minutes **MAKES:** 4 servings

- 1   pint lemon, lime, or orange sorbet
- ½   cup lemonade, limeade, or orange juice
- 1   12-ounce can lemon-lime carbonated beverage, chilled

one In a blender combine sorbet and lemonade. Cover and blend until smooth. Spoon into 4 glasses; top with lemon-lime beverage. Serve immediately.

NUTRITION FACTS PER SERVING: 193 cal., 0 g total fat (0 g sat. fat), 0 mg chol., 28 mg sodium, 49 g carbo., 1 g fiber, 0 g pro.

hot gingered cider

Mulling spice mix transforms ordinary
ingredients into an extraordinary beverage.

START TO FINISH: 15 minutes **MAKES:** 4 (8-ounce) servings

- 2   cups ginger ale
- 2   cups apple cider or apple juice
- 1   tablespoon lemon juice
- 2   tablespoons mulling spices*
- 1   1-inch piece fresh ginger, sliced

one In a medium saucepan combine ginger ale, apple cider, lemon juice, mulling spices, and fresh ginger. Cover and cook over medium-low heat for 5 to 10 minutes or until heated through (do not boil). Strain and discard the spices.

two To serve, ladle mixture into heatproof glass mugs or cups.

NUTRITION FACTS PER SERVING: 101 cal., 0 g total fat (0 g sat. fat), 0 mg chol., 12 mg sodium, 26 g carbo., 0 g fiber, 0 g pro.

*NOTE:** If purchased mulling spices are unavailable, use a mixture of 1 cinnamon stick, broken, and 1 tablespoon whole cloves.

5-ingredient
recipes

fast fondue

PREP: 10 minutes **BAKE:** 5 minutes **MAKES:** 8 servings

1   8-ounce wedge or round Cambozola, Camembert, or Brie cheese

     Coarsely ground mixed peppercorns

2   tablespoons chopped walnuts or pecans

     Sliced coarse-grain or crusty bread, toasted, or assorted crackers

one If using a cheese round, peel rind from top of cheese. Place cheese in a quiche dish or shallow baking dish. Sprinkle with peppercorns and nuts. Bake in a 450°F oven for 5 to 8 minutes or until cheese is softened and just begins to melt. Serve with toasted bread or crackers.

NUTRITION FACTS PER SERVING: 175 cal., 9 g total fat (5 g sat. fat), 20 mg chol., 411 mg sodium, 15 g carbo., 1 g fiber, 8 g pro.

artichoke dip with pretzels

START TO FINISH: 10 minutes **MAKES:** 40 servings

1   14-ounce can artichoke hearts, drained and finely chopped

1   8-ounce carton dairy sour cream

½   cup bottled chunky blue cheese salad dressing

¼   cup snipped chives or finely chopped green onion tops

Large pretzel rods, small pretzel knots, and/or melba toast rounds

one In a medium bowl stir together artichoke hearts, sour cream, salad dressing, and chives. Transfer to a serving bowl. Serve with pretzels and/or melba toast rounds for dipping.

NUTRITION FACTS PER SERVING: 31 cal., 3 g total fat (1 g sat. fat), 4 mg chol., 56 mg sodium, 1 g carbo., 0 g fiber, 1 g pro.

fresh fruit dip

START TO FINISH: 15 minutes **MAKES:** 6 servings

1	8-ounce carton vanilla low-fat yogurt
¼	cup unsweetened applesauce
⅛	teaspoon ground cinnamon, nutmeg, or ginger
3	cups assorted fresh fruit, such as pineapple chunks, strawberries, apple slices, and/or peach slices

one In a small bowl stir together yogurt, applesauce, and cinnamon. To serve, spear fruit with decorative picks and dip into yogurt mixture.

NUTRITION FACTS PER SERVING: 27 cal., 0 g total fat (0 g sat. fat), 1 mg chol., 9 mg sodium, 6 g carbo., 0 g fiber, 1 g pro.

layered black bean dip

PREP: 10 minutes **BAKE:** 20 minutes **MAKES:** 8 to 10 servings

1   15-ounce can black beans, rinsed and drained

¾   cup bottled salsa

2   cups shredded Monterey Jack cheese with jalapeño peppers or Monterey Jack cheese (8 ounces)

1   medium avocado, halved, seeded, peeled, and chopped
Tortilla chips

one In a large bowl mash beans with a fork. Stir in salsa and 1 cup of the cheese. Spread bean mixture in bottom of a 9-inch pie plate. Top with avocado and sprinkle with the remaining cheese. Bake, uncovered, in a 350°F oven for 20 minutes or until heated through and cheese is melted. Serve warm with tortilla chips.

NUTRITION FACTS PER SERVING: 291 cal., 18 g total fat (7 g sat. fat), 25 mg chol., 448 mg sodium, 25 g carbo., 6 g fiber, 12 g pro.

cheesy pecan quesadillas

3 ounces Brie or Muenster cheese, chopped (about ¼ cup)

2 8- to 9-inch flour tortillas

2 tablespoons chopped pecans or walnuts, toasted

2 tablespoons snipped fresh Italian parsley

Dairy sour cream

one Sprinkle cheese over half of each tortilla. Top with nuts and parsley. Fold tortillas in half, pressing gently. In a lightly greased 10-inch skillet or griddle, cook quesadillas over medium heat for 2 to 3 minutes or until lightly browned, turning once. Cut quesadillas into wedges. Serve with sour cream.

NUTRITION FACTS PER SERVING: 170 cal., 12 g total fat (6 g sat. fat), 27 mg chol., 202 mg sodium, 9 g carbo., 0 g fiber, 6 g pro.

toasted ravioli

PREP: 25 minutes **BAKE:** 15 minutes **MAKES:** 10 to 12 servings

- 1   9-ounce package refrigerated cheese-filled ravioli
- ½   cup Italian-seasoned fine dry bread crumbs
- ¼   cup milk
- 1   egg
- 1½ cups purchased pasta sauce

one In a large saucepan cook ravioli in boiling water for 3 minutes. Drain well; cool slightly. Place bread crumbs in a shallow dish. In another shallow dish beat together the milk and egg. Dip cooked ravioli in egg mixture; coat with bread crumbs. Place ravioli on a greased baking sheet.

two Bake in a 425°F oven for 15 minutes or until crisp and golden. Meanwhile, heat sauce in a small saucepan. Serve warm ravioli with sauce.

NUTRITION FACTS PER SERVING: 141 cal., 3 g total fat (1 g sat. fat), 32 mg chol., 391 mg sodium, 22 g carbo., 1 g fiber, 6 g pro.

toasted cheese pita chips

START TO FINISH: 25 minutes **MAKES:** 12 servings

3   pita bread rounds

3   tablespoons butter or margarine, melted

3   tablespoons grated Parmesan or Romano cheese

one Split pita bread rounds in half horizontally. Lightly brush the cut side of each pita bread half with melted butter. Cut each half into 6 wedges. Spread in a single layer on a baking sheet. Sprinkle with grated cheese. Bake in a 350°F oven about 10 minutes or until crisp. Cool. Transfer to an airtight container; store at room temperature for up to 1 week.

NUTRITION FACTS PER SERVING: 74 cal., 4 g total fat (2 g sat. fat), 9 mg chol., 135 mg sodium, 8 g carbo., 0 g fiber, 2 g pro.

parmesan or romano: You usually can use Parmesan and Romano cheeses interchangeably. Parmesan and Romano cheeses are pale yellow, hard cheeses that originated in Italy. Both have a sharp, rich flavor; Romano is slightly stronger. Parmesan cheese is made from cow's milk. Romano is often made with a blend of cow's and sheep's or goat's milk.

focaccia breadsticks

PREP: 15 minutes **BAKE:** 12 minutes **MAKES:** 10 breadsticks

¼   cup oil-packed dried tomatoes

¼   cup grated Romano cheese

2   teaspoons water

1½   teaspoons snipped fresh rosemary or
     ½ teaspoon dried rosemary, crushed

⅛   teaspoon cracked black pepper

1   10-ounce package refrigerated pizza dough

one Drain dried tomatoes, reserving oil; finely snip tomatoes. In a small bowl combine tomatoes, 2 teaspoons of the reserved oil, the cheese, water, rosemary, and pepper. Set aside.

two Unroll pizza dough. On a lightly floured surface, roll dough into a 10×8-inch rectangle. Spread tomato mixture crosswise over half of the dough. Fold plain half of dough over filling; press lightly to seal edges. Cut the folded dough lengthwise into ten ½-inch strips. Fold each strip in half and twist two or three times. Place on a lightly greased baking sheet. Bake in a 350°F oven for 12 to 15 minutes or until golden brown. Cool on a wire rack.

NUTRITION FACTS PER BREADSTICK: 113 cal., 3 g total fat (1 g sat. fat), 3 mg chol., 263 mg sodium, 18 g carbo., 1 g fiber, 5 g pro.

puff pastry cheese straws

PREP: 18 minutes **BAKE:** 12 minutes **MAKES:** 36 straws

1 17¼-ounce package frozen puff pastry, thawed

1 lightly beaten egg white

   Paprika

   Ground red pepper (optional)

1 cup finely shredded sharp cheese, such as aged cheddar, Asiago, or Parmesan (4 ounces)

one Open 1 sheet of puff pastry on a cutting board. Brush surface lightly with some of the beaten egg white. Sprinkle lightly with paprika and, if desired, red pepper. Sprinkle with half of the cheese. Roll a floured rolling pin over top to gently press the cheese into pastry.

two Cut puff pastry into long ½-inch strips; gently twist each strip several times. Lay strips 1 inch apart on a baking sheet lined with parchment paper. Repeat with remaining sheet of puff pastry and remaining ingredients. Bake in a 375°F oven for 12 to 14 minutes or until golden. Cool on a wire rack. Serve the same day.

NUTRITION FACTS PER STRAW: 73 cal., 5 g total fat (1 g sat. fat), 3 mg chol., 72 mg sodium, 5 g carbo., 0 g fiber, 1 g pro.

prosciutto-arugula roll-ups

START TO FINISH: 30 minutes **MAKES:** about 48 slices

1   5-ounce container semisoft cheese with garlic and herb

2   ounces soft goat cheese (chèvre)

⅓   cup pine nuts or chopped almonds, toasted

4   ounces thinly sliced prosciutto (8 slices)

1½ cups arugula or spinach leaves, stems removed (about 2½ ounces)

one Stir together cheeses and pine nuts. Spread about 2 tablespoons cheese mixture over each prosciutto slice. Top each with arugula. Roll up each slice from a short side. Cut into ½-inch slices. Serve immediately or cover and chill for up to 6 hours.

NUTRITION FACTS PER SLICE: 33 cal., 3 g total fat (1 g sat. fat), 4 mg chol., 55 mg sodium, 0 g carbo., 0 g fiber, 2 g pro.

tomato-pesto toast

PREP: 15 minutes **BROIL:** 3 minutes **MAKES:** 12 to 16 toasts

2	French-style rolls (about 6 inches long), cut into ½-inch slices
¾	cup purchased pesto
2	to 3 plum or Roma tomatoes, cut lengthwise into thin slices
⅓	cup crumbled feta cheese
	Coarsely cracked black pepper

one Arrange bread slices on the rack of an unheated broiler pan. Broil 4 to 5 inches from the heat about 1 minute on each side or until toasted. Spread a scant 1 tablespoon pesto on each slice of toasted bread; top each with a tomato slice. Crumble some of the cheese on top of each tomato slice. Sprinkle with pepper. Watching carefully, broil 4 to 5 inches from the heat for 1 to 2 minutes or until heated through.

NUTRITION FACTS PER TOAST: 160 cal., 9 g total fat (2 g sat. fat), 8 mg chol., 289 mg sodium, 15 g carbo., 1 g fiber, 6 g pro.

chicken & rice spring rolls

PREP: 25 minutes **CHILL:** 1 hour **MAKES:** 24 servings

8   8-inch round rice papers

16   thin asparagus spears, trimmed

1   cup finely chopped cooked chicken

1   cup cooked long grain rice

¾   cup bottled sweet-and-sour sauce

one Place some warm water in a shallow dish. Dip each rice paper in warm water and place between damp towels for 5 minutes.

two Meanwhile, cook asparagus spears in boiling water for 3 minutes. Drain; rinse with cold water. Drain again.

three In a medium bowl stir together chicken, rice, and ¼ cup of the sweet-and-sour sauce. Place 2 asparagus spears about 1 inch from the bottom edge of one of the rice papers. Place ¼ cup chicken mixture on top of asparagus. Fold up bottom edge of the rice paper over the filling. Fold in the sides; roll up. Repeat with remaining rice papers, asparagus, and chicken mixture.

four Cover and chill spring rolls for 1 to 2 hours. Cut each spring roll into thirds. Serve with remaining sweet-and-sour sauce.

NUTRITION FACTS PER SERVING: 56 cal., 1 g total fat (0 g sat. fat), 5 mg chol., 35 mg sodium, 12 g carbo., 1 g fiber, 3 g pro.

easy fresh lemonade

START TO FINISH: 15 minutes **MAKES:** 14 servings

8   cups water

2   cups sugar

4   cups ice

2   7½-ounce containers frozen lemon juice from concentrate, thawed

one For syrup, in a saucepan bring 2 cups of the water and the sugar to boiling over medium heat. Cook for 5 to 7 minutes or until sugar dissolves. Fill a large bowl with ice. Stir in syrup, lemon juice, and remaining water. Transfer to pitchers.

NUTRITION FACTS PER SERVING: 113 cal., 0 g total fat (0 g sat. fat), 0 mg chol., 6 mg sodium, 30 g carbo., 0 g fiber, 0 g pro.

orange cream punch

START TO FINISH: 15 minutes **MAKES:** 16 servings

1   14-ounce can sweetened condensed milk

1   12-ounce can frozen orange juice concentrate, thawed

Orange food coloring (optional)

2   1-liter bottles carbonated water or ginger ale, chilled

Orange sherbet

one In a punch bowl stir together sweetened condensed milk and orange juice concentrate. If desired, tint with orange food coloring. Slowly add carbonated water. Top with scoops of orange sherbet. Serve immediately.

NUTRITION FACTS PER SERVING: 164 cal., 3 g total fat (2 g sat. fat), 11 mg chol., 75 mg sodium, 33 g carbo., 0 g fiber, 3 g pro.

fancy fruit float

START TO FINISH: 10 minutes **MAKES:** 4 servings

2   cups cut-up fruit, such as sliced strawberries, halved grapes, sliced bananas, orange sections, or chopped apple

1   1-liter bottle low-calorie lemon-lime carbonated beverage or low-calorie ginger ale

2   cups fruit-flavored sherbet

one Divide the fruit among 4 tall glasses. Fill each glass three-quarters with carbonated beverage and top with a scoop of sherbet.

NUTRITION FACTS PER SERVING: 172 cal., 2 g total fat (1 g sat. fat), 5 mg chol., 83 mg sodium, 39 g carbo., 2 g fiber, 2 g pro.

berry-banana smoothies

START TO FINISH: 10 minutes **MAKES:** 2 servings

1   small banana, peeled, cut up, and frozen

¼   cup fresh or frozen assorted berries, such as raspberries, blackberries, and/or strawberries

1   cup orange juice

3   tablespoons vanilla low-fat yogurt

Fresh berries (optional)

one In a blender container combine all ingredients. Cover and blend until smooth. Pour into glasses. If desired, top with additional berries.

NUTRITION FACTS PER SERVING: 121 cal., 1 g total fat (0 g sat. fat), 2 mg chol., 18 mg sodium, 28 g carbo., 2 g fiber, 2 g pro.

ginger-lemon tea

START TO FINISH: 20 minutes **MAKES:** 6 servings

6 cups water

4 teaspoons sugar

1 1-inch piece fresh ginger, thinly sliced

8 lemon peel strips (2½ ×1 inch each)

8 green tea bags

one In a large saucepan combine the water, sugar, ginger, and lemon peel. Bring to boiling; reduce heat. Simmer, covered, for 10 minutes. Remove ginger and lemon strips with a slotted spoon; discard.

two Add tea bags to saucepan. Cover; let steep for 3 to 5 minutes. Remove tea bags; discard. Serve hot.

NUTRITION FACTS PER SERVING: 13 cal., 0 g total fat (0 g sat. fat), 0 mg chol., 7 mg sodium, 3 g carbo., 0 g fiber, 0 g pro.

hot caramel chocolate

START TO FINISH: 15 minutes MAKES: 6 servings

⅓   cup sugar

⅓   cup unsweetened cocoa powder

⅓   cup water

6   milk chocolate-covered round caramels

6   cups milk, half-and-half, or light cream

one In a large saucepan combine sugar, cocoa powder, and water. Cook and stir over medium heat until sugar is dissolved. Add caramels; stir until melted. Stir in the milk and heat through.

NUTRITION FACTS PER SERVING: 213 cal., 7 g total fat (4 g sat. fat), 19 mg chol., 133 mg sodium, 29 g carbo., 0 g fiber, 10 g pro.

mocha java

START TO FINISH: 10 minutes **MAKES:** 4 servings

4	cups strong coffee
½	cup semisweet chocolate pieces
¼	cup sugar
1	cup half-and-half or light cream

one In a small saucepan combine coffee, chocolate pieces, and sugar. Cook and stir over medium heat for 2 to 3 minutes or until chocolate is melted and sugar is dissolved. In another small saucepan heat half-and-half until steaming, stirring occasionally. Divide coffee mixture among 4 mugs. Add warm half-and-half.

NUTRITION FACTS PER SERVING: 232 cal., 13 g total fat (8 g sat. fat), 22 mg chol., 32 mg sodium, 29 g carbo., 1 g fiber, 3 g pro.

chai

START TO FINISH: 15 minutes **MAKES:** 8 servings

1¼	cups nonfat dry milk powder
¼	cup black tea leaves
12	cardamom pods
4	2-inch pieces stick cinnamon
2	teaspoons finely shredded lemon peel
8	cups water

one In a large saucepan combine all ingredients. Bring to boiling; remove from heat. Cover; let stand for 5 minutes. Strain through a sieve lined with 100-percent-cotton cheesecloth or a clean paper coffee filter.

NUTRITION FACTS PER SERVING: 40 cal., 0 g total fat (0 g sat. fat), 2 mg chol., 62 mg sodium, 6 g carbo., 0 g fiber, 4 g pro.

chicken & greens with pears

START TO FINISH: 15 minutes **MAKES:** 4 main-dish servings

- 6   cups packaged torn mixed greens or mesclun
- 10 to 12 ounces roasted or grilled chicken breast, diced
- ¾   cup bottled reduced-calorie or regular blue cheese salad dressing
- 2   pears, cored and sliced

    Freshly ground black pepper (optional)

one In a large bowl combine the greens, chicken, and dressing; toss gently to coat. Divide among 4 large salad bowls or dinner plates. Arrange pear slices on top of salads. Sprinkle with pepper, if desired.

NUTRITION FACTS PER SERVING: 225 cal., 6 g total fat (2 g sat. fat), 61 mg chol., 639 mg sodium, 16 g carbo., 3 g fiber, 26 g pro.

pasta-salami salad

PREP: 20 minutes **CHILL:** 4 to 24 hours **MAKES:** 6 main-dish servings

12   ounces rotini, cavatelli, or bow tie pasta

1   16-ounce package frozen pepper and onion stir-fry vegetables

4   ounces salami or cooked smoked sausage links

1   cup bottled Italian salad dressing

1   2¼-ounce can sliced pitted ripe olives (½ cup)

one Cook pasta according to package directions. Place frozen vegetables in a colander; pour pasta and cooking water over vegetables. Drain well.

two Cut salami into bite-size pieces. In a large bowl toss together pasta mixture, salami, dressing, and olives. Cover and chill for 4 to 24 hours. If necessary, stir in additional Italian dressing before serving.

NUTRITION FACTS PER SERVING: 498 cal., 27 g total fat (5 g sat. fat), 18 mg chol., 765 mg sodium, 52 g carbo., 3 g fiber, 13 g pro.

chicken taco salad

PREP: 10 minutes **COOK:** 10 minutes **MAKES:** 4 main-dish servings

- 1 9-ounce package frozen cooked Southwestern-seasoned chicken breast strips
- 1 15- to 16-ounce can pinto beans, rinsed and drained
- 1 cup frozen whole kernel corn
- ¾ cup salsa
  Tortilla chips

one In a medium saucepan stir together chicken, beans, corn, and salsa. Bring to boiling; reduce heat. Simmer, covered, for 10 minutes or until heated through, stirring occasionally. Serve with tortilla chips.

NUTRITION FACTS PER SERVING: 320 cal., 9 g total fat (2 g sat. fat), 30 mg chol., 1,066 mg sodium, 42 g carbo.,8 g fiber, 23 g pro.

pasta-chicken caesar salad

START TO FINISH: 20 minutes **MAKES:** 4 main-dish servings

6   ounces dried radiatore or large bow tie pasta
    (about 2¼ cups)

1   10-ounce package Caesar salad kit
    (includes lettuce, dressing, croutons, and cheese)

1   cup cherry tomatoes, halved

1   9-ounce package refrigerated cooked
    chicken breast strips

one Cook pasta according to package directions; drain well. Rinse with cold water; drain again. In a very large bowl combine cooked pasta, contents of salad package, and tomatoes; toss to combine. Divide among 4 serving bowls. Arrange chicken strips on top.

NUTRITION FACTS PER SERVING: 377 cal., 14 g total fat (3 g sat. fat), 49 mg chol., 868 mg sodium, 40 g carbo., 3 g fiber, 22 g pro.

quick & crunchy turkey salad

START TO FINISH: 10 minutes **MAKES:** 4 main-dish servings

1	16-ounce package shredded cabbage with carrot (coleslaw mix)
6	ounces cooked turkey breast, cubed (1¼ cups)
1	3-ounce package ramen noodles
⅔	cup bottled orange vinaigrette salad dressing
1	11- or 15-ounce can mandarin orange sections, drained

one In a large bowl combine coleslaw mix and turkey. Remove seasoning packet from noodles; reserve for another use. Crumble noodles; add to cabbage mixture. Pour dressing over salad; toss to coat. Gently stir in the orange sections.

NUTRITION FACTS PER SERVING: 527 cal., 23 g total fat (1 g sat. fat), 15 mg chol., 1,552 mg sodium, 67 g carbo., 3 g fiber, 17 g pro.

tortellini-pesto salad

PREP: 20 minutes **CHILL:** 2 hours **MAKES:** 4 main-dish servings

- 2 cups frozen or refrigerated cheese-filled tortellini (about 7 ounces)
- 4 ounces mozzarella cheese, cubed
- 1 cup coarsely chopped, seeded tomato
- ½ cup purchased pesto
- ¼ cup pine nuts or slivered almonds, toasted

one Cook tortellini according to package directions; drain. Rinse with cold water; drain well. In a large bowl combine tortellini, cheese, and tomato. Pour pesto over tortellini mixture; toss lightly to coat. Cover and chill 2 to 4 hours. Stir in pine nuts just before serving.

NUTRITION FACTS PER SERVING: 360 cal., 15 g total fat (4 g sat. fat), 51 mg chol., 453 mg sodium, 37 g carbo., 1 g fiber, 21 g pro.

strawberry-spinach salad

START TO FINISH: 20 minutes **MAKES:** 4 side-dish servings

- 4 cups torn spinach or 2 cups torn spinach and 2 cups torn salad greens
- 1 cup watercress
- 1 cup sliced fresh strawberries
- ½ of a small red onion, thinly sliced
- ½ cup bottled oil-and-vinegar salad dressing or poppy seed salad dressing

one In a large bowl combine spinach, watercress, strawberries, and onion. Pour dressing over salad; toss to coat.

NUTRITION FACTS PER SERVING: 168 cal., 16 g total fat (2 g sat. fat), 0 mg chol., 468 mg sodium, 8 g carbo., 2 g fiber, 2 g pro.

lemon sunshine salad

PREP: 30 minutes **CHILL:** 2 hours **MAKES:** 15 side-dish servings

½ cup acini di pepe (tiny, bead-shaped pasta)

1 4-serving-size package instant lemon pudding mix

1 29-ounce can peach slices in light syrup

2 11-ounce cans mandarin orange sections, drained

1 8-ounce container frozen whipped dessert topping, thawed

one Cook pasta according to package directions. Drain. Stir in pudding mix. Drain peaches, reserving ½ cup syrup; stir reserved syrup into pasta mixture. Cut peach slices into bite-size pieces. Fold peaches and orange sections into pasta mixture. Cover and chill for 2 hours. Just before serving, fold in whipped dessert topping.

NUTRITION FACTS PER SERVING: 150 cal., 3 g total fat (3 g sat. fat), 0 mg chol., 86 mg sodium, 30 g carbo., 1 g fiber, 1 g pro.

pea & peanut salad

START TO FINISH: 10 minutes **MAKES:** 4 to 6 side-dish servings

  1   10-ounce package frozen peas, thawed and drained

  1   cup Spanish or honey-roasted peanuts

  ¼   cup dairy sour cream

  2   tablespoons mayonnaise or salad dressing

  ½   teaspoon sugar

one In a medium bowl combine peas and peanuts. Stir together sour cream, mayonnaise, and sugar until combined. Stir into pea mixture until coated.

NUTRITION FACTS PER SERVING: 346 cal., 26 g total fat (5 g sat. fat), 9 mg chol., 131 mg sodium, 17 g carbo., 6 g fiber, 15 g pro.

fresh mozzarella salad

START TO FINISH: 10 minutes **MAKES:** 8 side-dish servings

- 4   medium tomatoes or 6 Roma tomatoes
- 4   ounces fresh mozzarella
- 2   tablespoons bottled balsamic vinaigrette salad dressing
- ½   cup loosely packed fresh basil leaves, thinly sliced

     Salt and fresh cracked black pepper

one Cut tomatoes into ½-inch slices. Cut mozzarella into ¼-inch slices. Arrange tomato and cheese slices on a platter. Drizzle with vinaigrette. Sprinkle basil on top. Sprinkle with salt and pepper.

NUTRITION FACTS PER SERVING: 64 cal., 4 g total fat (2 g sat. fat), 11 mg chol., 174 mg sodium, 4 g carbo., 1 g fiber, 3 g pro.

mediterranean-style pasta salad

PREP: 25 minutes **CHILL:** 4 hours **MAKES:** 4 to 5 side-dish servings

1½   cups dried mostaccioli pasta

1   cup halved cherry or grape tomatoes

⅓   cup sliced pitted kalamata or other ripe olives

1   4-ounce package crumbled feta cheese

½   cup bottled balsamic vinaigrette salad dressing

one Cook pasta according to package directions; drain. Rinse with cold water; drain well. In a large bowl combine the cooked pasta with remaining ingredients; toss to coat. Cover and chill for 4 to 8 hours. Stir gently before serving.

NUTRITION FACTS PER SERVING: 335 cal., 17 g total fat (5 g sat. fat), 25 mg chol., 792 mg sodium, 36 g carbo., 2 g fiber, 9 g pro.

barbecue meat loaf

PREP: 15 minutes **BAKE:** 45 minutes **MAKES:** 4 servings

1   beaten egg

¼   cup fine dry bread crumbs

½   cup bottled barbecue sauce

1   pound lean ground beef

2   4-inch pieces string cheese (about 2 ounces)

one In a medium bowl combine egg, bread crumbs, and ¼ cup of the barbecue sauce; add beef and mix well.

two In a 2-quart rectangular baking dish pat about two-thirds of the meat mixture into a 7×3-inch rectangle. Place the cheese lengthwise in the center of the rectangle. Pat remaining meat mixture on top, sealing it around the cheese. Bake, uncovered, in a 350°F oven for 40 to 45 minutes or until center of the loaf registers 160°F on an instant-read thermometer. Spoon remaining barbecue sauce over loaf; bake for 5 minutes more.

NUTRITION FACTS PER SERVING: 394 cal., 25 g total fat (10 g sat. fat), 144 mg chol., 735 mg sodium, 13 g carbo., 0 g fiber, 26 g pro.

instant-read thermometers: Instant-read thermometers are used to check the internal temperature of food toward the end of cooking time. They should not be left in food as it cooks in the oven or microwave. To use a digital instant-read thermometer, insert the thermometer tip into the food at least ¼ inch for 10 seconds. For a dial instant-read thermometer, insert the tip into the food to a depth of 2 to 3 inches.

taco pizza

PREP: 15 minutes **BAKE:** 20 minutes **MAKES:** 6 slices

- 8 ounces lean ground beef and/or bulk pork sausage
- 1 medium green sweet pepper, chopped (¾ cup)
- 1 11½-ounce package refrigerated corn bread twists
- ½ cup purchased salsa
- 3 cups shredded taco cheese (12 ounces)

one In a skillet cook beef and pepper over medium heat until meat is brown; drain. Set aside.

two Unroll corn bread dough (do not separate into strips). Press dough into the bottom and up the edges of a greased 12-inch pizza pan. Spread salsa on top of dough. Sprinkle with meat mixture and cheese. Bake in a 400°F oven about 20 minutes or until bottom of crust is golden brown. Cut into wedges.

NUTRITION FACTS PER SLICE: 465 cal., 30 g total fat (15 g sat. fat), 73 mg chol., 870 mg sodium, 27 g carbo., 1 g fiber, 22 g pro.

meatball oven dinner

PREP: 5 minutes **BAKE:** 45 minutes **MAKES:** 8 servings

16 1-ounce frozen cooked Italian-style meatballs, thawed

2 cups purchased three-cheese pasta sauce

8 frozen cheddar-garlic biscuits or one
10-ounce package refrigerated flaky buttermilk
biscuits (10)

one Cut meatballs in half and place in the bottom of a 2-quart rectangular baking dish. Pour pasta sauce over meatballs. Bake, covered, in a 375°F oven for 20 to 25 minutes or until sauce is bubbly. Top meatball mixture with biscuits. Bake, uncovered, about 25 minutes more for frozen biscuits (about 20 minutes more for refrigerated biscuits) or until biscuits are golden brown.

NUTRITION FACTS PER SERVING: 402 cal., 24 g total fat (12 g sat. fat), 49 mg chol., 1,424 mg sodium, 29 g carbo., 4 g fiber, 18 g pro.

thai beef stir-fry

PREP: 10 minutes **COOK:** 5 minutes **MAKES:** 4 servings

4	ounces rice noodles
1	16-ounce package frozen pepper and onion stir-fry vegetables
2	tablespoons cooking oil
12	ounces beef stir-fry strips
½	cup bottled Thai peanut stir-fry sauce

one Prepare noodles according to package directions. Drain and set aside. In a large skillet cook vegetables in 1 tablespoon hot oil over medium-high heat for 2 to 3 minutes or until just tender. Drain; transfer vegetables to a bowl. In the skillet cook and stir beef strips in remaining oil for 2 to 3 minutes or until desired doneness. Return vegetables to skillet; add sauce. Stir to combine; heat through. Serve over noodles.

NUTRITION FACTS PER SERVING: 404 cal., 16 g total fat (4 g sat. fat), 50 mg chol., 597 mg sodium, 39 g carbo., 3 g fiber, 23 g pro.

stir-fry time-saver: Stir-fries are quick and convenient one-dish meals. You can get dinner on the table even more quickly when you use meats and poultry that are precut by your supermarket's butcher. If you must cut your own beef strips for the recipe above, the task is easier if you partially freeze the meat first. Place it in the freezer for 30 minutes before cooking time, then cut thin strips.

spinach-stuffed flank steak

PREP: 20 minutes **BROIL:** 10 minutes **MAKES:** 4 servings

¼   cup dried tomatoes (not oil-packed)

1   1-pound beef flank steak or top round steak, trimmed of separable fat

1   10-ounce package frozen chopped spinach, thawed and well drained

2   tablespoons grated Parmesan cheese

2   tablespoons snipped fresh basil

one In a small bowl soak dried tomatoes in enough hot water to cover for 10 minutes. Drain. Snip into small pieces.

two Meanwhile, make shallow diagonal cuts at 1-inch intervals in a diamond pattern on both sides of steak. Place steak between 2 pieces of plastic wrap. Pound into 12×8-inch rectangle. Discard plastic wrap.

three Spread spinach over steak. Sprinkle with tomatoes, cheese, and basil. Starting from a short side, roll up steak. Secure with toothpicks at 1-inch intervals, starting ½ inch from one end. Cut between toothpicks into eight 1-inch slices.

four Place slices, cut sides down, on the unheated rack of a broiler pan. Broil 3 to 4 inches from the heat to desired doneness, turning once. (Allow 10 to 12 minutes for medium rare or 12 to 16 minutes for medium.) Remove toothpicks.

NUTRITION FACTS PER SERVING: 281 cal., 9 g total fat (4 g sat. fat), 45 mg chol., 521 mg sodium, 18 g carbo., 12 g fiber, 37 g pro.

easy elegant beef roast

PREP: 15 minutes **ROAST:** 1¾ hours **MAKES:** 10 to 12 servings

- 1   4- to 6-pound beef rib roast
      Salt and black pepper
- 2   tablespoons olive oil
- 1   tablespoon dried minced onion
- 2   teaspoons bottled minced garlic

one Cut 1-inch pockets on fat side of the roast at 3-inch intervals. Sprinkle roast with salt and pepper. In a small bowl combine the remaining ingredients; rub onto roast and into pockets.

two Place roast, fat side up, in a roasting pan. Insert an oven-safe meat thermometer into the thickest portion of meat without touching fat or bone. Roast in a 350°F oven for 1¾ to 2¼ hours for medium rare (135°F) or 2¼ to 2¾ hours for medium (150°F). Transfer to serving platter; cover with foil. Let stand for at least 15 minutes before carving (temperature will rise 5° F during standing).

NUTRITION FACTS PER SERVING: 296 cal., 18 g total fat (7 g sat. fat), 91 mg chol., 83 mg sodium, 1 g carbo., 0 g fiber, 31 g pro.

stroganoff-sauced beef roast

PREP: 15 minutes **COOK:** 15 minutes **MAKES:** 3 to 4 servings

1   16-ounce package cooked beef pot roast with gravy

2   cups shiitake, crimini, or button mushrooms

½   cup dairy sour cream French onion dip

2   cups hot cooked noodles

one Transfer beef with gravy to a large skillet (leave meat whole). Remove stems from shiitake mushrooms; halve or quarter mushrooms. Add mushrooms to skillet. Cook, covered, over medium-low heat for 15 minutes or until heated through, stirring mushrooms once and turning roast once. Break meat into bite-size pieces. Stir onion dip into meat mixture; heat through (do not boil). Stir in noodles.

NUTRITION FACTS PER SERVING: 542 cal., 7 g total fat (11 g sat. fat), 99 mg chol., 787 mg sodium, 46 g carbo., 4 g fiber, 8 g pro.

speedy beef stew

PREP: 15 minutes **COOK:** 10 minutes **MAKES:** 4 servings

1	17-ounce package refrigerated cooked beef roast au jus
2	10¾-ounce cans condensed beefy mushroom soup
1	16-ounce package frozen mixed vegetables
4	teaspoons snipped fresh basil or 1½ teaspoons dried basil, crushed
1½	cups milk

one Cut beef into bite-size pieces, if necessary. In a 4-quart Dutch oven combine beef and au jus, soup, vegetables, and dried basil, if using. Bring to boiling; reduce heat. Simmer, covered, for 10 minutes. Stir in milk and fresh basil, if using. Heat through. Ladle into soup bowls.

NUTRITION FACTS PER SERVING: 386 cal., 15 g total fat (7 g sat. fat), 80 mg chol., 1,688 mg sodium, 33 g carbo., 5 g fiber, 33 g pro.

oven-barbecued beef sandwiches

PREP: 10 minutes **BAKE:** 2 hours **MAKES:** 6 to 8 servings

- 1   10¾-ounce can condensed cream of chicken or mushroom soup
- 1¼ cups bottled barbecue sauce
- 1   4- to 6-pound beef roast, such as boneless chuck
- 1   1-ounce envelope dry onion soup mix

      Onion buns or kaiser rolls, toasted

one In a roasting pan pour soup and barbecue sauce over roast. Sprinkle dry soup mix over roast. Bake, covered, in a 350°F oven about 2 hours or until tender enough to slice. (For shredded meat, cook about 3 hours or until very tender.)

two Drain off fat and remove any bones from roast. Slice or shred the meat and serve on buns. Spoon sauce over meat.

NUTRITION FACTS PER SERVING: 887 cal., 53 g total fat (20 g sat. fat), 179 mg chol., 1,446 mg sodium, 42 g carbo., 2 g fiber, 56 g pro.

greek-style pitas

PREP: 15 minutes **CHILL:** 1 hour **MAKES:** 4 servings

   1   cup deli creamy cucumber and onion salad

  ½   cup chopped tomato

   1   teaspoon snipped fresh dill

   4   wheat or white pita bread rounds, halved crosswise

  12   ounces thinly sliced cooked deli roast beef

one In a bowl combine salad, tomato, and dill; cover and chill 1 hour. Line pita halves with roast beef. Spoon salad mixture into each pita half.

NUTRITION FACTS PER SERVING: 380 cal., 10 g total fat (3 g sat. fat), 82 mg chol., 427 mg sodium, 39 g carbo., 1 g fiber, 34 g pro.

bigger & better saucy pork chops

PREP: 10 minutes **BAKE:** 2 hours **BROIL:** 10 minutes **MAKES:** 6 servings

6 center-cut pork loin rib chops, cut 1½ inches thick (about 3 pounds)

⅓ cup packed brown sugar

¼ cup hot water

½ cup bottled chili sauce

⅓ cup ketchup

1 teaspoon dry mustard

one Trim fat from chops. Arrange chops in a single layer on a rack in a roasting pan. Pour hot water into bottom of pan up to the level of the rack. Cover pan with foil. Bake in a 350°F oven for 2 hours or until chops are tender.

two For the sauce, stir together brown sugar and the ¼ cup hot water. Stir in remaining ingredients. Spoon sauce generously over chops. Place chops on the unheated rack of a broiler pan. Broil 5 to 6 inches from the heat for 10 to 12 minutes or until sauce begins to glaze chops, turning once. Heat any remaining sauce and pass with chops.

NUTRITION FACTS PER SERVING: 421 cal., 12 g total fat (4 g sat. fat), 135 mg chol., 529 mg sodium, 20 g carbo., 1 g fiber, 55 g pro.

brown sugar-glazed ham

PREP: 10 minutes **BAKE:** 1 hour 35 minutes **MAKES:** 16 to 20 servings

1	5- to 6-pound cooked bone-in ham (rump half or shank portion)
1½	cups packed brown sugar
1½	cups red wine vinegar
4	sprigs fresh mint

one If desired, score ham by making diagonal cuts 1 inch apart in fat in a diamond pattern. Place on a rack in a shallow roasting pan. Insert an oven-safe meat thermometer so it does not touch bone. Bake in a 325°F oven until thermometer registers 125°F. For rump, allow 1¼ to 1½ hours; for shank, allow 1¾ to 2 hours.

two Meanwhile, for glaze, in a medium saucepan stir together remaining ingredients. Bring to boiling; reduce heat. Boil gently, uncovered, about 30 minutes or until reduced to 1 cup. Remove from heat. Remove and discard mint. Brush ham with some of the glaze.

three Bake ham for 20 to 30 minutes more or until thermometer registers 135°F, brushing occasionally with additional glaze. Let stand for 15 minutes before carving. (The meat temperature will rise 5°F during standing.) Bring any remaining glaze to boiling; serve with ham.

NUTRITION FACTS PER SERVING: 232 cal., 8 g total fat (3 g sat. fat), 51 mg chol., 1,305 mg sodium, 22 g carbo., 0 g fiber, 20 g pro.

ham & cheese calzones

PREP: 15 minutes **BAKE:** 15 minutes **MAKES:** 4 servings

1	10-ounce package refrigerated pizza dough
¼	cup coarse-grain mustard
6	ounces sliced Swiss or provolone cheese
8	ounces cubed cooked ham (1½ cups)
½	teaspoon caraway seeds

one Line a baking sheet with foil; lightly grease foil. Unroll pizza dough. On a lightly floured surface roll or pat dough into a 15×10-inch rectangle. Cut dough in half crosswise and lengthwise to make 4 rectangles. Spread mustard over rectangles. Divide half of the cheese among rectangles, placing cheese on half of each and cutting or tearing to fit as necessary. Top with ham and sprinkle with caraway seeds. Top with remaining cheese. Brush edges with water. Fold dough over filling to opposite edge, stretching slightly if necessary. Seal edges with a fork.

two Place calzones on the prepared baking sheet. Prick tops to allow steam to escape. Bake in a 400°F oven about 15 minutes or until golden brown. Let stand for 5 minutes before serving.

NUTRITION FACTS PER SERVING: 421 cal., 21 g total fat (10 g sat. fat), 72 mg chol., 1,390 mg sodium, 28 g carbo., 1 g fiber, 30 g pro.

smoked sausage pasta bake

PREP: 25 minutes **BAKE:** 15 minutes **MAKES:** 4 servings

- 12 ounces cavatelli or rotini pasta
- 1 26- to 28-ounce jar purchased spicy tomato pasta sauce
- 6 ounces cooked smoked sausage, halved lengthwise and sliced
- ¾ cup bottled roasted red sweet peppers, drained and coarsely chopped
- 1 cup shredded provolone or mozzarella cheese (4 ounces)

one Cook pasta according to package directions; drain well. Return pasta to pan. Stir sauce, sausage, and roasted peppers into pasta, tossing gently to coat. Spoon pasta mixture into four greased 14- to 16-ounce casseroles. Sprinkle with cheese. Bake in a 375°F oven for 15 to 20 minutes or until cheese is melted and pasta mixture is heated through.

NUTRITION FACTS PER SERVING: 654 cal., 25 g total fat (12 g sat. fat), 38 mg chol., 995 mg sodium, 77 g carbo., 6 g fiber, 26 g pro.

honey-mustard lamb chops

PREP: 10 minutes **BROIL:** 10 minutes **MAKES:** 2 servings

4	lamb chops, cut 1 inch thick (about 1 pound)
2	small zucchini, halved lengthwise
1	tablespoon Dijon-style mustard
1	tablespoon honey
1½	teaspoons snipped fresh rosemary or ½ teaspoon dried rosemary, crushed

one Trim fat from chops. Arrange chops and zucchini, cut sides up, on the unheated rack of a broiler pan. In a small bowl stir together the remaining ingredients. Spread some of the mustard mixture on top of the chops.

two Broil chops and zucchini 3 to 4 inches from the heat for 5 minutes. Turn chops and zucchini; spread more of the mustard mixture on the chops. Broil for 5 to 10 minutes more to desired doneness (160°F for medium) and until zucchini is tender, spreading the remaining mustard mixture on zucchini the last 3 minutes of broiling.

NUTRITION FACTS PER SERVING: 182 cal., 6 g total fat (2 g sat. fat), 60 mg chol., 99 mg sodium, 12 g carbo., 1 g fiber, 21 g pro.

french-onion baked chicken

PREP: 20 minutes **BAKE:** 35 minutes **MAKES:** 4 servings

2	pounds chicken thighs or drumsticks
⅓	cup creamy ranch salad dressing or French salad dressing
¼	teaspoon bottled hot pepper sauce
1	2.8-ounce can French-fried onions, crumbled
½	cup crushed cornflakes

one Skin chicken. In a shallow bowl stir together salad dressing and hot pepper sauce. In another bowl combine onions and cornflakes.

two In a 3-quart rectangular baking dish with a rack arrange chicken pieces, meaty side up. Brush with salad dressing mixture. Sprinkle with onion mixture, pressing mixture onto chicken.

three Bake, uncovered, in a 425°F oven for 35 to 40 minutes or until chicken is tender and no longer pink (180°F), covering loosely the last 10 minutes, if necessary, to prevent overbrowning.

NUTRITION FACTS PER SERVING: 408 cal., 24 g total fat (3 g sat. fat), 108 mg chol., 558 mg sodium, 18 g carbo., 0 g fiber, 28 g pro.

old-fashioned fried chicken

PREP: 10 minutes **COOK:** 25 minutes **MAKES:** 4 to 6 servings

½ cup all-purpose flour

½ teaspoon each salt and black pepper

1 5-ounce can evaporated milk

⅔ cup water

2 cups cooking oil

2½ to 3 pounds meaty chicken pieces (breasts, thighs, and drumsticks)

one In a shallow dish stir together flour, salt, and pepper. Set aside. In a bowl stir together milk and water; set aside. In a 12-inch skillet over medium heat, heat ½ inch of oil. Dip chicken pieces in milk mixture; roll in flour mixture.

two Cook chicken, uncovered, in hot oil for 10 minutes or until golden on the bottom. Turn and cook pieces 15 minutes more or until chicken is tender and no longer pink (170°F for breasts; 180°F for thighs and drumsticks). Remove chicken from skillet; drain on paper towels. Serve warm.

NUTRITION FACTS PER SERVING: 495 cal., 32 g total fat (8 g sat. fat), 125 mg chol., 419 mg sodium, 15 g carbo., 0 g fiber, 34 g pro.

oven-fried coconut chicken

PREP: 10 minutes **BAKE:** 45 minutes **MAKES:** 6 servings

- ½   cup flaked coconut
- ¼   cup fine dry seasoned bread crumbs
- 2½ to 3 pounds meaty chicken pieces (breasts, thighs, and drumsticks)
- ¼   cup butter or margarine, melted

one In a shallow bowl stir together coconut and bread crumbs; set aside. Brush chicken pieces with melted butter. Roll chicken pieces in coconut mixture to coat all sides. In a 15×10×1- or a 13×9×2-inch baking pan arrange chicken, skin side up, so pieces don't touch. Drizzle any remaining butter over chicken. Bake in a 375°F oven for 45 to 50 minutes or until chicken is tender and no longer pink (170°F for breasts; 180°F for thighs and drumsticks). Do not turn.

NUTRITION FACTS PER SERVING: 332 cal., 21 g total fat (10 g sat. fat), 108 mg chol., 284 mg sodium, 6 g carbo., 0 g fiber, 29 g pro.

tuscan chicken

START TO FINISH: 50 minutes **MAKES:** 4 servings

- 2 to 2½ pounds meaty chicken pieces (breasts, thighs, and drumsticks)
- 2 tablespoons olive oil
- 1¼ teaspoons pesto seasoning
- ½ cup whole kalamata olives
- ½ cup dry white wine or chicken broth

one In a 12-inch skillet cook chicken pieces in hot oil over medium heat for 15 minutes, turning to brown evenly. Reduce heat. Drain excess oil. Sprinkle seasoning evenly over chicken. Add olives. Pour white wine over all. Cover tightly and cook for 25 minutes. Uncover; cook for 5 to 10 minutes more or until chicken is tender and no longer pink (170°F for breasts; 180°F for thighs and drumsticks).

NUTRITION FACTS PER SERVING: 334 cal., 18 g total fat (4 g sat. fat), 104 mg chol., 280 mg sodium, 2 g carbo., 1 g fiber, 34 g pro.

blue ribbon cranberry chicken

PREP: 15 minutes **BAKE:** 1½ hours **MAKES:** 4 to 6 servings

- 1   16-ounce can whole cranberry sauce
- 1   cup Russian salad dressing or French salad dressing
- 1   envelope (½ of a 2-ounce package) onion soup mix
- 2½   to 3 pounds meaty chicken pieces (breasts, thighs, and drumsticks)

     Hot cooked rice (optional)

one In a bowl stir together cranberry sauce, salad dressing, and soup mix. Skin chicken, if desired. Arrange chicken pieces, meaty side down, in a 3-quart rectangular baking dish. Pour cranberry mixture over chicken pieces.

two Bake, uncovered, in a 325°F oven about 1½ hours or until the chicken is tender and no longer pink (170°F for breasts; 180°F for thighs and drumsticks), stirring glaze and spooning over chicken once or twice. Serve over hot cooked rice.

NUTRITION FACTS PER SERVING: 803 cal., 47 g total fat (9 g sat. fat), 141 mg chol., 919 mg sodium, 53 g carbo., 1 g fiber, 43 g pro.

balsamic chicken over greens

PREP: 15 minutes **MARINATE:** 1 hour **BROIL:** 12 minutes **MAKES:** 4 servings

4   skinless, boneless chicken breast halves
    (about 1¼ pounds)

1   cup bottled balsamic vinaigrette salad dressing

3   cloves garlic, minced

¼   teaspoon crushed red pepper

8   cups torn mixed salad greens

one Place chicken in a self-sealing plastic bag set in a shallow dish. For marinade, stir together ½ cup of the vinaigrette, the garlic, and red pepper. Pour marinade over chicken; close bag. Marinate in the refrigerator for 1 to 4 hours, turning occasionally.

two Drain chicken, reserving marinade. Place chicken on the unheated rack of a broiler pan. Broil 4 to 5 inches from heat for 12 to 15 minutes or until chicken is tender and no longer pink (170°F), turning once and brushing once with marinade halfway through broiling. Discard any remaining marinade.

three Arrange greens on serving plates. Cut chicken into strips. Place chicken on top of greens. Drizzle with remaining vinaigrette.

NUTRITION FACTS PER SERVING: 284 cal., 13 g total fat (2 g sat. fat), 82 mg chol., 525 mg sodium, 7 g carbo., 1 g fiber, 34 g pro.

pepper & peach fajita chicken

START TO FINISH: 30 minutes **MAKES:** 4 servings

4	skinless, boneless chicken breast halves (about 1¼ pounds)
1½	teaspoons fajita seasoning
2	tablespoons olive oil or butter
1½	cups sweet pepper strips
1	medium fresh peach or nectarine, cut into thin slices, or 1 cup frozen peach slices, thawed

one Sprinkle both sides of chicken with seasoning. In a large skillet cook chicken in 1 tablespoon of the oil over medium heat for 12 to 14 minutes or until chicken is tender and no longer pink (170°F), turning once. Transfer chicken to a serving platter; keep warm.

two Add remaining oil to skillet. Add pepper strips. Cook and stir for 3 minutes or until pepper strips are crisp-tender. Gently stir in peach slices. Cook for 1 to 2 minutes more or until heated through. Spoon pepper strips and peach mixture over chicken.

NUTRITION FACTS PER SERVING: 243 cal., 9 g total fat (1 g sat. fat), 82 mg chol., 150 mg sodium, 7 g carbo., 2 g fiber, 33 g pro.

skillet chicken alfredo

START TO FINISH: 20 minutes **MAKES:** 4 servings

1   10-ounce package frozen broccoli or asparagus spears

12   ounces skinless, boneless chicken breast halves or turkey breast tenderloins

1   tablespoon cooking oil

1   10- or 12-ounce container Alfredo pasta sauce

4   English muffins or bagels, split and toasted

one Cook broccoli according to package directions; drain and keep warm. Meanwhile, cut chicken crosswise into ½-inch strips. In a large skillet cook chicken in hot oil over medium-high heat for 3 to 4 minutes or until tender and no longer pink (170°F). Drain fat. Stir in pasta sauce. Simmer for 2 to 3 minutes or until sauce is heated through. Place toasted muffin or bagel halves on plates. Arrange broccoli spears on top. Spoon chicken and sauce over all.

NUTRITION FACTS PER SERVING: 497 cal., 28 g total fat (1 g sat. fat), 85 mg chol., 573 mg sodium, 33 g carbo., 4 g fiber, 30 g pro.

mustard-puff chicken

PREP: 5 minutes **BROIL:** 9 minutes **MAKES:** 4 servings

4 skinless, boneless chicken breasts halves (about 1¼ pounds)

⅓ cup mayonnaise or salad dressing

1 tablespoon Dijon-style mustard

1 tablespoon sliced green onion

   Dash ground red pepper

one Place chicken on the unheated rack of a broiler pan. Broil 4 to 5 inches from the heat for 5 minutes. Meanwhile, in a small bowl stir together remaining ingredients. Turn chicken; brush liberally with mayonnaise mixture. Broil for 4 to 6 minutes more or until chicken is tender and no longer pink (170°F).

NUTRITION FACTS PER SERVING: 265 cal., 17 g total fat (2 g sat. fat), 72 mg chol., 182 mg sodium, 1 g carbo., 0 g fiber, 27 g pro.

ranch-style chicken strips

PREP: 15 minutes **BAKE:** 12 minutes **MAKES:** 4 servings

Nonstick cooking spray

2 cups crushed cornflakes

2 tablespoons snipped fresh basil or
1 teaspoon dried basil, crushed

1 8-ounce bottle buttermilk ranch salad dressing

12 ounces skinless, boneless chicken breast halves,
cut into thin strips

one Lightly coat a 15×10×1-inch baking pan with cooking spray; set aside. In a shallow dish combine the cornflakes and basil. In another dish place ½ cup of the dressing. Dip chicken strips into dressing, roll in crumb mixture to coat. Arrange strips in prepared pan. Bake in a 425°F oven for 12 to 15 minutes or until chicken is tender and no longer pink (170°F). Serve with remaining dressing.

NUTRITION FACTS PER SERVING: 543 cal., 32 g total fat (5 g sat. fat), 54 mg chol., 928 mg sodium, 38 g carbo., 0 g fiber, 24 g pro.

barbecued chicken pizza

PREP: 20 minutes **BAKE:** 19 minutes **MAKES:** 6 servings

1	10-ounce package refrigerated pizza dough
½	of a 32-ounce container shredded cooked chicken in barbecue sauce (about 2 cups)
1	8-ounce package shredded four-cheese pizza blend
¼	cup snipped fresh cilantro

one In a greased 15×10×1-inch baking pan unroll pizza dough. Using your hands, press dough into a 12×10-inch rectangle. Build up the edges slightly. Bake dough in a 425°F oven for 7 minutes. Remove from oven.

two Spread chicken evenly over hot crust. Sprinkle with cheese and cilantro. Bake for 12 to 15 minutes more or until lightly brown. Cut into wedges.

NUTRITION FACTS PER SERVING: 324 cal., 13 g total fat (6 g sat. fat), 39 mg chol., 683 mg sodium, 33 g carbo., 1 g fiber, 20 g pro.

nutty turkey tenderloins

PREP: 15 minutes **BAKE:** 18 minutes **MAKES:** 4 servings

- 2 turkey breast tenderloins, halved horizontally (about 1 pound)
- ¼ cup creamy Dijon-style mustard blend
- 1 cup corn bread stuffing mix
- ½ cup finely chopped pecans
- 2 tablespoons butter, melted

one Brush turkey generously with the mustard blend. In a shallow dish combine the stuffing mix and pecans; dip turkey in stuffing mixture to coat both sides. Place in a shallow baking pan. Drizzle with melted butter. Bake, uncovered, in a 375°F oven for 18 to 20 minutes or until turkey is no longer pink (170° F).

NUTRITION FACTS PER SERVING: 395 cal., 21 g total fat (5 g sat. fat), 84 mg chol., 566 mg sodium, 21 g carbo., 1 g fiber, 30 g pro.

turkey-avocado quesadillas

PREP: 10 minutes **COOK:** 4 minutes **MAKES:** 3 servings

3   7- or 8-inch flour tortillas

3   tablespoons bottled peppercorn ranch salad dressing

1   cup bite-size pieces cooked turkey breast or
     one 5-ounce can chunk-style turkey, drained

1   avocado, halved, pitted, peeled, and sliced

¾   cup shredded Monterey Jack cheese (3 ounces)

one Spread one side of each tortilla with salad dressing. Arrange turkey and avocado slices over half of each tortilla. Sprinkle cheese over turkey and avocado. Fold in half, pressing gently (tortillas will be full).

two On a large nonstick griddle cook quesadillas over medium heat for 2 minutes per side or until lightly brown and cheese melts.

NUTRITION FACTS PER SERVING: 437 cal., 29 g total fat (9 g sat. fat), 69 mg chol., 481 mg sodium, 20 g carbo., 3 g fiber, 26 g pro.

quick turkey tetrazzini

PREP: 20 minutes **BAKE:** 15 minutes **MAKES:** 4 servings

Nonstick cooking spray

6 ounces spaghetti

1 19-ounce can ready-to-serve chunky creamy chicken with mushroom soup

6 ounces cooked turkey breast, chopped (about 1 cup)

½ cup finely shredded Parmesan cheese (2 ounces)

2 tablespoons sliced almonds

one Lightly coat a 2-quart square baking dish with cooking spray; set aside. Cook spaghetti according to the package directions; drain and return to pan. Add soup, turkey, and half of the cheese; heat through. Transfer spaghetti mixture to baking dish. Sprinkle with almonds and remaining cheese. Bake in a 425°F oven for 12 to 15 minutes or until top is golden.

NUTRITION FACTS PER SERVING: 413 cal., 13 g total fat (5 g sat. fat), 59 mg chol., 752 mg sodium, 43 g carbo., 2 g fiber, 28 g pro.

raspberry-smoked turkey pockets

START TO FINISH: 15 minutes **MAKES:** 4 servings

8   ounces smoked turkey breast, cut into thin strips

2   cups shredded romaine or spinach

¾   cup raspberries or sliced strawberries

¼   cup bottled raspberry vinaigrette salad dressing

2   large pita rounds, split

one In a large bowl gently toss together turkey strips, romaine, raspberries, and vinaigrette until combined. Divide mixture among pita halves.

NUTRITION FACTS PER SERVING: 192 cal., 6 g total fat (1 g sat. fat), 25 mg chol., 935 mg sodium, 24 g carbo., 3 g fiber, 13 g pro.

simple salsa fish

START TO FINISH: 15 minutes **MAKES:** 4 servings

1 pound fresh or frozen skinless orange roughy or red snapper fillets, ½ to 1 inch thick

⅓ cup salsa

1 clove garlic, minced

1 14-ounce can vegetable broth

1 cup quick-cooking couscous

one Thaw fish, if frozen. Rinse fish; pat dry. Set aside. In a small bowl, combine salsa and garlic; set aside. In a saucepan bring the broth to boiling. Stir in couscous; cover and remove from heat. Let stand for 5 minutes or until liquid is absorbed.

two Place fish on the greased unheated rack of a broiler pan. Broil about 4 inches from the heat until fish flakes easily when tested with a fork (allow 4 to 6 minutes per ½-inch thickness of fish). Turn 1-inch-thick fillets over halfway through broiling. Spoon salsa mixture over fish; broil about 1 minute more or until salsa is heated through. Serve fish on couscous mixture.

NUTRITION FACTS PER SERVING: 295 cal., 3 g total fat (0 g sat. fat), 42 mg chol., 549 mg sodium, 39 g carbo., 7 g fiber, 30 g pro.

almond walleye

START TO FINISH: 20 minutes MAKES: 4 servings

    4   8- to 10-ounce fresh or frozen walleye pike fillets or
         other fish fillets

    ½   cup all-purpose flour

    ¼   cup ground almonds (1 ounce)

    ¼   teaspoon each salt and black pepper

    ¼   cup olive oil

one Thaw fish, if frozen. Rinse fish; pat dry. In a shallow pan or dish stir together flour, almonds, salt, and pepper. Coat fish with flour mixture. In a large skillet, cook 2 of the fillets in 2 tablespoons hot oil over medium heat for 4 to 6 minutes on each side or until coating is golden and fish flakes easily when tested with a fork. Remove from skillet; keep warm. Repeat with remaining fillets and oil.

NUTRITION FACTS PER SERVING: 423 cal., 20 g total fat (3 g sat. fat), 194 mg chol., 261 mg sodium, 12 g carbo., 1 g fiber, 46 g pro.

crunchy catfish & zucchini

PREP: 15 minutes **BAKE:** 12 minutes **MAKES:** 4 servings

1	pound fresh or frozen catfish fillets
1	medium zucchini or yellow summer squash
4	cups cornflakes
1	cup bottled ranch salad dressing
2	teaspoons bottled hot pepper sauce

one Thaw fish, if frozen. Rinse fish; pat dry. Cut fish into 1-inch strips. Cut zucchini in half crosswise. Cut each half lengthwise into 6 wedges.

two Place cornflakes in a large self-sealing plastic bag. Seal and crush slightly; set aside. In a large mixing bowl combine dressing and hot pepper sauce. Reserve half for dipping sauce; set aside. Add catfish and zucchini strips to remaining dressing in bowl; stir gently to coat.

three Add one-third of the zucchini and fish to the bag with the crushed cornflakes. Seal; shake to coat. Place coated zucchini and fish in a single layer on a greased 15×10×1-inch baking pan. Repeat with remaining zucchini and fish.

four Bake in a 425°F oven for 12 to 15 minutes or until fish flakes easily with a fork and crumbs are golden. Serve with reserved dipping sauce.

NUTRITION FACTS PER SERVING: 545 cal., 40 g total fat (7 g sat. fat), 58 mg chol., 779 mg sodium, 24 g carbo., 0 g fiber, 20 g pro.

honey-mustard lamb chops
Recipe on page 334

ginger-lemon tea
Recipe on page 305

focaccia breadsticks
Recipe on page 296

blue ribbon cranberry chicken
Recipe on page 339

pesto & cheese tomato melt
Recipe on page 377

simple salsa fish
Recipe on page 350

barbequed chicken pizza
Recipe on page 345

sweet-and-sour shrimp
Recipe on page 368

beer-battered cod

START TO FINISH: 35 minutes MAKES: 4 servings

Cooking oil for deep-fat frying

6 4- to 6-ounce fresh or frozen cod fillets

2 cups self-rising flour

½ teaspoon each salt and black pepper

1 12-ounce can beer

one In a heavy 3-quart saucepan or deep-fat fryer heat 2 inches of oil to 365°F.

two Meanwhile, thaw fish, if frozen. Rinse fish; pat dry. In a large bowl stir together flour, salt, and pepper. Sprinkle both sides of fish with 2 tablespoons of the flour mixture. Add beer to remaining flour mixture and stir until combined. Dip fish pieces, one at a time, into the batter, coating well (batter will be thick).

three Carefully lower fish into hot oil. Fry 1 or 2 pieces at a time for 4 to 6 minutes or until golden and fish flakes easily when tested with a fork. Drain on paper towels; keep warm in a 300°F oven while frying remaining fish.

NUTRITION FACTS PER SERVING: 635 cal., 29 g total fat (4 g sat. fat), 72 mg chol., 1,181 mg sodium, 50 g carbo., 2 g fiber, 37 g pro.

fish fillets au gratin

PREP: 10 minutes **BAKE:** 23 minutes **MAKES:** 4 servings

1	pound fresh or frozen skinless fish fillets, ¾ inch thick
¼	cup fine dry bread crumbs
2	teaspoons snipped fresh dill or ½ teaspoon dried dill
¼	teaspoon lemon-pepper seasoning
½	cup shredded cheddar cheese (2 ounces)

one Thaw fish, if frozen. Rinse fish; pat dry. Cut fish into 4 serving-size portions, if necessary. Place fillets in a greased shallow baking dish; set aside. In a small bowl stir together bread crumbs, dill, and seasoning. Spoon over fish.

two Bake, uncovered, in a 400°F oven for 20 to 25 minutes or until fish flakes easily when tested with a fork. Sprinkle with cheese; bake for 3 to 5 minutes more or until cheese melts.

NUTRITION FACTS PER SERVING: 169 cal., 6 g total fat (33 g sat. fat), 63 mg chol., 350 mg sodium, 4 g carbo., 0 g fiber, 24 g pro.

parmesan baked fish

PREP: 15 minutes **BAKE:** 12 minutes **MAKES:** 4 servings

4   4-ounce fresh or frozen skinless salmon fillets or
    other firm-textured fish fillets, ¾ to 1 inch thick

    Nonstick cooking spray

¼   cup light mayonnaise dressing or salad dressing

2   tablespoons grated Parmesan cheese

1   tablespoon snipped fresh chives or sliced green onion

1   teaspoon white wine Worcestershire sauce

one Thaw fish, if frozen. Rinse fish; pat dry. Coat a 2-quart baking dish with cooking spray. Arrange fillets in dish. In a small bowl stir together remaining ingredients; spread over fillets. Bake, uncovered, in a 450°F oven for 12 to 15 minutes or until fish flakes easily when tested with a fork.

NUTRITION FACTS PER SERVING: 252 cal., 16 g total fat (3 g sat. fat), 77 mg chol., 200 mg sodium, 2 g carbo., 0 g fiber, 25 g pro.

smoked salmon pizza

PREP: 10 minutes **BAKE:** 11 minutes **MAKES:** 6 to 8 servings

1   16-ounce Italian bread shell (Boboli®)

2   medium tomatoes, very thinly sliced

4   ounces sliced provolone cheese

3   ounces thinly sliced smoked salmon (lox-style)

½   cup crumbled semisoft goat cheese or
    garlic-and-herb feta cheese

one Place bread shell on a baking sheet. Arrange tomatoes, provolone cheese, and salmon on top. Sprinkle with goat cheese. Bake in a 400°F oven for 11 to 13 minutes or until heated through.

NUTRITION FACTS PER SERVING: 316 cal., 12 g total fat (5 g sat. fat), 24 mg chol., 899 mg sodium, 35 g carbo., 2 g fiber, 18 g pro.

tuna & noodles

START TO FINISH: 20 minutes MAKES: 4 to 6 servings

1 12-ounce package dried egg noodles (6 cups)

1 10¾-ounce can condensed cream of celery soup

6 ounces American cheese, cubed, or
   process Swiss cheese slices, torn

½ cup milk

1 12-ounce can solid white tuna (water- pack), drained

one In a 4-quart Dutch oven cook noodles according to package directions; drain. In the same pan combine soup, cheese, and milk. Cook and stir over medium heat until bubbly. Stir tuna into soup mixture. Gently stir in noodles. Cook for 2 to 3 minutes more until heated.

NUTRITION FACTS PER SERVING: 645 cal., 23 g total fat (11 g sat. fat), 162 mg chol., 1,476 mg sodium, 68 g carbo., 3 g fiber, 40 g pro.

tuna salad with a twist

START TO FINISH: 15 minutes **MAKES:** 4 servings

- 1 12-ounce can chunk white tuna (water-pack), drained
- 1/3 cup bottled creamy Italian salad dressing
- 1/3 cup finely chopped fresh or drained, canned pineapple
- 4 Boston lettuce leaves
- 2 sourdough, sesame, or plain bagels, halved and toasted

one In a medium bowl combine drained tuna, dressing, and pineapple. Place lettuce leaves on toasted bagel halves. Spoon tuna mixture over the lettuce leaves.

NUTRITION FACTS PER SERVING: 276 cal., 10 g total fat (2 g sat. fat), 38 mg chol., 902 mg sodium, 22 g carbo., 1 g fiber, 24 g pro.

shrimp with basil on linguine

PREP: 20 minutes **COOK:** 2 minutes **MAKES:** 4 servings

1   pound fresh or frozen peeled, deveined medium
    shrimp (1½ pounds in shell)

6   ounces spinach linguine or fettuccine

2   teaspoons snipped fresh basil or tarragon or
    1 teaspoon dried basil or tarragon, crushed

2   tablespoons butter or margarine

one Thaw shrimp, if frozen. Rinse shrimp; pat dry. Prepare linguine according to package directions. In a large skillet cook shrimp and basil in hot butter over medium-high heat for 2 to 3 minutes or until shrimp turn opaque, stirring frequently. Serve warm over linguine.

NUTRITION FACTS PER SERVING: 332 cal., 9 g total fat (4 g sat. fat), 189 mg chol., 231 mg sodium, 33 g carbo., 1 g fiber, 29 g pro.

sweet-and-sour shrimp

START TO FINISH: 15 minutes **MAKES:** 4 servings

¾ pound fresh or frozen peeled, deveined shrimp

⅓ cup bottled stir-fry sauce

¼ cup pineapple-orange juice

Nonstick cooking spray

3 cups assorted fresh stir-fry vegetables

one Thaw shrimp, if frozen. Rinse shrimp; pat dry. In a small bowl, combine stir-fry sauce and juice.

two Coat an unheated nonstick wok or large skillet with cooking spray. (Add oil, if necessary, during cooking.) Heat wok or skillet over medium-high heat. Add vegetables; cook and stir for 3 to 5 minutes or until crisp-tender. Remove from wok. Add shrimp; cook and stir for 2 to 3 minutes or until shrimp turn opaque. Push shrimp to side of wok.

three Add sauce mixture to wok. Stir in vegetables; heat through.

NUTRITION FACTS PER SERVING: 119 cal., 1 g total fat (0 g sat. fat), 131 mg chol., 666 mg sodium, 11 g carbo.,2 g fiber, 17 g pro.

buttery bay scallops

START TO FINISH: 10 minutes **MAKES:** 3 or 4 servings

- ¾   pound fresh or frozen bay scallops
- 1   clove garlic, minced
- ⅛   teaspoon dried tarragon, crushed
- 2   tablespoons butter or margarine

    Salt and black pepper

one Thaw scallops, if frozen. Rinse scallops; pat dry. In a skillet cook garlic and tarragon in hot butter over medium heat for 1 minute. Remove from heat. Add scallops. Sprinkle lightly with salt and pepper. Cook over medium heat about 4 minutes or just until opaque, turning occasionally.

NUTRITION FACTS PER SERVING: 173 cal., 9 g total fat (5 g sat. fat), 59 mg chol., 362 mg sodium, 3 g carbo., 0 g fiber, 19 g pro.

oven omelets with pesto

START TO FINISH: 35 minutes **MAKES:** 6 servings

2	cups desired frozen vegetables
3	tablespoons purchased basil pesto
	Nonstick cooking spray
3	cups refrigerated or frozen egg product, thawed, or 12 eggs
¼	cup water
⅛	teaspoon each salt and black pepper

one Cook vegetables according to package directions. Drain. Cut up any large pieces. Stir in pesto. Meanwhile, coat a 15×10×1-inch baking pan with cooking spray; set aside.

two In a mixing bowl combine egg product, water, salt, and pepper. Using a fork or rotary beater, beat until combined but not frothy. Place prepared pan on center oven rack. Pour egg mixture into pan. Bake, uncovered, in a 400°F oven about 8 minutes or until mixture is set but still has a shiny surface.

three Cut baked eggs into six 5-inch squares. Invert omelet squares onto warm serving plates. Spoon cooked vegetables on half of each omelet; fold other half over, forming a triangle.

NUTRITION FACTS PER SERVING: 142 cal., 7 g total fat (2 g sat. fat), 4 mg chol., 290 mg sodium, 5 g carbo., 1 g fiber, 15 g pro.

chipotle-bean enchiladas

PREP: 25 minutes **BAKE:** 30 minutes **MAKES:** 5 servings

10	6-inch corn tortillas
1	15-ounce can pinto beans or black beans, rinsed and drained
1	tablespoon chopped chipotle pepper in adobo sauce
2	cups shredded four-cheese Mexican-style blend (8 ounces)
2	10-ounce cans enchilada sauce

one Stack tortillas; wrap tightly in foil. Bake in a 350°F oven for 10 minutes or until warm. Meanwhile, for filling, combine beans, chipotle, 1 cup of the cheese, and ½ cup of the enchilada sauce. Spoon about ¼ cup filling onto one edge of each tortilla. Roll up each tortilla. Arrange tortillas, seam side down, in a greased 2-quart rectangular baking dish. Top with remaining sauce. Bake, covered, in a 350°F oven for 25 minutes or until heated through. Sprinkle with remaining cheese. Bake, uncovered, about 5 minutes more until cheese melts.

NUTRITION FACTS PER SERVING: 487 cal., 19 g total fat (8 g sat. fat), 40 mg chol., 1,091 mg sodium, 63 g carbo., 14 g fiber, 23 g pro.

chipotle chile peppers: A chipotle chile is a dried, smoked jalapeño that's milder than a fresh jalapeño and has a smoky, almost chocolaty flavor. In addition to the dried form, they also come canned in adobo sauce—a mixture of ground chiles, herbs, and vinegar. They're available at local supermarkets or Hispanic food markets.

black bean cakes

PREP: 10 minutes COOK: 8 minutes MAKES: 4 servings

1   15-ounce can black beans with cumin and chili spices
    or black beans, undrained

1   cup bottled salsa

2   tablespoons lime juice

1   8½-ounce package or
    ½ of a 15-ounce package corn bread and muffin mix

    Nonstick cooking spray

½   cup dairy sour cream Mexican-style dip

one In a medium bowl slightly mash undrained beans. Stir in ½ cup of the salsa and the lime juice. Stir in corn bread mix just until moistened.

two Coat a large nonstick skillet or griddle with cooking spray; heat skillet over medium heat. For each cake, spoon about ¼ cup batter into hot skillet. Use the back of a spoon to spread batter into a 4-inch circle. Cook for 1 to 2 minutes on each side or until browned. Repeat with remaining batter. Serve with remaining salsa and sour cream dip.

NUTRITION FACTS PER SERVING: 429 cal., 12 g total fat (5 g sat. fat), 1 mg chol., 1,314 mg sodium, 65 g carbo., 11 g fiber, 12 g pro.

tortilla lasagna

PREP: 10 minutes **BAKE:** 35 minutes **MAKES:** 8 servings

1	7-ounce package Spanish rice mix
1	11-ounce can whole kernel corn with sweet peppers
2	15-ounce cans black beans
10	6-inch corn tortillas
2	cups shredded Monterey Jack cheese with jalapeño peppers (8 ounces)

one Prepare the rice according to package directions, except substitute undrained corn for ½ cup of the liquid. In a medium bowl slightly mash undrained beans.

two Place 5 tortillas in the bottom of a greased 3-quart rectangular baking dish, overlapping and placing slightly up the sides of the dish (cut tortillas as necessary to fit). Spoon beans evenly over tortillas. Sprinkle with 1 cup of the cheese. Top with the remaining tortillas. Spoon cooked rice over tortillas.

three Bake, covered, in a 400°F oven for 30 minutes. Uncover and sprinkle with remaining cheese. Bake 5 minutes more or until cheese is melted. Let stand for 10 minutes before serving.

NUTRITION FACTS PER SERVING: 406 cal., 12 g total fat (7 g sat. fat), 34 mg chol., 1,101 mg sodium, 60 g carbo., 11 g fiber, 20 g pro.

gardener's pie

PREP: 15 minutes BAKE: 45 minutes MAKES: 4 servings

1   16-ounce package loose-pack frozen vegetable medley, thawed

1   11-ounce can condensed cheddar cheese soup

½   teaspoon dried thyme, crushed

1   20-ounce package refrigerated mashed potatoes

1   cup shredded smoked cheddar cheese (4 ounces)

one In a 1½-quart casserole, combine vegetables, soup, and thyme. Stir mashed potatoes to soften. Spread carefully over vegetable mixture to cover surface. Bake, covered, in a 350°F oven for 30 minutes. Uncover and bake 15 minutes more or until heated through, topping with cheese the last 5 minutes of baking.

NUTRITION FACTS PER SERVING: 349 cal., 17 g total fat (8 g sat. fat), 39 mg chol., 1,031 mg sodium, 40 g carbo., 4 g fiber, 15 g pro.

bread bowl potato soup

PREP: 5 minutes **COOK:** 15 minutes **MAKES:** 4 servings

1   14-ounce can reduced-sodium chicken broth

1   20-ounce package refrigerated diced potatoes with onions

1   cup milk

1   10-ounce package soy-based vegetarian smoked sausage, halved lengthwise and sliced

4   purchased bread bowls (optional)

one In a large saucepan bring chicken broth to boiling. Add potatoes; return to boiling. Reduce heat. Simmer, covered, for 10 minutes or until potatoes are very tender. Remove from heat. Cool slightly.

two Place half of the potato mixture in a food processor/blender container. Cover and blend until almost smooth, leaving some pieces of potato. Remove to a large bowl. Repeat with remaining potato mixture. Return all to saucepan. Stir in milk and sausage. Heat through. If desired, serve in bread bowls.

NUTRITION FACTS PER SERVING: 724 cal., 11 g total fat (2 g sat. fat), 5 mg chol., 2,401 mg sodium, 121 g carbo., 10 g fiber, 32 g pro.

linguine with gorgonzola sauce

START TO FINISH: 20 minutes **MAKES:** 3 servings

1   9-ounce package refrigerated linguine

1   pound asparagus, cut into bite-size pieces

1   cup half-and-half or light cream

½   cup crumbled Gorgonzola or other blue cheese (2 ounces)

2   tablespoons chopped walnuts, toasted

one Cook pasta according to package directions, adding asparagus to the water with pasta; drain. Return pasta and asparagus to pan.

two Meanwhile, in a medium saucepan combine half-and-half and cheese. Bring to boiling over medium heat; reduce heat. Simmer, uncovered, for 3 minutes. Pour sauce over pasta mixture; toss gently to coat. Transfer to a warm serving dish. Sprinkle with nuts.

NUTRITION FACTS PER SERVING: 478 cal., 22 g total fat (10 g sat. fat), 62 mg chol., 365 mg sodium, 54 g carbo., 2 g fiber, 19 g pro.

pesto & cheese tomato melt

PREP: 10 minutes **BROIL:** 2 minutes **MAKES:** 2 servings

¼   cup purchased basil pesto

2   tablespoons chopped nuts

4   1-inch slices sourdough French bread, toasted

¼   cup oil-packed dried tomatoes, drained and chopped

1   cup shredded mozzarella cheese (4 ounces)

one In a small bowl stir together pesto and nuts. Spread over toasted bread slices. Top with tomatoes and cheese. Place on a baking sheet. Broil 4 inches from the heat for 2 to 3 minutes or until cheese melts.

NUTRITION FACTS PER SERVING: 587 cal., 34 g total fat (6 g sat. fat), 36 mg chol., 918 mg sodium, 44 g carbo., 2 g fiber, 25 g pro.

asian noodle bowl

START TO FINISH: 25 minutes **MAKES:** 4 servings

8   ounces dry buckwheat soba noodles, udon noodles, or vermicelli noodles

2   cups vegetable broth

½   cup bottled peanut sauce

2   cups Chinese-style frozen stir-fry vegetables

½   cup dry roasted peanuts, chopped

one Cook noodles according to package directions. Drain but do not rinse. Set aside. In the same pan, combine broth and peanut sauce. Bring to boiling. Stir in frozen vegetables and cooked noodles. Return to boiling; reduce heat. Simmer for 2 to 3 minutes or until vegetables are heated through. Divide noodles and broth among 4 bowls. Sprinkle with peanuts.

NUTRITION FACTS PER SERVING: 403 cal., 15 g total fat (2 g sat. fat), 0 mg chol., 1,326 mg sodium, 59 g carbo., 4 g fiber, 15 g pro.

fresh tomato pizza with pesto

START TO FINISH: 15 minutes **MAKES:** 4 servings

½ cup purchased pesto

1 16-ounce Italian bread shell (Boboli)

3 medium ripe tomatoes, thinly sliced

1 2¼-ounce can sliced, pitted ripe olives, drained (about ⅔ cup)

2 cups shredded Monterey Jack or mozzarella cheese (8 ounces)

one Spread pesto over bread shell. Place on a large pizza pan or baking sheet. Arrange tomato slices on top. Sprinkle with olives and cheese. Bake in a 425°F oven for 10 to 15 minutes or until cheese melts. Cut into wedges.

NUTRITION FACTS PER SERVING: 776 cal., 48 g total fat (11 g sat. fat), 60 mg chol., 1,265 mg sodium, 60 g carbo., 4 g fiber, 32 g pro.

couscous & pine nut-stuffed peppers

PREP: 15 minutes **COOK:** 5 minutes **BAKE:** 25 minutes **MAKES:** 4 servings

1	5.6-ounce package pine nut couscous mix
½	cup purchased shredded carrot
2	large sweet peppers
½	cup shredded Italian-style cheese blend (2 ounces)
1½	cups purchased olive pasta sauce

one Prepare couscous mix according to package directions, except omit oil and add the shredded carrot with the couscous.

two Meanwhile, cut peppers in half lengthwise; remove seeds and membranes. Cook pepper halves in boiling water for 5 minutes. Drain on paper towels. Place peppers, cut side up, in a 2-quart rectangular baking dish. Spoon cooked couscous mixture into pepper halves.

three Bake, covered, in a 350°F oven for 20 to 25 minutes or until filling is heated through and peppers are tender. Sprinkle cheese over peppers. Bake, uncovered, 5 minutes more or until cheese is melted. Meanwhile, in a small saucepan heat the pasta sauce. Serve peppers with sauce.

NUTRITION FACTS PER SERVING: 259 cal., 6 g total fat (3 g sat. fat), 10 mg chol., 801 mg sodium, 42 g carbo., 7 g fiber, 11 g pro.

chipotle rub

START TO FINISH: 10 minutes
MAKES: Enough for 2½ pounds of pork, chicken, or turkey

- 1 teaspoon ground coriander
- ¼ teaspoon paprika
- ¼ to ½ teaspoon ground black pepper
- 1 small dried chipotle pepper, seeded and crushed, or ⅛ to ¼ teaspoon ground red pepper

one In a small bowl stir together all ingredients. Rub evenly onto meat. Cook as desired.

beer marinade

PREP: 10 minutes **MARINATE:** 4 to 24 hours
MAKES: Enough for 3 pounds of beef or pork

1 cup beer (measured after foam has subsided) or apple cider

2 tablespoons brown sugar

1 tablespoon Worcestershire sauce

2 teaspoons chili powder

1 clove garlic, minced

one In a small bowl stir together all ingredients. Pour over meat; turn to coat. Marinate in the refrigerator for 4 to 24 hours, turning occasionally. Drain, discarding marinade. Cook as desired.

savory-balsamic marinade

PREP: 10 minutes **MARINATE:** 2 to 4 hours
MAKES: Enough for 1 pound of beef, pork, lamb, chicken, turkey, or fish

¼ cup balsamic vinegar

1 tablespoon snipped fresh savory or
  1 teaspoon dried savory, crushed

½ teaspoon black pepper

one In a small bowl stir together all ingredients. Pour over meat, poultry, or fish; turn to coat. Marinate in the refrigerator for up to 2 hours for fish, up to 4 hours for meat, turning once. Drain, discarding marinade. Cook as desired.

mustard-horseradish sauce

START TO FINISH: 5 minutes **MAKES:** about ½ cup.

- 1 tablespoon Dijon-style mustard
- ⅓ cup dairy sour cream, mayonnaise, or salad dressing
- 1 green onion, finely chopped
- 1 to 2 teaspoons prepared horseradish

one In a small bowl stir together all ingredients. Serve with beef, pork, lamb, chicken, or turkey.

NUTRITION FACTS PER TABLESPOON: 20 cal., 2 g total fat (1 g sat. fat), 4 mg chol., 16 mg sodium, 1 g carbo., 0 g fiber, 0 g pro.

strawberry salsa

START TO FINISH: 10 minutes **MAKES:** 2 cups

¼   cup apricot jam or preserves

¼   teaspoon ground cinnamon

2   cups chopped fresh strawberries

one In a medium bowl combine jam and cinnamon; stir in strawberries. Let stand a few minutes to blend flavors. Serve over waffles, pancakes, French toast, or hot cereal, or stir into yogurt.

NUTRITION FACTS PER ½ CUP: 78 cal., 0 g total fat (0 g sat. fat), 0 mg chol., 7 mg sodium, 19 g carbo., 2 g fiber, 1 g pro.

herbed mayonnaise

PREP: 10 minutes **CHILL:** 1 hour **MAKES:** 1¼ cups

½ cup mayonnaise or salad dressing

½ cup dairy sour cream

3 tablespoons snipped fresh dill

2 tablespoons snipped fresh parsley

1 clove garlic, minced

one In a food processor/blender combine all ingredients. Cover and blend until almost smooth. Cover and chill for at least 1 hour or up to 24 hours. Serve with beef, pork, lamb, chicken, turkey, or fish.

NUTRITION FACTS PER TABLESPOON: 50 cal., 5 g total fat (1 g sat. fat), 5 mg chol., 34 mg sodium, 0 g carbo., 0 g fiber, 0 g pro.

asparagus with citrus mayonnaise

START TO FINISH: 25 minutes **MAKES:** 4 servings

1 pound fresh asparagus spears or
one 10-ounce package frozen asparagus spears

2 tablespoons plain fat-free yogurt

2 tablespoons light mayonnaise dressing or
salad dressing

½ teaspoon finely shredded orange peel

Dash ground red pepper

one Snap off and discard woody bases from asparagus.
In a medium saucepan cook fresh asparagus, covered, in
a small amount of boiling water for 4 to 6 minutes or until
crisp-tender. (Or cook frozen asparagus according to package
directions.) Drain; keep warm. Meanwhile, in a small bowl stir
together remaining ingredients. Spoon over hot asparagus.

NUTRITION FACTS PER SERVING: 46 cal., 3 g total fat (1 g sat. fat), 3 mg chol.,
60 mg sodium, 3 g carbo., 2 g fiber, 2 g pro.

green beans & bacon

START TO FINISH: 30 minutes **MAKES:** 12 servings

7	slices bacon
2	9-ounce packages frozen whole green beans, thawed
6	medium carrots, cut into 3- to 4-inch strips
2	tablespoons butter or margarine
2	cloves garlic, minced

one In a large skillet cook bacon over medium heat for 8 to 10 minutes or until just crisp, turning occasionally. Remove bacon, reserving 2 tablespoons drippings in skillet; drain bacon on paper towels.

two Add remaining ingredients to reserved drippings in skillet. Cook and stir over medium-high heat about 5 minutes or until vegetables are crisp-tender. Transfer to a serving bowl. Crumble bacon; sprinkle over beans.

NUTRITION FACTS PER SERVING: 67 cal., 4 g total fat (2 g sat. fat), 8 mg chol., 98 mg sodium, 6 g carbo., 2 g fiber, 2 g pro.

broccoli corn bread

PREP: 10 minutes **BAKE:** 30 minutes **MAKES:** 16 servings

1	8½-ounce package corn muffin mix
3	eggs
2	cups shredded cheddar cheese (8 ounces)
1	10-ounce package frozen chopped broccoli, thawed and well drained
½	cup chopped onion

one In a large bowl combine corn muffin mix and eggs. Stir in remaining ingredients. Spoon into a greased 9×9×2-inch baking pan. Bake in a 350°F oven about 30 minutes or until a toothpick inserted near the center comes out clean. Serve corn bread warm.

NUTRITION FACTS PER SERVING: 138 cal., 7 g total fat (3 g sat. fat), 55 mg chol., 209 mg sodium, 12 g carbo., 1 g fiber, 6 g pro.

sweet saucy carrots & pecans

START TO FINISH: 20 minutes **MAKES:** 4 servings

1   pound peeled baby carrots

2   tablespoons orange marmalade

1   tablespoon butter or margarine

½   teaspoon salt

2   tablespoons pecan pieces, toasted

one In a large saucepan cook carrots, covered, in a small amount of boiling water for 8 to 10 minutes or until crisp-tender. Drain. Return carrots to pan. Stir in orange marmalade, butter, and salt until carrots are coated. Top with pecans.

NUTRITION FACTS PER SERVING: 124 cal., 6 g total fat (2 g sat. fat), 8 mg chol., 365 mg sodium, 19 g carbo., 4 g fiber, 2 g pro.

corn on the cob with herb butter

PREP: 15 minutes **CHILL:** 1 hour **COOK:** 5 minutes **MAKES:** 16 servings

- 1 cup butter or margarine
- 1 tablespoon each snipped fresh thyme and marjoram or 2 tablespoons snipped fresh basil
- 16 ears of corn

  Salt and black pepper

one Stir together butter and herb. Cover and chill for at least 1 hour or up to 24 hours before serving to allow flavors to blend.

two Remove husks from corn. Scrub with a stiff brush to remove silks; rinse. Cook, covered, in enough boiling water to cover for 5 to 7 minutes or until tender. Serve with herb butter. Sprinkle with salt and pepper.

NUTRITION FACTS PER SERVING: 185 cal., 13 g total fat (8 g sat. fat), 33 mg chol., 137 mg sodium, 17 g carbo., 2 g fiber, 3 g pro.

ranch fries

PREP: 25 minutes **BAKE:** 40 minutes **MAKES:** 6 servings

Nonstick cooking spray

3 pounds baking potatoes

1 2-ounce package ranch salad dressing mix

one Lightly coat 2 baking sheets with cooking spray. Scrub potatoes and cut into 2×¼-inch pieces. Combine potatoes and dressing mix in large bowl. Spread half of the potatoes in a single layer on each prepared baking sheet. Lightly coat with cooking spray; bake in a 400°F oven for 20 minutes. Toss potatoes with metal spatula; spray again with cooking spray. Switch positions of pans; bake for 20 minutes more or until golden and crisp.

NUTRITION FACTS PER SERVING: 191 cal., 0 g total fat (0 g sat. fat), 0 mg chol., 678 mg sodium, 42 g carbo., 4 g fiber, 5 g pro.

vegetable rice pilaf

PREP: 15 minutes **COOK:** 45 minutes **MAKES:** 6 servings

1	cup finely chopped celery
⅓	cup chopped onion
¼	cup butter or margarine
1½	cups brown rice
3¾	cups chicken broth or reduced-sodium chicken broth

one In a large saucepan, cook celery and onion in butter until tender. Add rice; cook until lightly brown. Carefully stir in chicken broth. Bring mixture to boiling; reduce heat. Simmer, covered, about 45 minutes or until rice is tender and all liquid is absorbed.

NUTRITION FACTS PER SERVING: 268 cal., 11 g total fat (6 g sat. fat), 22 mg chol., 729 mg sodium, 38 g carbo., 2 g fiber, 5 g pro.

crunchy pound cake slices

PREP: 15 minutes **BROIL:** 2 minutes **MAKES:** 4 servings

 4   ½-inch slices purchased pound cake

 ¼   cup chocolate hazelnut spread

 ½   cup roasted mixed nuts, coarsely chopped

 1   pint caramel or cinnamon ice cream

one Place pound cake slices on a baking sheet. Broil 3 to 4 inches from heat for 1 minute on each side or until lightly brown. Cool slightly. Spread one side of each slice with chocolate hazelnut spread. Sprinkle with nuts; pat gently to form an even layer. Transfer each slice to a dessert plate and top with a scoop of ice cream. Serve immediately.

NUTRITION FACTS PER SERVING: 763 cal., 45 g total fat (22 g sat. fat), 206 mg chol., 421 mg sodium, 82 g carbo., 2 g fiber, 12 g pro.

mocha pears

PREP: 10 minutes **COOK:** 15 minutes **CHILL:** 4 hours **MAKES:** 6 servings

2   16-ounce cans or one 29-ounce can pear halves in heavy syrup (12 pear halves)

2   teaspoons instant coffee crystals

1   teaspoon vanilla

¾   cup vanilla low-fat yogurt

Miniature semisweet chocolate pieces

one Drain pears, reserving syrup. Place pears in a bowl; set aside. In a saucepan combine reserved syrup and coffee crystals. Bring to boiling; reduce heat. Simmer, uncovered, about 15 minutes or until mixture is slightly thickened and reduced to ½ cup. Stir in vanilla. Pour coffee mixture over pears. Cover; refrigerate for at least 4 hours, turning pears once.

two Use a slotted spoon to remove pear halves from coffee mixture. Place 2 pear halves into each of 6 dessert dishes; drizzle with coffee mixture. Top with yogurt and chocolate pieces.

NUTRITION FACTS PER SERVING: 168 cal., 2 g total fat (1 g sat. fat), 2 mg chol., 30 mg sodium, 37 g carbo., 3 g fiber, 2 g pro.

stirred custard

PREP: 15 minutes **CHILL:** 2 hours **MAKES:** 8 servings

5	beaten egg yolks
1½	cups milk
¼	cup sugar
1½	teaspoons vanilla
	Fresh fruit, such as blueberries, blackberries, or strawberries (optional)

one In a medium heavy saucepan use a wooden spoon to stir together egg yolks, milk, and sugar. Cook over medium heat, stirring constantly with a wooden spoon, until mixture just coats the back of a clean metal spoon. Remove pan from heat. Stir in vanilla.

two Quickly cool custard by placing saucepan in a large bowl of ice water for 1 to 2 minutes, stirring constantly. Pour custard mixture into a bowl. Cover surface with plastic wrap. Chill for at least 2 hours or until serving time. Do not stir. If desired, serve custard over fresh fruit.

NUTRITION FACTS PER SERVING: 85 cal., 4 g total fat (2 g sat. fat), 136 mg chol., 27 mg sodium, 8 g carbo., 0 g fiber, 3 g pro.

chocolate cookie cheesecakes

PREP: 20 minutes **BAKE:** 20 minutes **CHILL:** 1 to 24 hours
MAKES: 12 servings.

- 12 chocolate sandwich cookies with white filling
- 2 8-ounce packages cream cheese, softened
- ½ cup sugar
- 1 teaspoon vanilla
- 2 eggs

one Split each cookie, keeping filling intact on 1 cookie half. Line twelve 2½-inch muffin cups with foil bake cups. Place a cookie half with filling in each cup, filling side up. In a medium mixing bowl beat cream cheese, sugar, and vanilla until smooth. Add eggs. Beat on low speed just until combined. Spoon mixture into cups. Crush remaining cookies; sprinkle over filling.

two Bake in a 325°F oven for 20 to 25 minutes or until set (top may indent slightly). Cool. Cover and chill for at least 1 hour or up to 24 hours. To serve, remove bake cups.

NUTRITION FACTS PER SERVING: 223 cal., 16 g total fat (9 g sat. fat), 77 mg chol., 183 mg sodium, 16 g carbo., 0 g fiber, 4 g pro.

peanut butter s'more tarts

PREP: 15 minutes **CHILL:** 2 to 24 hours **MAKES:** 6 servings **STAND:** 30 min.

1	cup semisweet chocolate pieces (6 ounces)
½	cup peanut butter
1½	cups miniature marshmallows
½	cup chopped peanuts
1	4-ounce package graham cracker tart shells (6)

one In a small saucepan melt chocolate pieces over low heat, stirring constantly. Remove from heat. Stir in peanut butter until smooth. Stir in marshmallows and peanuts. Spoon into tart shells. Cover and chill for 2 hours or overnight. Let stand at room temperature for 30 minutes before serving.

NUTRITION FACTS PER SERVING: 505 cal., 31 g total fat (8 g sat. fat), 0 mg chol., 257 mg sodium, 42 g carbo., 7 g fiber, 10 g pro.

parfait pie with coconut shell

PREP: 20 minutes **BAKE:** 20 minutes **CHILL:** 4 hours **MAKES:** 8 servings

2   cups flaked coconut

3   tablespoons butter or margarine, melted

1   10-ounce package frozen red raspberries, thawed

1   3-ounce package raspberry-flavored gelatin

1   pint vanilla ice cream

one In a medium bowl combine coconut and melted butter. Press evenly into the bottom and sides of a 9-inch pie plate. Bake in a 325°F oven for 20 minutes. Cool on a wire rack.

two Drain raspberries, reserving syrup. Set aside. Add enough water to the syrup to measure 1¼ cups. In a medium saucepan combine the gelatin and the syrup mixture. Heat and stir until gelatin is dissolved. Remove from heat.

three Add the ice cream by spoonfuls to syrup mixture; stir until melted. Cover and chill until mixture mounds when spooned. Fold in raspberries. Pour into coconut shell. Refrigerate for at least 4 hours or until set.

NUTRITION FACTS PER SERVING: 291 cal., 14 g total fat (10 g sat. fat), 27 mg chol., 114 mg sodium, 40 g carbo.,2 g fiber, 3 g pro.

double berry soup

START TO FINISH: 20 minutes **MAKES:** 4 servings

2 cups frozen unsweetened blueberries

1 10-ounce package frozen sliced strawberries in syrup

½ teaspoon finely shredded orange peel (optional)

¾ cup orange juice

2 cups orange or other fruit sorbet or sherbet

one In a medium saucepan combine frozen blueberries with their syrup, half of the frozen strawberries with their syrup, the orange peel (if using), and orange juice. Cook over medium heat, stirring occasionally, for 4 to 5 minutes or just until the berries are thawed. Remove from heat. Stir in remaining frozen strawberries; let stand for 5 minutes. Ladle soup into 4 shallow dessert bowls. Top each with a scoop of sorbet.

NUTRITION FACTS PER SERVING: 262 cal., 2 g total fat (1 g sat. fat), 5 mg chol., 37 mg sodium, 63 g carbo., 8 g fiber, 2 g pro.

index

D-J

Q-R

S

T-Z

metric information

The charts on this page provide a guide for converting measurements from the U.S. customary system, which is used throughout this book, to the metric system.

Product Differences

Most of the ingredients called for in the recipes in this book are available in most countries. However, some are known by different names. Here are some common American ingredients and their possible counterparts:
- Sugar (white) is granulated, fine granulated, or castor sugar.
- Powdered sugar is icing sugar.
- All-purpose flour is enriched, bleached or unbleached white household flour. When self-rising flour is used in place of all-purpose flour in a recipe that calls for leavening, omit the leavening agent (baking soda or baking powder) and salt.
- Light-colored corn syrup is golden syrup.
- Cornstarch is cornflour.
- Baking soda is bicarbonate of soda.
- Vanilla or vanilla extract is vanilla essence.
- Green, red, or yellow sweet peppers are capsicums or bell peppers.
- Golden raisins are sultanas.

Volume and Weight

The United States traditionally uses cup measures for liquid and solid ingredients. The chart below shows the approximate imperial and metric equivalents. If you are accustomed to weighing solid ingredients, the following approximate equivalents will be helpful.
- 1 cup butter, castor sugar, or rice = 8 ounces = ½ pound = 250 grams
- 1 cup flour = 4 ounces = ¼ pound = 125 grams
- 1 cup icing sugar = 5 ounces = 150 grams
- Canadian and U.S. volume for a cup measure is 8 fluid ounces (237 ml), but the standard metric equivalent is 250 ml.
- 1 British imperial cup is 10 fluid ounces.
- In Australia, 1 tablespoon equals 20 ml, and there are 4 teaspoons in the Australian tablespoon.
- Spoon measures are used for smaller amounts of ingredients. Although the size of the tablespoon varies slightly in different countries, for practical purposes and for recipes in this book, a straight substitution is all that's necessary. Measurements made using cups or spoons always should be level unless stated otherwise.

Common Weight Range Replacements

Imperial / U.S.	Metric
½ ounce	15 g
1 ounce	25 g or 30 g
4 ounces (¼ pound)	115 g or 125 g
8 ounces (½ pound)	225 g or 250 g
16 ounces (1 pound)	450 g or 500 g
1¼ pounds	625 g
1½ pounds	750 g
2 pounds or 2¼ pounds	1,000 g or 1 Kg

Oven Temperature Equivalents

Fahrenheit Setting	Celsius Setting	Gas Setting
300°F	150°C	Gas Mark 2 (very low)
325°F	160°C	Gas Mark 3 (low)
350°F	180°C	Gas Mark 4 (moderate)
375°F	190°C	Gas Mark 5 (moderate)
400°F	200°C	Gas Mark 6 (hot)
425°F	220°C	Gas Mark 7 (hot)
450°F	230°C	Gas Mark 8 (very hot)
475°F	240°C	Gas Mark 9 (very hot)
500°F	260°C	Gas Mark 10 (extremely hot)
Broil	Broil	Grill

*Electric and gas ovens may be calibrated using celsius. However, for an electric oven, increase celsius setting 10 to 20 degrees when cooking above 160°C. For convection or forced air ovens (gas or electric), lower the temperature setting 25°F/10°C when cooking at all heat levels.

Baking Pan Sizes

Imperial / U.S.	Metric
9×1½-inch round cake pan	22- or 23×4-cm (1.5 L)
9×1½-inch pie plate	22- or 23×4-cm (1 L)
8×8×2-inch square cake pan	20×5-cm (2 L)
9×9×2-inch square cake pan	22- or 23×4.5-cm (2.5 L)
11×7×1½-inch baking pan	28×17×4-cm (2 L)
2-quart rectangular baking pan	30×19×4.5-cm (3 L)
13×9×2-inch baking pan	34×22×4.5-cm (3.5 L)
15×10×1-inch jelly roll pan	40×25×2-cm
9×5×3-inch loaf pan	23×13×8-cm (2 L)
2-quart casserole	2 L

U.S. / Standard Metric Equivalents

⅛ teaspoon = 0.5 ml	
¼ teaspoon = 1 ml	
½ teaspoon = 2 ml	
1 teaspoon = 5 ml	
1 tablespoon = 15 ml	
2 tablespoons = 25 ml	
¼ cup = 2 fluid ounces = 50 ml	
⅓ cup = 3 fluid ounces = 75 ml	
½ cup = 4 fluid ounces = 125 ml	
⅔ cup = 5 fluid ounces = 150 ml	
¾ cup = 6 fluid ounces = 175 ml	
1 cup = 8 fluid ounces = 250 ml	
2 cups = 1 pint = 500 ml	
1 quart = 1 litre	